A Curious History
of Vegetables

Also by Wolf Storl

Healing Lyme Disease Naturally: History, Analysis, and Treatments

The Herbal Lore of Wise Women and Wortcunners: The Healing Power of Medicinal Plants

Culture and Horticulture: The Classic Guide to Biodynamic and Organic Gardening

A Curious History *of* Vegetables

Aphrodisiacal and Healing Properties,
Folk Tales, Garden Tips, and Recipes

Wolf D. Storl

North Atlantic Books
Berkeley, California

Published by
North Atlantic Books
Berkeley, California

Originally published as *Bekannte und vergessene Gemüse* by AT Vorlag. Translated from the original German by Christine Reindal-Storl. Garden tips by Larry Berger and Wolf D. Storl; recipes by Paul Silas Pfyl.

Cover art by Barbara Hanneder
Original color illustrations by Barbara Hanneder
Cover design by John Yates
Book design by Suzanne Albertson

Printed in the United States of America

A Curious History of Vegetables: Aphrodisiacal and Healing Properties, Folk Tales, Garden Tips and Recipes is sponsored and published by the Society for the Study of Native Arts and Sciences (dba North Atlantic Books), an educational nonprofit based in Berkeley, California, that collaborates with partners to develop cross-cultural perspectives, nurture holistic views of art, science, the humanities, and healing, and seed personal and global transformation by publishing work on the relationship of body, spirit, and nature.

Garden tips by Larry Berger and Wolf D. Storl; recipes by Paul Silas Pfyl.

MEDICAL DISCLAIMER: The following information is intended for general information purposes only. Individuals should always see their health care provider before administering any suggestions made in this book. Any application of the material set forth in the following pages is at the reader's discretion and is his or her sole responsibility.

North Atlantic Books' publications are available through most bookstores. For further information, visit our website at www.northatlanticbooks.com or call 800-733-3000.

Library of Congress Cataloging-in-Publication Data

Names: Storl, Wolf-Dieter, author.
Title: A curious history of vegetables : aphrodisiacal and healing
    properties, folk tales, garden tips, and recipes / Wolf D. Storl.
Other titles: Bekannte und vergessene Gemèuse. English
Description: Berkeley, California : North Atlantic Books, 2016. | Originally
    published as: Bekannte und vergessene Gemèuse; translated from the
    original German by Christine Reindal-Storl. | Includes bibliographical
    references and index.
Identifiers: LCCN 2016009397 | ISBN 9781623170394
Subjects: LCSH: Vegetables—History. | Vegetables—Social aspects. |
    Vegetables—Therapeutic use. | Vegetable gardening. | Cooking (Vegetables)
Classification: LCC SB320.5 .S77 2016 | DDC 635—dc23
LC record available at http://lccn.loc.gov/2016009397

1 2 3 4 5 6 7 8 UNITED 21 20 19 18 17 16

"Brahman is food.
Only he who knows that he is eating God,
truly eats."

—TAITTIREYA UPANISHAD

CONTENTS

Forgotten, Rare, and Less-Known Vegetables 271

*Illustration 1. The Hindu god Ganesha, "the guardian of the threshold";
silk-paper print I got in a shop in Katmandu, Nepal, some thirty years ago.*

Introduction

Plants that "Dance with Humanity," or Anthropochores

Our lives and those of all animals are entirely dependent on the green world of plants. In the Vedas of ancient India, the oldest scriptures of Hinduism, wise seers wrote that plants feed us as mothers feed their children; or, to say the least, they care for us like wiser, elder siblings. What a different vision this is compared to a scientific worldview that reduces plants to physical, spiritless, and soulless protoplasmic structures! Anyone who asks people who still live close to nature—the last hunters and gatherers, shamans of indigenous tribes, or even long-time gardeners—about the nature of plant life will hear there is very much more to plants than meets the eye, much more than superficial and external observation reveals. They will probably even speak of a sentient plant soul, a conscious plant spirit, and tell us that, because this plant "spirit" or "soul" is not as obvious and does not express itself as overtly as human beings or animals do, we can only approach it in ways that are beyond the external senses. These plant friends will tell us that we can see deeply into the plant world with "inner senses." When we are quiet and listen, we can see the plant world mirrored in our own inner world and we can learn from the plants; the plants themselves will show us about their deeper nature and their healing abilities. We can come to experience various plant species as mighty personalities, as wise beings that mediate between heaven and earth in their own particular way and that have a very, very long history—much longer than ours! A plant, even a garden vegetable, can definitely be a good friend, a benefactor, or even a guide into a beautiful parallel world.

Indigenous peoples who are intimately connected to their natural environment communicate with plants, as they do with animals, spirits, and gods. In the first book of the Bible we are told that the first human beings, Adam and Eve, talked to the other creatures. Shamans and native peoples who live in nature's midst still have this ability even though modern circumstances—being submerged in all sorts of technology and living at a fast, usually machine-driven pace—make it difficult to find the quiet and inner peace to "hear" and communicate with nature and spirits. But we do not need to be shamans or mystically inclined to recognize plants as personalities. We can learn very much about plants by patiently observing them, for instance, while gardening. All that is necessary to develop appreciation for plants is plain and simple interest.

In this book we will explore the history and characteristics of many of the plants that we encounter in our daily lives: the plants we grow in vegetable gardens and consume with our meals. These are extremely friendly plants: *anthropochores*, as botanists call them—plants that "dance with humanity."

From Wild Gardens to Plant Zoos

The vegetation that characterizes a landscape is typically an expression of the formative forces of altitude, the seasons, the climate, the bedrock and soil, and temperature and its fluctuations. The survival of aboriginal peoples everywhere was dependent on the immediate environment, the local plants and animals. The surrounding nature influenced and resonated with the folk customs, festivities, habits—even the spiritual views of the people.

Nowadays things are very different. We are not meshed with our natural surroundings in the same way. We witness continuing globalization in the supermarket, and even our modern gardens display a potpourri of plants originating from all over the world. In a single vegetable garden one may see, for example, Chinese cabbage originally from East Asia, tomatoes and beans from the jungle areas of South America, Jerusalem artichokes or "sun chokes," from the North American prairie, eggplant from India, and okra from Africa. Many of them are giants compared to their original wild form; they have bigger cells and less cellulose than did their wild relatives, and most have lost their bitter or poisonous aspects, stickers, or thorns. Because they have given themselves over to human care, gardeners must indeed carefully tend to their needs; they must water them, protect them from being eaten by animals, and keep the comparatively more robust weeds from stifling them. And though this tending takes effort, most modern people believe that gardening is quite an improvement over hunting and gathering in the wild. They proudly point out that human beings have very successfully changed plant forms through breeding and selection in order to create optimal crops for themselves. But I sometimes wonder if plants did not "outsmart" us human beings. Did they "train" us to take care of them—and thus make it possible for them to thrive in places they never could have without our help?

According to cultural anthropologists and ethnobotanists, primitive hunters and gatherers had a more leisurely life than sedentary gardening populations did. Even the Shoshone or the bushmen in Africa, whose environments were dry or desert-like, worked not more than two hours a day to cover their daily food needs (Sahlins 1972)—and they still had a well-balanced diet. The whole countryside was their "garden," the gods and nature spirits were the "gardeners." The "harvest" meant the clan merrily swarmed out to gather whatever was ripe at the time. If they even occasionally planted anything themselves, thereby changing the digging stick into a dibble, it was usually in order to cultivate consciousness-changing (psychotropic) plants.

The ancestors of the northern Europeans were similar. Roman historian Publius Cornelius Tacitus (56–117 AD) wrote in his work *Germania* (originally titled *On the Origin and Situation of the Germanic Peoples*) that the uncouth barbarians who lived in the forests north of the Alps were not interested in gardening:[1] "For they strive not to bestow labour proportionable to the fertility and compass of their lands, by planting orchards, by enclosing meadows, by watering gardens. From the earth, corn [grain] only is exacted." About their foods he wrote, "The meals are simple; wild fruit, fresh meat, or cottage cheese" (Tacitus 2012, 23, 26). Grains were preferably eaten as porridge or made into beer. "The Germani," he wrote, "serve an extract of barley and rye as a beverage that somehow resembles an inferior wine." The vegetables these people ate were mostly wild plants and herbs of the season, which were gathered in meadows or on the forest's edge. The seeds of wild plants like plantain seeds, which are rich in protein, were also gathered as "grains."[2]

Nonetheless, the women of these tribes north of the Alps did tend simple gardens, the so-called "leek gardens" (Anglo-Saxon *leac-tún*). All green, juicy plants that were strengthening, especially those believed to increase male potency, were referred to as "leeks" (Old Norse *laukr*). These gardens were fenced off with interwoven hazelnut and willow branches in order to keep out animals, which, for the most part, roamed freely. In addition to leeks these Alpine gardeners grew bear's garlic, peas, Good King Henry (the leaves were used like spinach), lentils, rape, turnips, parsnips, chives, and chard. They also cultivated fruit trees, herbs and greens for seasoning and healing, and poppies for the seeds. The gardens could also have fiber and dyeing plants, such as hemp, linseed, reseda, and woad. It was only after contact with the Romans that the northern peoples developed a real garden culture where they cultivated new kinds of vegetables, such as field beans (or fava beans), red beets, and onions. As the northern cultures became Christianized and came under the reign of Charlemagne (742–814), ever more Mediterranean plants appeared in their gardens. After the discovery of America and the colonizing of many other parts of the world, numerous new and ever more varieties of vegetables came into gardens, settling into them as if nothing could be more natural.

In this book we will take a close look at most of our vegetables, and offer some recipes for whoever would like to try something new. It goes without saying that naturally, organically grown vegetables are the ones that can best unfold their qualities. Vegetables that have been artificially fertilized and doused with herbicides and pesticides, possibly also grown in greenhouses without direct exposure to the sun, moon, and stars, will not have the same full-bodied power as do naturally grown ones.

Food as Medicine: The Healing Power of Common and Rare Vegetables and Wild Plants

Just as cars need to be fueled, occasionally lubricated, and filled with antifreeze in the winter, the human being has to keep his or her bio machine regularly furnished with the right fuel. Despite general awareness regarding mass-produced "junk food," some still claim that it does not matter whether the energy sources (carbohydrates and fats), bodybuilders (proteins) and supplements (vitamins and minerals) come from a fast-food hut, a gourmet restaurant, or an expensive natural health food store—claiming that all that matters is that all necessary nutritional building blocks are present in a balanced meal. According to this mechanistic view—which is, incidentally, still taught in the schools—the main nutritional focus is on the basic ingredients. Such a mechanistic view might work very well for machines, but is it an adequate explanation for the function and nature of living organisms?

A fundamental truth is forgotten in the flood of detailed information, in the elaborate charts showing nutritional values expressed in complicated weights and numbers, and in the often contradictory recommendations of experts. That truth: the food that gives life to animals and people consists of plant substance or, more specifically, of the energy of sunlight that plants absorb with the help of light-sensitive chlorophyll. Green leaves can be described as literal "light traps." The sun's radiant power enables plants to split the carbon dioxide that animals, microorganisms, and fungi exhale into its constituent elements: oxygen (O_2) and carbon (C); and then to combine the carbon with water in order to synthesize it into energy-laden glucose, which is the basis of all organic molecules and the very foundation of all nourishment. By this process an estimated 200 billion tons of biomass are created yearly in the biosphere of our planet.

Aristotle and other ancient Greek philosophers spoke about primal matter as dark, amorphous ur-substance, as *Chaos*. By contrast, they defined *Cosmos* as the orderly, formative power of the heavens. When the instreaming cosmic light permeates Chaos, matter is shaped, formed, and harmonized, and becomes animated and alive.

By the above definition we can understand the role vegetation plays in the drama of creation. Plants are intermediaries. They mediate between heavenly Cosmos and material Chaos. They capture the energy of cosmic light, and use it to vitalize, inform, and animate raw, "nonliving" earthly matter consisting of the primordial elements fire, air, water, and earth. These vitalized elements, in turn, can serve as nourishment for all other living beings. (The harmonizing structuring influence of sunlight on living things can be seen, for example, when we observe how potatoes sprout in dark cellars: pale, deformed, and without direction, they twine about until they happen upon a beam of light coming through a crack; then suddenly the sprouts turn green, straighten up, and begin to grow in an orderly way.)

The moon and the planets also impart structuring impulses. When we eat grains, fruits, and vegetables that have grown in a natural way, i.e., in organic soil and natural sunlight, the structuring photonic energy is also transmitted to our bodies, which, in turn, affects our thoughts and feelings. Obviously, our inner world is not separated from our physical bodies; we are what we eat.

This wonderful process, which science calls photosynthesis, was interpreted in ancient India as a form of meditation: plant entities find themselves in a state of *samadhi*, the blissful state of deepest meditation and oneness with divine origin. Motionless, silent, and rooted in the earth, they surrender themselves completely to the sky and

Illustration 2. San Bushmen (Basarwa): hunter and gatherer in nature's garden

absorb with their green foliage the light that shines down from the sun, moon, and stars. They are thus in a constant state of divine and eternal harmony. According to the *Upanishads,* plants consume cosmic and stellar energies and, in turn, offer themselves for others to eat. "The creatures that live on the earth come into being through food; they live through food and finally they merge into food" (*Anandavalli Upanishad*). Whenever humans beings or animals satisfy their hunger with fruits, roots, leaves, stems, or seeds of a plant, quanta of cosmic light and warmth are converted not just into body warmth, but also into the warmth of feelings, the heat of passion, and at last the inward light of consciousness.

Ultimately, the Rishis and seers in old India interpreted the cosmic light that plants absorb as the shining light of divine love: "Brahma is food. Only he who realizes that he is eating God, truly eats" (*Taittireya Upanishad*). This cosmic light that the plants are constantly meditating on was also perceived as *om,* the primordial, all-pervasive sound emanating from the sun. This primordial light and sound divides, splits, and shatters into countless vibrations—which constitute cosmic harmony. According to these ancient seers, in each vibration a godly being, a deva (the spiritual entity that expresses itself in the plant),[3] or angel, incarnates. In the vision of the seers, cosmic beings can enter the material world in the form of plants. Each kind of plant, each species, is a manifestation of a deva. When people prepare certain plants as meals, healing mixtures, or psychedelics, they make it possible for a certain deva to temporarily leave the macrocosm (external nature) and enter the human or animal microcosm. There it can unfold its properties. In the human microcosm these "angels" and "gods" manifest in various nuances as good health, moods, dreams, thoughts, intuition, and inspiration.

According to this old Vedic belief, even the spirits of the ancestors who wish to reincarnate on earth find their way from the beyond through the vegetables and grains eaten by the man and woman who will beget them. If things are really as the ancient Rishis claim, then it is not surprising how carefully most traditional peoples cultivate and prepare their food. It is not just a matter of assembling the necessary material nutrients: it is a matter of religion, of bonding with the gods, the ancestors, even with the godly Self. The Ayurvedic nutritional doctrine distinguishes three different characteristics (*gunas*) of nourishment, as follows:

1. *Sattva:* foods that are pure and full of cosmic light and also feed the soul with cosmic harmony. Such foods grow in wild nature or are cultivated in an organic vegetable garden. Honey, milk, and dairy products—from naturally held, healthy cows (cows that are free to enjoy sunlight and green pastures, and have not been maltreated with hormones and antibiotics, or had their horns removed)—also belong to this category. It is the proper food of those who meditate and live a quiet life.

2. *Rajas:* foods that further an active life, providing strength and energy. Meat and strong spices fall into this category. It is the nourishment of energetic and active people, including warriors and athletes. Onions, garlic, peppers, and tomatoes are all considered rajasic.

3. *Tamas:* foods that make the body sluggish and the spirit dull. For example, meat from animals that have not been well cared for and are terrified when slaughtered is considered tamasic (to the extreme). Also, vegetables raised under artificial lights and with the help of herbicides and pesticides are tamasic. These are the foodstuffs that sustain the low side of our nature—or even the demonic side. Most assuredly genetically "improved" foods fit into this category as well, since the cosmic influence has been interrupted and chaoticized; such degraded food can only communicate noncosmic information to our bodies.

To a large degree we have the freedom to choose what we eat and which influences we avail ourselves of. It is in our hands to determine whether angels (*devas*) or demons (*rakshasas*) enter our microcosm. Correctly understood, the food we eat has karma in store for us. With *satvic* food (i.e., pure and wholesome), we advance our spiritual development; with *tamasic* food (i.e., old, foul, or unpalatable), we do just the opposite: we promote pessimism, ignorance, laziness, criminal tendencies, and doubt.

Such insights are not unique to Asian cultures, however. There have often enough been voices in Western cultures that verify such maxims. "Show me what you eat, and I will tell you who you are," said the French novelist and gastronomist, Jean Anthelme Brillat-Savarin (1755–1826). In Shakespeare's *Julius Caesar* Cassius asks, regarding Caesar, "Now, in the name of all the gods at once, upon what meat does this our Caesar feed that he is grown so great?" In a lecture a few years ago, the Dutch artist and botanist Herman de Vries listed all the plants to whom he owes his personality and being. The lecture,

Illustration 3. Shiva, who harmoniously incorporates the three Ayurvedic characteristics (gunas) of nourishment—sattva, rajas, tamas

consisting of nothing but plant names—from apple to zucchini—lasted a couple hours. He concluded, "These are the plants that I have eaten and that have made me who I am today." And Rudolf Steiner, the founder of anthroposophy, once said, "We not only eat that which we see before our physical eyes, but we also eat the spiritual essence, which is hidden behind the physical manifestation."

Each plant species, thus, has its own characteristic vibrations that are transmitted to the person who eats them. The elements, the soil, the water, and especially the sun are the basis of these vibrations. The formative forces are obvious: some plants prefer shade, others prefer direct sunlight; some like cool temperatures and others prefer the heat; some open their blossoms early in the morning, others late in the afternoon, and even some wait until after sunset.

We know that the sun has different qualities and effects depending on the time of year or the sign it is in. When it is in Scorpio, Sagittarius, or Capricorn, it is less powerful than when it is in Gemini, Cancer, or Leo. So called "short-day" plants—such as rice, millet, cotton, dahlia, Jerusalem artichoke, chrysanthemum, or soybean—blossom when the sun reaches Virgo and the days start to grow shorter than the nights. Long-day plants—such as carrots, cabbage, fava beans, beets, spinach, or lettuces—need, by contrast, more than twelve hours of sun each day in order to be able to blossom. For this reason, they never reach the blossom stage in the tropics.

Though most plants flower in the summer and bear fruit in the fall, some plants show curious shifts. Food plants, especially grains and fruits, are in harmonious unison with the yearly sun cycle and therefore have a harmonious and energizing effect on us. Plants that blossom in fall and winter, such as autumn crocus and helleborne, have fallen out of the cosmic rhythm—so much so they often prove to have a poisonous, destructive effect on our body rhythms. Under certain circumstances, however, these kinds of plants can be used medicinally, such as to bring on a severe somatic reaction.

The daily cycle is also important for plants. The light spectrum varies with the movement of the sun across the sky. Thus, its effect on the vegetation is different in the early morning hours than it is at other times of day. Plants go into sleep or wake positions, and flowers open or close their buds, or emanate their fragrance or not—all depending on the position of the sun. Traditional herb gatherers and gardeners know this and harvest accordingly. Swedish botanist Carl Linnaeus (1707–1778) planted a floral clock in his garden in Uppsala that was based on this principal; he could tell the exact time of day with it. Similarly there are also "fragrance clocks."

Vegetation is also influenced by its location, especially in terms of its longitude and latitude and the angle of the sunrays hitting it. German poet and plant enthusiast Johann Wolfgang von Goethe (1749–1832) recognized this on his extensive trip to Italy in the late eighteenth century, where he noted that familiar plants growing there looked very different from those in his homeland. More subtle influences are also at work in plant expression, such as conjunctions, oppositions, trigons (triangle constellations), and the position of the moon and the other planets. Indeed, alchemists and medieval doctors drew up entire plant taxonomies on the basis of planetary signatures. By keenly observing the physiognomy of the plants, they recognized which planetary forces—or even which planetary gods—were at work in the respective plant. According to this classification, for example, the red beet was described as belonging to Mars, with a tinge of Jupiter and Saturn involved. The swallowwort or greater celandine, which contains yellow juice that tastes like bile, was ascribed to Jupiter, whose organ is the liver. The sedative effect of this juice was attributed to a slight lunar (Moon) influence. Herbs rich in mucilage, like the mallow or comfrey (*Symphytum*), belonged to Mercury, though, as a bone healer, comfrey was also associated with Saturn. All told, what to us may seem to be a mere expression of superstition was in fact once a useful astrological system of plant classification, one that unfortunately has not survived to today.

Shamanistic Food

We have seen that each plant species has its own specific relationship to the cosmic formative forces manifested in the instreaming light. Each species absorbs a different quality of this light, building it into its cells and tissues along the process of developing its full capacity as, say, a plant for healing, or dyeing, or eating. Philosophers and keen plant observers from many different cultures have concluded that each plant species has its own energies and its own influence on our soul and spirit. For this reason shamans, ascetics (called "*sadhus*" in India), and medicine people are careful to not reduce their diet to a limited plant assortment—and especially not to just what the supermarket shelf has to offer. On the contrary, they very consciously consume a wide spectrum of herbs and vegetables, because they know that a very diverse diet provides a wider spectrum of "information," which makes them more perceptive, more alive, and more healthy.

Anthropological studies indicate the universality of the belief—which is actually more an inner experience than a belief—that each kind of food causes a specific resonance or "attunement" in whoever eats it.

- **Seasonal, Local Vegetable Foods:** If human beings eat what grows in their immediate and natural environment with each season, they will be better able to tune into the invisible and subtle forces that are at work in their ecotope. Such a diet connects with the "spirit" of the land, allowing them to live in harmony with it. This is very important for shamans, who believe that many human diseases result from angered local nature spirits or animals. As such, if we are in tune with our surroundings, we are less likely to be afflicted by the ailments that could befall us.

- **Ancestral Foods:** If people eat the food their ancestors ate (some might call this "soul food"), they will be able to tune into their ancestral spirits, receiving their inspiration and intuition. It is important to be reconciled with our ancestors, who live on in our psyche whether we are conscious of it or not, as this alignment influences our spiritual and physical health. For example, consider how the modern Japanese maintain this tradition. Though they could import less expensive rice, they eat only their own traditional rice. Rice symbolizes a direct connection to their ancestors: each household and Shinto temple offers sake and rice to the ancestors and the gods who, in return, send health, fertility, and vitality. Another example: Dr. D. C. Jarvis, author of the best-selling *Folk Medicine,* advises his fellow New Englanders to eat rye bread, oatmeal, and herring in order to maintain their cultural ethos *and* stay healthy.

The peasant philosopher Arthur Hermes (1890–1986), who taught me so much about these things, made these insights a cornerstone of his life. His garden, which became ever more jungle-like as the summer advanced, had a fantastic variety of vegetables, including rare and formally "extinct" varieties. He talked to the plants, speaking to them in a loud voice as naturally as he did with people. In his cosmology each kind of plant represented a spiritual entity. He sowed and planted in harmony with the stars. Plants meant to develop strong roots, such as carrots and celeriac, were sown and planted when the moon was in an earth sign. Plants that should bring forth fruit and seeds, such as broccoli and sunflowers, were sown and planted when the moon was in a fire sign. Cabbage and leafy vegetables were put in the ground when the moon was in a watery sign, so they would grow lushly. For fertilizer he used only compost, homemade liquid manure (made from nettle or comfrey), and ashes from his wooden fire (in which he burnt nothing unnatural). He never used artificial fertilizer, and often repeated:

> Vegetables that have been pepped up with artificial fertilizer weigh more; they are more waterlogged, which is more interesting for sale by the pound, but they have less divine light-energy. Light has no weight, but it makes the difference in such qualities as nutritive value, natural storage life, and the ability to reproduce. Artificially grown vegetables cannot give us the strength we need in order to think profoundly and with true insight. Such foods have been desensitized to the inherent order they would otherwise assimilate through cosmic light. They also contribute to our own desensitization to cosmic order when we eat them.

He also emphasized, "Sun! The plants need a lot of sunshine! Not only the sun in the sky, but also the 'sun' that shines in our hearts." This "inner sun" consists of the loving thoughts and the tender care we bestow upon the plants. Our interest, our admiration for their beauty, and our appreciation of their fragrance together constitute a kind of "spiritual fertilizer."

Arthur Hermes's garden did not stop at the end of the garden beds; instead it continued on over the hedge and into the nearby meadows and fields where he collected wild plants and herbs for salads and soups. (This approach is similar to the gardening practices of Native Americans and other indigenous peoples.) In his universe "weeds" did not exist; all plants were useful as food, seasoning, or healing. All were the gift of Mother Earth. He valued especially the virtues of these wild plants, and spent time meditating their effect on body and soul. Like a shaman—or a homeopathic doctor testing the healing properties of various plants— he gained new and valuable insights through his meditation: one kind of plant "cools," another kind "warms"; this plant stimulates digestion,

Illustration 4. Sami shaman, Lapland (Johannes Sheffer, A History of Lapland, 1673)

and that plant tones tissue; yet another plant is astringent or calming, and so on.

Another figure who made sure to eat as many wild plants as possible was Bill Tall Bull, medicine man of the Tsistsistas (Cheyenne). He sees each plant, just like each human being, as having four "souls." To his mind the bloated crops that grow in the white man's fields have only three, or sometimes merely two, such souls. Commercial agricultural crops that manage to survive only due to herbicides, pesticides, fungicides, and artificial irrigation are remarkably weak, entirely inadequate for nourishing all four souls of the human being. Whoever eats only such inferior foods will inevitably become dull; though such a person can still function, their finer senses will atrophy. For this reason, according to the old Cheyenne, civilized modern people have no more visions; they cannot understand the language of the animals, or the language of the spirits.

If Arthur Hermes and the old Cheyenne medicine man are right, then the tidings don't bode well for modern humanity. Ethnobotanists tell us that the majority of us derive our sustenance from less than a dozen kinds of domesticated plants. The four most important sources of carbohydrates—wheat, rice, corn, and potatoes—feed more people than the next twenty-six carbohydrate-rich plant species added together, and 90 percent of the earth's population nourishes itself mainly from only twenty plant species. The average American here in the U.S. eats thirty plant species per year and less than fifty in his or her entire life—and that despite the fact that fifteen thousand edible plants grow in the United States (Hartmann, 2000, 58). And as the range of vegetables becomes ever smaller, the packaging becomes ever more colorful and varied. In the last few decades, international oil corporations have bought out most of the smaller independent seed producers. They have since standardized the seeds they cultivate; in doing so they have reduced genetic variety for their economic benefit at the expense of our nutritional benefit—essentially, to our own detriment.

The foodplants that keep us alive have traditionally always had a religious mystique to them. Many food taboos and food preferences are part of one's cultural identity; for instance: the strict vegetarianism of the Indian Jains, the ban on eating meat or beans by the Pythagoreans, or the kosher rules of the Orthodox Jews. Our industrialized refined foodstuffs—TV dinners, microwave meals, fast food, and all the mass-produced, artificially fertilized, pest-controlled, globally transported and genetically "improved" agricultural products—all have their cultural effects too. How? Their consumption supports the officially sanctioned positivistic, materialistic ideology that permeates our society, as these industrial products are hardly capable of opening our spirits to the subtle dimensions of our existence. Fast food and designer foods hamper communication with nature spirits, ancestral spirits, angels, and plant devas, such as are known—according to anthropologists—to traditional cultures all over the world. It follows, then, that anyone interested in opening "chakras" or in maintaining a spiritual view should become aware of this dimension of food. Naturally grown vegetables and wild plants as part of the diet will be helpful, even essential, in such quests. But then again, most people are afraid of such openness.

The Garden

Most full-blooded gardeners have a sort of magical charisma about them. Indeed, gardens themselves are magical places. Despite the popularity of science and agricultural chemicals, many gardeners still plant according to the moon and "talk" to their plants. They like to brew strange liquid manures and place terra cotta figures of gnomes, dwarves, or elves in their gardens, claiming that these give visible expression to invisible elemental forces that help the plants grow and flourish. Gardens are usually fenced off from "the rest of the world," and pathways often lead to a well or a megalith that symbolizes the heart of the garden.

Gardens, vegetable gardens included, reflect the inner character of the gardener and how he or she relates to nature. An old saying goes, "Show me your garden, and I will tell you who you are." In their work gardeners project their souls into their garden, creating, according to Arthur Hermes, a haven for elemental beings and devas. The sight of such a garden can touch the heart of the observer and elicit liberating gasps of appreciation. A well-tended garden pleasantly astonishes, with both its beauty and its healing potential.

Vegetable gardens, like ornamental gardens or parks, ought to be esthetic places, full of blossoms attracting butterflies and songbirds alike. But the intention isn't just for show; in this there is ecological and even utilitarian value as well. The nectar of the flowers, for example, lures hovering flies that devour aphids (plant lice); links such as this contribute to a vibrant, hardy ecosystem.

One way to look at a vegetable garden is to see it as a "landing site" for beings of another (spiritual) dimension to manifest themselves. In harmony with the sun's yearly cycle, the plant beings take on a physical body, grow, go to seed, and disappear again when winter comes. Of course, this is an unusual, rather poetic perspective, but it's also a shared one. Many native horticultural societies have similar views, seeing gardens as places where heavenly beings incarnate in the form of food plants, thus sacrificing themselves so that humans might live. Anthropologists speak in this regard of the "Hainuwele Complex," a concept derived from native horticultural societies in West Ceram, Melanesia. Their myth tells of a heavenly girl named Hainuwele, a goddess, who came down from heaven to visit the earliest humans. During a dancing festival they sacrificed, dismembered, and buried her in the moist earth. Each body part turned into an edible plant. The Iroquois tell a similar tale. Three divine maidens turned into corn, beans, and pumpkins after they fell from the heavens onto the earth. Similar concepts were held by Neolithic Europeans, who saw in their staple crops the sacrifice of the children of the Earth Goddess. At its core even Christianity contains the ancient belief of the sacrifice of the solar divinity and his resurrection into bread and wine.

Illustration 5. Gardener on an old woodcarving

For full-fledged materialists, tales such as these are nothing but superstitious nonsense. But whoever has dealt with plants intensively knows they are very much more than scientific botany—which restricts itself to only external empirical data—can explain. Plants are, as the great plant enthusiast Goethe declared, both sensory and extrasensory beings. They can "talk" to our souls; they can communicate with us in our dreams. They have a very long history of interaction with human beings. The garden vegetables readily lend themselves to being interpreted as plant devas, ones especially friendly to humans.

The Healing Power of Vegetables

The commonly known vegetable plants in our gardens are much more than just primitive life forms capable of producing and storing various carbohydrates, proteins, and compounds that feed and heal us. Plants, be they incarnations of devas or not, have a long history of interaction with our culture. As Richard Grossinger aptly declared in *Planet Medicine* in regard to curative herbs, plants do not just have a botanical identity; each also has a cultural and linguistic identity inseparable from its medical qualities (1990, 33). This is just as true for the vegetables in our gardens. From one generation to the next, traditional kitchen knowledge is passed

Illustration 6. The joy of gardening

on regarding both the nutritional and healing aspects of the garden's produce. For example, women cooked celeriac and served it to their men in order to activate their sexual prowess. Borrage was used to create a cheerful mood as well as for flavoring, and lettuce was cooked to calm members of the household. In other words, gardens were apothecaries full of tried and true cures.

Each vegetable, each herb, even each flower and "weed" can be a healing plant. Each plant that we consume, if correctly prepared, affects our body and how we feel. And as far as our inward bodily balance is concerned, each plant tips the scale in one way or the other. Plants that appeal to us personally deserve our special attention; we should get to know them well, as we never know what we may discover within them.

Join me in getting to know the aphrodisiacal and healing properties, folk tales, garden tips, and recipes of the curious collection of vegetables to be found in these pages.

A NOTE ON ASTROLOGICAL CLASSIFICATION

Since classical antiquity herbalists and gardeners have practiced planetary classification. They categorized plants according to both external characteristics and "signatures"—such as firmness, appearance, and color, as well as the plants' preferred locale—and to inner characteristics like flavor and the physical and mental effect on those who consume them. These herbalists and gardeners then related these impressions to the seven visible planets: Mercury, Venus, Earth, Mars, Jupiter, Saturn, and the moon. (Note that this calculation of "seven" deems the moon a planet, though we classify it as our planet's natural satellite. And as for Uranus, Neptune,

Illustration 7. Meals are sacred rituals celebrating life (late-nineteenth-century print)

and Pluto: as they weren't yet visible, and were thus unknown, they were not part of the astrology of the time.) This volume will use the traditional classification. (More can be read on the subject in my book, *Culture and Horticulure: A Philosophy of Gardening.*) And while each plant obviously has all seven planets at work in it, one planet usually predominates with greater influence. Plus, note that when different authorities discussing a certain plant emphasize one planet more than others, this often concerns a specific use or purpose. For example, a doctor might emphasize one aspect of a plant more than would the gardener, the philosopher, or the dye master—as all have their own special areas of interest.

Common Vegetables

The aim with this book is to provide the reader with a holistic view of the vegetable residents of our gardens. To do this we'll want to consider vegetables in all aspects: their botanical peculiarities, their family membership, the symbology and meaning bestowed upon them in different cultures, the myths and stories concerning them, and their healing potential and general traditional uses. We will do this in parts, starting with common vegetables—from asparagus to Jerusalem artichoke to tomato—before discussing the forgotten, rare, and less-known: both of vegetables (such as burdock, Good King Henry, and skirret) and of lettuce greens (such as miner's lettuce, purslane, and rampion).

For readers fortunate enough to call a vegetable patch their own, I have included invaluable Garden Tips from my friend Larry Berger, a pioneer organic gardening expert with many years of experience. His advice is labeled with an "LB"; those with no label are my own. For those who like to cook, another friend of mine, Swiss gourmet cook Paul Silas Pfyl, has created some novel recipes that perfectly bring out the spirit to be found within each vegetable or lettuce—from both the common as well as the lesser-known varieties.

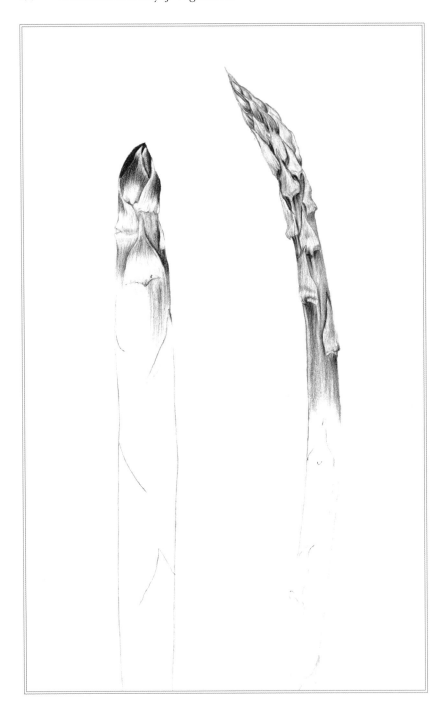

Asparagus (*Asparagus officinalis*)

Plant Family: Asparagaceae: asparagus family; formerly Liliaceae: lily family

Other Names: garden asparagus, sparrowgrass

Healing Properties: cleanses blood, especially for those suffering from rheumatism or bladder, kidney, or heart ailments; rejuvenates energy; promotes urination (diuretic)

Symbolic Meaning: nobility, wealth, refined eroticism; signature of the goddess of love: Aphrodite/Venus, Kamadeva

Planetary Affiliation: mainly Venus and Mars; also Jupiter

In northern Europe asparagus season is a very special time of year. Easter and Pentecost (Whitsuntide), which are celebrated as joyously as is Christmas, would not be complete without a dish of buttered asparagus. As such there are many recipes highlighting this culinary delight.

In early spring, when fresh asparagus begins to appear in the markets in northern Europe, everyone knows that warmer days are just around the corner. This vegetable somehow bears within it the promise of warm summer days after the long, cold winter. The way that asparagus has always been eaten—and in some cases is eaten still—surely makes it what anthropologists call "ceremonial" food: food eaten in a special context. The delicate, fast-growing spring shoots of this Liliaceae family member fit perfectly to the image of nature finally awakening in the spring and to the Easter festival when the Savior was "resurrected." For the Easter dinner asparagus is usually served with ham, and for good reason; while their flavors do complement each other, there is an archaic symbolic

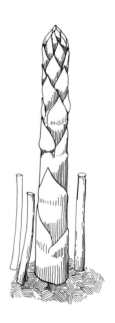

Illustration 8. Asparagus (illustration by Molly Conner-Ogorzaly, from B. B. Simpson and M. Conner-Ogorzaly, Economic Botany, *1986, 120)*

element to the pairing as well. Pigs were once considered a symbol of life, joy, and fertility for the Celtic-Germanic-Slavic northern Europeans. On certain special occasions, Germanic tribes sacrificed a pig or a wild boar for Freyr, the phallic god of fertility and brother of the beautiful goddess Freya. The celestial twins were believed to ride over the countryside in a wagon in the spring, Freya all the while strewing flowers from the carriage. In pre-Christian times people celebrated an orgiastic May festival during the time of the full moon. They raised the phallic maypole, danced rounds, and indulged in ecstatic sensual love. After the Christianization of Europe, this festival was changed into Whitsuntide or Pentecost, celebrating the Holy Spirit who descended upon the people such that they spoke in tongues. For this reason, the Pentecost Sunday meal usually consists of cooked (cow) tongue served with asparagus.

This lacy plant of the lily family is definitely an aristocrat. Cookbooks praise it as the finest of vegetables, and it has been lauded throughout the ages. Modern-day plant expert Fritz-Martin Engel reports: "Pharaohs, emperors, kings, generals, and great spiritual leaders, princely poets such as Goethe and gourmands like Brillat-Savarin—all of them ate and eat asparagus with great enthusiasm." It follows that old astrological herbal doctors saw in asparagus the signature of the god Jupiter, lord and enjoyer of all sensual pleasures.

For the ancient Egyptians asparagus was a sacred food; for this reason they included it in offerings to the gods. Archeologists have found valuable dishware during excavations at the Pyramid of Sakkara (Saqqara) that had food traces clearly identifiable as asparagus. Bundles of asparagus tips—alongside figs, melons, and other sumptuous foods—were also found in the graves of rich Egyptians buried some five thousand years ago. At around the same time in China, honored guests were treated to a relaxing asparagus footbath upon their arrival. Ancient Greeks harvested wild asparagus; the ancient Romans went further, having developed the necessary painstaking garden methods to cultivate this vegetable. Caesar Augustus is supposed to have been especially fond of asparagus—perhaps because the shoots were regarded as one of the greatest aphrodisiacs—and what the emperor does, everyone else does. And historical chronicles report that Emperor Charles V (1500–1558), the ruler of the Habsburg Empire, paid an unexpected visit to Rome during the time of fasting. Since there were not many supplies at hand at such short notice, the cardinal in charge had an idea that saved the day. He had the cooks prepare three different asparagus dishes, served on three different perfumed tablecloths along with three different exquisite wines. It is said that the emperor praised these delicacies for years on end. Asparagus dishes were also cherished at the court of

Illustration 9. In eastern Europe icons are decorated with feathery asparagus fronds (illustration by Molly Conner-Ogorzaly, from B. B. Simpson and M. Conner-Ogorzaly, Economic Botany, *1986, 236)*

the "Sun King," Louis XIV. Whoever wanted to win over Madame de Maintenon, the king's second wife, only had to bring her a new asparagus recipe. She wrote all of the recipes into a book; asparagus *soup à la Maintenon* is still common knowledge for gourmands.

Much of the aura of asparagus concerns its reputation as a rejuvenating aphrodisiac. Indeed, backing this description is the belief that the fast-growing, phallic shoots will increase sexual desire and potency. The ancient Greeks ascribed asparagus to the goddess of love, Aphrodite. The Boeotians made wreaths for brides out of asparagus fronds. The poet Apuleius, author of *The Golden Ass,* is supposed to have won over the heart of the wealthy widow Pudentilla with a love potion containing asparagus, crab tails, fish eggs, dove blood, and a bird's tongue. (The marriage earned him a court case for witchcraft, but he was acquitted.)

Though this fine vegetable was placed under the rule of Jupiter, it does not reside there exclusively. Medieval doctors, not surprisingly, also attributed it to Venus, the planetary goddess who rules over urinary and sexual organs. Consequentially, these doctors prescribed cooking the root in water or wine and drinking it "to increase semen" and stimulate libido. (Galenic *humoral* doctors also prescribed the plant for "obstructions of the liver, spleen, and kidneys," as well as for kidney stones since it was considered "dilutive, diuretic, and dividing.")

Asparagus was regarded as a sex tonic in other cultures as well. The Hindus ascribed it to their "cupid," Kamadeva, who could help a beautiful maiden, young Parvati, beguile even the highest ascetic god, Shiva; this he did by aiding Parvati in distracting the ash-covered ascetic god just long enough for him to fall in love with her. Though he later married Parvati, the extreme yogi Shiva was furious at having his deep meditation interrupted, and burned Kamadvea to ashes with his fiery third eye. Shocked, the goddesses begged Shiva to bring the god of love and sensual desire back to life. Shiva finally conceded and revived Kamadeva, but as he no longer had a body he became even trickier, especially when invisibly shooting his honeyed arrows into hapless hearts.

Traditional Medicinal Use

In the Indian Ayurveda medical tradition, although wild asparagus (*satavar* or *satamuli; sat* = one hundred, *muli* = roots) is also used as a heart and brain tonic, it's generally considered a healing plant for sexual ailments and infertility, especially in that it's thought to increase *ojas*, general life energy. The juice of the roots is cooked with clarified butter (*ghee*), lemon juice, honey, long pepper (*Piper langum*), and milk to create an aphrodisiac that increases semen, increases mother's milk, and tones the uterus. In a similar tradition, Muslims cook the roots (*safed musli*) in milk as a substitute for *salep,* the famous elixir made of orchid bulbs for increasing masculine prowess and for "thickening and increasing semen" (de Vries 1989, 303). And in China, asparagus (known for over five thousand years by the name *Tien men Tong*) is used as a diuretic and expectorant. Asparagus came to America with the European settlers; it escaped from gardens to become a rampant wild plant, an invader growing along roadsides and railroad tracks.

In the seventeenth century asparagus began to be cultivated in central Europe as a vegetable and a medicinal plant; from that time forward it finds mention in herbal books. In the apothecaries the root was called "*official*"—from which comes the botanical name *officinalis*—which means it was in the *officinarum*, the workroom of the apothecaries. This also means that asparagus root was recognized by the Galenic doctors as a proper medicine, specifi-

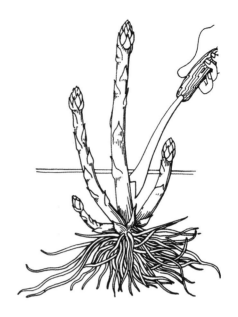

Illustration 10. Aristocratic vegetable asparagus (illustration by Molly Conner-Ogorzaly, from B. B. Simpson and M. Conner-Ogorzaly, Economic Botany, *1986, 236)*

cally for "blood thinning," for "hip pain" (rheumatism, sciatica), hepatitis, kidney stones, and urinary disorders. Pietro Andrea Mattioli (1501–1577), the personal physician of the Habsburg emperor, wrote in his 1544 herbal book: "Asparagus makes men have pleasant desires," a belief also shared among the simpler folk, as a tongue-in-cheek Swabian folk saying goes: "The pastor knows very well why he has asparagus in his garden." In Transylvania it was known as "spindle in the pants." In Styria, Austria, the former home of Arnold Schwarzenegger, wine with asparagus seeds was prescribed for infertility.

In modern phytotherapy, asparagus is still considered to be an effective diuretic. Preparations from the rootstock are made for renal gravel, edema, arthritis, rheumatism, gout, cardiac insufficiency, and liver and spleen ailments. As such, it's effective for diabetes, heart ailments, and lesser kidney ailments.

Garden Tips

Cultivation: Given how difficult it is to grow, asparagus is understandably a costly deluxe vegetable. Each asparagus plant—like a typical aristocrat—needs much more room than do other ordinary vegetables. Because the plant is originally from the eastern Mediterranean, it also needs plenty of sun and warmth. Asparagus grows best in any kind of environment where vineyards thrive. From the sowing of the seeds, which only reluctantly germinate, until the first harvest, four whole years have to pass. In the first year, in "kindergarten," the seeds grow into small plants with buds and thick outrunner roots that look like tarantulas. Each of these spider-like formations should be planted about two feet apart from each other and almost a foot deep. They should then be well covered with sand and humus. The best fertilizer is composted dove or pigeon dung—I can testify for this out of my own gardening experience. (Note that doves are also under the rule of Venus.) At this stage, it is important to make sure the beds remain free of weeds.

Not until three years have passed will this plant of the Liliaceae family finally blossom. Its greenish white blossoms develop into coral red berries, which attract birds. The seeds of the berries, which pass through the birds undamaged, have been thus distributed throughout America, South Africa, and Australia. The red berries hint that Mars, Venus's lover, is also in the plant signature. Occultists and advanced Harry Potter adepts are mindful to collect the berries in the new moon. *Magister Botanicus*, the classic German handbook on plants, reports that in inside circles the berries are sold as "Ferrari testosterone."

In the fourth spring the first harvest begins. And though it is tempting to want it all, it is important to not be too greedy; be sure to leave at least half of the shoots so the plant can strengthen with the sunlight. By summer the shoots develop into four-foot-tall, beautifully delicate fronds. In eastern Europe these fronds are used to decorate religious icons. In Livonia asparagus is called "God's plant"; in Lithuania it is called "sacred plant."

Asparagus can usually be harvested for up to fifteen years before it gets too worn out—at which point one can begin again with a new garden bed and new plants.

Soil: Though it takes a few years to establish a producing asparagus bed—even when grown from roots rather than seeds—if cared for properly an asparagus bed can last for up to fifteen years. The plant prefers a loose, sandy, and somewhat alkaline soil that is also rich in humus, yet it will do well in heavier soils as long as they drain well. Select a sunny corner of your garden, one with rich, deep soil. And note: the heroic measures formerly taken to plant asparagus on soil mounds in eighteen-inch-deep trenches are no longer considered necessary; roots (of the young plants) planted two to eight inches deep do just as well. These planting beds should be well prepared with plenty of powdered limestone and well-rotted manure. Mulch the bed and wait a year before planting, which should produce your first two-to-three-week harvest. After five years, your harvests will likely last for up to ten weeks.

Recipes

Asparagus Dessert with Mallow Blossoms • 4 Servings

3 cups yogurt • 1 pound green asparagus • 2 tablespoons raisins
• 3 tablespoons honey • 2 tablespoons ground hazelnuts
• 1 pinch saffron • 30 mallow blossoms

Put the yogurt in cheesecloth (or a dishcloth) and drain for 12 hours at room temperature. Cut the asparagus into small wheels and steam until soft. Let cool. In a large bowl mix the drained yogurt with the raisins, honey, ground nuts, saffron, and the asparagus wheels. Garnish with mallow blossoms and serve.

Asparagus Tureen with Rhubarb Sauce • 4 Servings

Tureen: 2 pounds (905 grams) green or white asparagus
• 1 pinch marrow from a vanilla bean • herbal salt • pepper
• 7 tablespoons cheddar cheese, grated • 2 eggs, plus 2 egg yolks,
whisked together • ½ cup (115 milliliters) cream (18% fat)

Rhubarb Sauce: 1 cup rhubarb, cubed • 2 tablespoons butter
• 1 tablespoon honey • 1 tablespoon apple vinegar

• ½ cup (115 milliliters) vegetable broth • herbal salt
• pepper • ½ cup (115 grams) sweet basil leaves

TUREEN: Preheat the oven to 350 °F (175 °C). Steam the asparagus with the vanilla and herbal salt until tender. Set aside 8 asparagus spears. Purée the remaining asparagus in a large bowl and pepper to taste. Cool for about 30 minutes. Once it's cool, mix into the asparagus purée the cheese, eggs, egg yolks, and cream. Place the 8 asparagus spears in a 9 by 13-inch ovenproof dish. Cover the spears with the asparagus purée. Place the dish in a larger pan with sides higher than the dish; add water to the height of the contents of the dish. Bake in this water bath, covered, at 350 °F (175 °C) for about 40 minutes. It's ready when golden brown on top. Transfer to a serving tureen.

SAUCE: In a medium pan sauté the rhubarb in butter until nicely blended, about 5 minutes. Add honey. Season with herbal salt and pepper. Add the vinegar and vegetable broth and let simmer for about 20 minutes. Stir in the basil and serve with the asparagus tureen.

Bean (*Phaseolus vulgaris, Phaseolus coccineus, Vicia faba*)

Plant Family: Fabaceae, Leguminosae, or Papilionaceae: bean, legume, or pea family

Other Names or Varieties: navy beans, pinto beans, black beans, kidney beans, lima beans

Phaseolus vulgaris: common bean, green bean, French bean

Phaseolus coccineus: runner bean, scarlet runner bean, pole bean

Vicia faba: fava bean, broad bean, Windsor bean, horse bean, pigeon bean

Healing Properties: lowers damaging LDL cholesterol; regulates the large intestine; promotes urination (diuretic); beneficial for adult-onset diabetes

Symbolic Meaning: souls of the dead, death and rebirth, sexuality, poverty, foolishness

Planetary affiliation: Venus, Saturn

Our common green beans were originally climbers in the South American tropics. Even today, the indigenous natives in South American jungles gather wild beans (*P. aborigineus*) to eat. And yet the bean is actually a poisonous plant. Eating the beans pods or the seeds raw can cause acute stomach cramps, after which the body will try to rid itself of the toxic proteins through vomiting and diarrhea. In the very worst case, the poisoning can lead to a circulatory collapse—and even death.

One would assume that humans would avoid such a toxic plant, but South American natives are absolute masters of plant pharmacology. They've long known how to make poisonous manioc roots (cassave, *Manihot esculenta*), a spurge containing prussic acid, into a main staple. They also boil complicated plant mixtures down to potent arrow poison (curare).[1] And from the bark and leaves of the Ayahuasca liana (*Banisteriopsis esculenta*) they make one of the most potent shaman brews, one that opens the user to the world of the spirits and makes genuine telepathy possible. The magic brew works only when Ayahuasca liana is boiled with other herbs and roots that also contain DMT (Dimethyltryptamine); none of the single ingredients alone has psychedelic properties. The brew is so incredibly complicated in its composition and effect that it cannot have been the result of experimentation, and its secret was not revealed to others until Western researchers cracked it the 1970s. The indigenous people, however, have no use for laboratories and equipment. As ethnologists report, shamans have the ability to communicate directly with the spirit of the plants and inquire of their secrets—be they for medicinal purposes or for the purely nutritional, such as beans being an excellent source of protein.

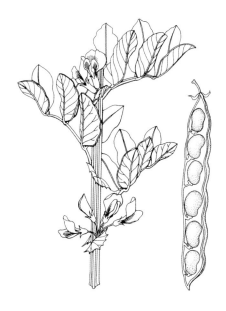

Illustration 11. Original European fava bean (illustration by Molly Conner-Ogorzaly, from B. B. Simpson and M. Conner-Ogorzaly, Economic Botany, *1986, 195)*

The cultivation of the bean was a very long process that took several thousand years to spread over the entire Western Hemisphere. The oldest findings in Peru date back to 6000 BC. Through careful selection, ever more kinds, sizes, and colors were developed over time. It is not surprising that beans in combination with corn became basic daily food of many Amerindian cultures, as they complement each other perfectly. Together they contain all of the essential amino acids needed for nutrition, a combination that can even substitute for meat. This factor greatly benefitted the Aztecs, as the needs of their population eventually outgrew the animal protein that was available, which was mostly turkey and Chihuahuas. (In addition, the warrior class of Aztec society augmented their protein intake with "sacred" cannibalism: war captives whose hearts had been offered to the sun.) To this day beans (*habituelas*) and corn—in the form of *tortillas, enchiladas,* or *tacos*—are the daily fare of Mexicans. *Frijoles,* a kind of baked beans, belong to the culinary identity of Mexico in the same way that hamburgers and fries belong to the United States, or *roesti* (a plate-sized hash brown) to the Swiss.

North American Woodland Culture Indians planted beans, corn, and pumpkins in raised mounds; the corn served as climbing poles for the beans. In the fall, larders were full to the brim with corn, beans, and squash. These natives saw the three cultivated plants as philanthropic goddesses who had fallen from the sky to the earth and taken on plant bodies. The "three heavenly sisters" were celebrated in sacred winter ceremonies. And the Algonquian Indian succotash—corn kernels and beans cooked together—is still a typically American dish, just like roast turkey, corn bread, and pumpkin pie. East Coast baked beans also come to us from Native Americans, who stewed a pot of kidney beans with woodchuck or bear meat (or, later, pig meat) in a pit of hot coals covered with earth, where it was left to bake for twelve or more hours.

As of the sixteenth century the South American "welsh" bean (meaning "foreign" bean) conquered gardens of the Old World. It even slowly but surely replaced the old European fava bean (*Vicia faba*) or broad bean, which had been a crop since the late Neolithic in the Near East and was even identified in the Bible. Fava beans were found in ancient lake dwellings in the foothills of the Alps. Germanic and Celtic peoples grew them in pre-Roman times as both food for people and fodder for animals; this was true especially in the coastal regions where the soil was too salty for peas to thrive (peas being the other favorite source of protein). With the arrival of Indian beans, fava beans became nothing more than fodder for livestock and were degraded to the status of "pig beans," "sow beans," or "cow beans." (It wasn't until the twentieth century that fava beans were rediscovered as cooking beans.) The banishment of the fava bean became even more complete when the whole folklore and healing lore surrounding the Old World species—including the clownish bean songs at festivals celebrating beans during the winter solstice—were also transferred to the new Indian beans.

In Europe beans are generally associated with stupidity, craziness and foolishness. A British expression reflects it: "His beans are in full bloom!" In Northern Germany, a drunkard or crazed person is said to be "in the beans" (*Er ist in den Bohnen*). In English something "isn't worth a bean" or someone is "full of beans." Indeed, the British comedian Rowan Atkinson is well known for his appropriately named Mr. Bean character. And why does the bean have a seam? . . . Because it laughed so hard that it burst and had to be sewn.

The tradition of holding bean festivals at the close of the year dates as far back as the Saturnalia festival in ancient Rome. In very ancient Roman times, the Saturnalia King (the one who got the piece of cake with a bean it in) was chosen one month before the end of the festival. Once taking office, he was celebrated as the incarnation of a god, allowed to indulge his desires, passions, and moods without restraint. The drawback to this ritual was that on the evening of the festival his reign ended, at which point he had to cut his throat as a sacrifice in front of the altar of Saturn! The Saturnalia is an obvious extension of the archaic chaos and fertility festivals known from pre-Roman Mediterranean cultures—which include sacrifices and orgies that we cannot understand from our modern perspective. During such festivals, borders between our human world and the extrasensory world, this world and "the other world," are obliterated. The dead come closer to the living, transmitting energies and power necessary for new life and reincarnation.

Saturnalia was also a time when usual taboos were suspended. Masters and slaves traded places, men and women changed roles, all rules were broken, and there was no lack of sensual joy and abandon—with orgies not uncommon during the festivities. For the old Romans, the merriment was dedicated to the grandfather of the gods, Saturn. Saturn carries a bag of seeds and a scythe, as he had given people the first seeds and taught them agriculture. He also rules over times of downfall, whether in world epochs, in the yearly cycle, or in the life of the individual.

Other agriculture peoples celebrated similar festivals to ensure the fertility of the fields, the cows, and the tribe. For example, the Iroquois and Algonquian had a midwinter fools festival during which the invisible gods of the food plants possessed the people, temporarily robbing them of their senses.

Carnival-like festivals similar to the old Roman Saturnalia are still celebrated in all of western Europe around the time of the winter solstice. In Holland, for Three Kings' Day or Epiphany (January 6) a cake is baked with a bean in it. Whoever gets the piece with the bean becomes Bean King or Queen; the lucky one chooses a mate, and the two get royal treatment during the evening's dancing and feasting. The partygoers freely consume alcohol and enjoy pranks and tomfoolery, and everyone enjoys laughing about the whole scale of human stupidity on display. Like with Saturnalia, the usual taboos are lifted, including sexual ones. A verse of a bean song from eighteenth century Hamburg goes like this: "You young fellows, you don't have to try to ensnare those young ladies with your beans and the taut ham between your thighs" (*Ihr Junggesellen müsst nicht den Jungfern Netze stellen mit euren Bohnen und wohl gar mit eurem prallen Schinkenpaar*). An Alemannic bean song ends each verse with the refrain: "Now go on and get the heck out of the beans." In Germany people still say, "That goes even beyond the bean song (*Das geht übers Bohnenlied*)" when something has gone over and beyond what is socially acceptable. In modern European bean celebrations the participants might lift up the bean king so that he can write, with chalk on a ceiling beam, CBM (the initials of Caspar, Balthazar, a ritual believed to drive off all the bad spirits). This custom was originally dedicated to the Celtic *Matronae*, the three goddesses, who blessed all homes at the end of winter solstice celebration.

In modern carnivals there remain only a few remnants referring to beans and the role they used to play. In such festivities a carnival king and queen are usually chosen via a method particular to the region, and many comedians present sketches about stupidity—much of which is televised. Such events are still considered a time for the social vent—when people can joke about taboos and say things they might otherwise not to say. In all, very few know the prominent role the bean once played during the festivities of former times—though in some areas a bean baked in a cake still determines the lot, and some bean songs have survived to this day.

Illustration 12. The bean king (Otto von Reinsberg-Düringsfeld, Traditions et Légendes de la Belgique, 1870)

In many places beans were considered appropriate food offerings for the spirits of the dead. Beans were found in Egyptian graves (Fifth Dynasty, 2500 BC) as well as in prehistoric burial sites in Peru. Beans, along with peas, millet, hazelnuts, and hempseed, were also the preferred food offerings for the dead of the Germanic, Celtic, Baltic, and Slavic peoples. They were also convinced that the enjoyment of pulses—the edible seeds of various legumes—increased carnal desire in the living, thus making it easier for the departed ancestors to reincarnate.

After the Christianization of these cultures, though broad beans became a major food for the time of fasting (Lent), they were otherwise not favored. Until long past the Middle Ages people avoided eating beans during the time of the winter solstice—even though the legume had formerly been such a favorite food at that time of year. In a curious shift in belief, beans were thought to cause infertility or dreadful nightmares. An old superstition deems that dreaming of beans announces hardship, discord, or even death in the family. If a bean plant suddenly got white leaves (chlorosis), it meant a death would occur in the family. It was believed that one could even curse an enemy to death with the help of dried beans. To do this, one chanted a spell for seven weeks, throwing three beans each day over the shoulder and onto the dung pile where they—just like the unfortunate target—would rot.

Beans were an integral part of ancient death rituals throughout history. For the Greeks, bean blossoms were a symbol of death. Homer called beans "the nourishment of (fallen) heroes." In the evening of the May full moon, when the spirits of the dead (*lemures*) descend down to the earth, the Roman head of the household walked through his house strewing nine black beans while saying: "With this, I buy myself and my kin free!" Another Roman bean festival, Fabaria, celebrated on the first day of June, honored Carna, the goddess of death. The Romans offered her beans and bacon so that she might protect them from vampires of the night seeking to suck out their lives in their sleep.

Because of the long-held association of beans with sexuality and the dead—it was generally believed that beans contained the souls of the dead—priests of old considered them impure. Indeed, Egyptian priests were not allowed to touch beans, and Roman flamen—priests who maintained the fires at sacrificial ceremonies—weren't allowed to even mention them. And both Orphic priests and Pythagoreans were forbidden to eat beans, as these mystics claimed that eating beans would be "like eating the head of one's own parents." The sense of taboo was so strong that a group of Pythagoreans even let themselves be mowed down by soldiers rather than escape by running through a bean field. Given this context, we can better understand a comment of the philosopher Diogenes of Sinope (412–323 BC): "Beans are mainly made up of the substance which accounts for animation in human beings."

In ancient Greece voting was conducted with white and black pebbles or beans; winners were those granted the most white beans. (Consider too the phrases "spill the beans" and "bean counter.") Beans were particularly used in the elections of magistrates. Why? Because the dead were believed to live in them, and the wise ancestors, who know much that remains unknown to the living, should help decide who is worthy of office. But how did the Greeks and other peoples come to presume that souls live in beans? The French ethnobotanist and classicist Jacques Brosse (1922–2008) would reply that one need merely to open a bean pod to find the answer, as beans looks like embryos. Indeed, the Greek word for bean, "*kyamos*," comes from the verb "*kyeo*" (to carry in the womb).

Not surprisingly, beans played a part in choosing the victim in the archaic Hellenic tradition of sacrificing one of their own at year's end—a tribute to the dying year that looked to life's revival out of the earth in the coming spring. As drawing the lot of the bean determined who would be sacrificed, it was believed that the spirits of the dead themselves influenced the selection. After all, the bean symbolized the "embryo" of the New Year—the "New Year's Baby"—whose life on earth begins after the winter solstice.

Rudolf Steiner (1861–1925) wrote that beans have something animated, something "astral" (ensouled) about them. The roots of beans and other legumes have little knots in which live symbiotic nitrogen-binding bacteria (mycorrhizae). Steiner calls nitrogen (N), which legumes greedily absorb, "incarnation substance for astral realms" since no animated beings, no soul, can incarnate without this element. Indeed, "animals" are animated souls (from the Latin *anima*). The proteins in animals contain large amounts of nitrogen—in contrast to plants, who are mostly made of carbohydrates: that is, carbon, hydrogen, and oxygen.

Illustration 13. Oldest sketch of the bean plant (Leonhart Fuchs, De Historia Stirpium Commentarii Insignes, *1543)*

Generally, plant "souls" remain nonincarnated and in "other realms"; only when flowering do plant souls fleetingly take on physical appearance. But beans and other legumes contain so much protein that one could call them "animal plants"—and, as mentioned earlier, that they can be a nourishing substitute for meat.

Beans (Fabaceae), whether *Phaseolus* or *Vicia,* reveal themselves as especially animated ("astralized") in other ways, too. They do not blossom actinomorphically (in round disks) like, for example, daisies or sunflowers. Instead they bloom zygomorphically (with double symmetry), having a top and bottom, a front and back, like orchids or pansies—and more like animals. The corolla of the Fabaceae blossom reminds us of a butterfly. Indeed, that is why the scientific name of this plant family is also *Papilionaceae,* from the Latin word for butterfly, "*papilio.*" But the similarity to animals extends beyond just appearance. Though we associate mobility, or animation, with animals, not plants, beans present an exception to this rule. Pole beans, which grow quickly, spiral around vertical supports, and the leaves fold up at night. Their filaments, which carry pollen-bearing anthers, are also capable of animal-like movement so they can pollinate the pistil when insects fail to do so. Interestingly, it's the sheer fact that these plants are animated, or astralized, to this extent that makes them usually poisonous; as such they are best not eaten raw or undercooked.[2]

Traditional Medicinal Use

What kind of healing energy is contained in this unusual garden dweller? Medieval doctors saw the signature of Venus—the planetary goddess who rules over the urinary and sexual organs and is also responsible for physical beauty—in the white blossoms and the shape of the seeds (which look like kidneys, embryos, or testicles). The English herbal doctor Nicholas Culpeper (1616–1654) noted about preparations with fava beans (*Vicia*): "The distilled water of the flowers is good to cleanse the skin and face from spots and wrinkles. The water distilled from the green husks is held to be effectual against the stone, and to provoke urine. . . . Bean flour, boiled to a poultice with wine and vinegar and some oil put thereto, easeth both pains and swelling of the testicles." He recommends an external application of ground beans mixed with fenugreek seeds and honey for rashes, bruises, and contusions. He also ascribes a diuretic and kidney strengthening effect to the "French bean" (*Phaseolus*).

These indications are basically still true today. Phytotherapists prescribe a diuretic, uric acid–reducing decoction from the dried pods of green beans (*Phaseolus*) for rheumatism and fluid retention. Such a decoction is also still used today against the onset of adult diabetes; the guanidine derivative has an insulin-like effect. Bean flour poultices (mixed with honey and oil) are still used successfully today for all kinds of swellings and lumps. Skin rashes can be treated with dried and ground bean pods applied as a fine powder. Native Americans treated lumbago with hot poultices of cooked, mashed beans.

Recent research shows that beans are good for us in other respects, too. Beans can cause gas ("Beans, beans, the musical fruit . . ."), but they also help regulate the function of the large intestine, prevent constipation, and help prevent hemorrhoids. They help reduce damaging LDL cholesterol and blood sugar levels, and like many pulses they contain cancer-inhibiting protease, which gets released once they reach the intestines.

Garden Tips

Cultivation: Pole beans have preferences similar to bush beans. Pole beans require a longer time to mature, but the yield is higher and they need less space.

Before planting, briefly presoak your beans for a few hours in water with the addition of a nitrogen inoculant, such as in water in which a cow pie has been soaking. This will ensure that the beans sprout faster and continue to grow steadily. When plants are about three inches high, thin them to about four to six inches apart. Cultivate lightly with a hoe so as not to disturb the shallow roots. Light mulch may be applied after the plants are thriving. For best texture and flavor, beans should be picked before they are fully mature. Regular picking is important since the plant will stop producing if the seed is allowed to mature. The traditional method of planting pole beans is to drive seven-foot stakes into the ground, mounding up some soil around the base, and planting six (inoculated) seeds in the hill around each pole.

Soil: Bush beans, also called snap beans, can thrive in almost any soil from light sand to heavy clay. Pole beans have the same requirements but can withstand even heavier soils than can bush beans. Bush beans are a most rewarding crop, as they are easy to grow, productive, and simple to harvest. Note that bean seeds need warm soil in order to sprout; in cold soil they will rot.

Of Special Note: Instead of making one large planting of beans, make several plantings at two-week intervals. This will assure a continuous supply of beans throughout summer and early fall. All beans fix nitrogen in the soil and therefore are valuable soil builders. When clearing the finished bean plants, cut them off at soil level and leave the roots in the ground. As the nitrogen is fixed in the roots, in the following year one can grow nitrogen-loving vegetables where the beans had been. (LB)

Recipes

Green Bean, Potato, and Dried Prune Stew • 4 Servings

1 pound (455 grams) potatoes, peeled or unpeeled, diced
• 12 onions, coarsely chopped • 2 tablespoons butter
• 2 pounds (905 grams) green beans
• 1 quart (945 milliliters) vegetable broth
• some fresh summer savory • 12 dried prunes
• 1 to 2 garlic cloves, to taste • sea salt • black pepper

Sauté the potatoes and onions in butter for about 10 minutes, until golden brown. Add beans and sauté briefly together, then add broth, summer savory, dried prunes, and garlic. Cook on low heat until done. Add salt and pepper to taste.

TIP: The stew tastes best if steeped for about an hour after cooking, but should still be served hot.

Green Beans in Garlic Butter • 4 Servings

20 (or fewer) whole peeled garlic cloves • 6 tablespoons butter
• 2 pounds (905 grams) green beans • ½ cup (115 milliliters) vegetable
broth • sea salt, pepper • 4 tablespoons sour cream • 1 teaspoon paprika

Gently sauté garlic in butter for about 20 minutes. Add the beans and vegetable broth, cover, and let simmer for about 30 minutes or until tender. Add salt and pepper to taste, then stir in sour cream and paprika.

TIPS: Leave garlic cloves whole as they taste better this way and develop their full aroma. • Try long pepper instead of common black pepper; it has a fine smoky flavor and smells delicately of cinnamon, clove, and nutmeg. • This dish pairs nicely with baked potatoes.

Broad Beans with Goat Cheese and Stinging Nettle or other Wild Greens • 4 Servings

1 pound (455 grams) broad beans/fava beans (removed from husks)
• 1 tablespoon red wine vinegar • 3 tablespoons olive oil
• 1 medium onion, finely chopped • chives, finely chopped (to taste)
• herbal salt • black pepper • 1½ cups (340 grams) fresh goat cheese
(or cottage cheese) • 4 tablespoons stinging nettle (or cress),
very finely chopped • cress, finely chopped (for garnish)

Put beans in boiling, salted water for 4 to 6 minutes, then drain. Put drained beans in fresh water and bring to a boil. When the beans are tender, remove them from the pot and let cool; pour out the water. While the beans cool, add vinegar and olive oil to the pot and mix; add onions, chives, and salt and pepper to taste. Add the beans to this mixture and marinate for 1 hour. If using fresh goat cheese: shape the cheese into small patties; roll them in stinging nettle or cress until well covered. (If using cottage cheese: mix the herbs into the cottage cheese and serve as a side dish.) After the beans have marinated, place them on a plate and garnish with the cress; serve with the goat cheese patties or herbal cottage cheese.

TIP: This dish pairs nicely with freshly baked dark bread.

Bell Pepper and Chili Pepper (*Capsicum annuum, C. fructescens*)

Family: *Solanacea:* nightshade family

Other Names: green pepper, sweet pepper, cayenne pepper, ornamental pepper

Healing Properties: taken externally: topical applications warm and relax muscle tissues, reduce pain; ideal for rheumatism and lumbago taken internally: stimulates blood circulation, thins the blood; increases stomach digestive juices and lessens nausea (as such supports alcohol withdrawal); induces sweating; lowers fever; reduces pain; strengthens the immune system

Symbolic Meaning: incarnates the fire power of hot summer: awakens zest for life; generates inner cleansing; protects against evil eye/ sadness; stokes creative energy

Planetary affiliation: Mars

How to describe peppers? Some are colorful—bright yellow to deep red— crispy, fleshy pepper fruits that make a feast for the eyes. Some are the more or less hot and spicy peppers that pep up soups and meats. They are abundantly available in supermarkets and are found in the plots or green houses of enthusiastic gardeners who pamper them into thriving. The many kinds of *Capsicum*—from those with lip-burning long pods to the fleshy sweet ones and mild—all belong to the same genus as part of the nightshade family. They love the summer heat and need a temperature of at least 66 °F (19 °C) in order to blossom—otherwise there will be no fruit. In the tropics they are perennials, just as tomatoes are, but in northern climates they are annual plants perforce. The "pods," which are actually berries, contain plenty of vitamins—mainly vitamin C and provitamin A—and the spicy substance capsaicin (from the Greek *capto,* to bite), which can still be tasted in dilutions of 1:2,000,000.

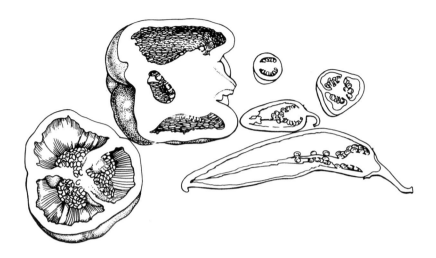

Illustration 14. Bell pepper and chili pepper cut in half

Many people associate the pepper with Hungary—and for good reason. The word "paprika" is Hungarian, though it derives from the Serbo-Croatian word "*papar*" (pepper). Indeed, paprika is at least as intimately connected to the Hungarian soul as, for example, cucumber with the Polish soul, cabbage with the German soul, or potato with the Irish soul. Peppers—some pale and mild, some bright and hot—are echoed in Hungarian music, which often ranges from soft and melancholy to passionate, even ecstatic. And the character of this plant fits very well with the formerly wild, shamanistic horse-riding people from the western Asian steppes that settled in the Danube River area in between agricultural Slavs and Germanics. The Hungarians believe that peppers protect from the evil eye and wicked vampires. For example, pepper pods are put under the pillows of women in childbirth in order to protect them. But the strongest association derives from the fact that paprika is the Hungarian national seasoning, used in their famous goulash, salami, and gypsy schnitzel. Hungarian gardeners naturally cultivated a whole pallet of various kinds of paprika, and Hungarian scientists have vigorously studied their "soul plant." In fact, Albert Szent-Györgyi (1893–1986), director of the Institute of Medical Chemistry at the University in Szeged, was the first to prove that paprika contains four to six times the vitamin C found in lemons or oranges.

Despite all of this, pepper did not come to Hungary until shortly before the eighteenth century. Legend tells that a Hungarian water-carrier named Ilona smuggled some of the "Turkish pepper" fruits from Ottoman governor Pasha Mehmed's flower garden in Buda. The Turks, who also cherish the fiery plant, had gotten it from the Spanish, Sicilians, or Portuguese in the sixteenth or seventeenth centuries—and they, in turn, had learned of pepper from Native Americans.

Toward the end of the Middle Ages Europeans were addicted to exotic spices, especially black pepper. But the export trade in spices was controlled by middlemen Arabs, who monopolized the ports of Venice and Genoa and charged shockingly high prices. It was precisely high demand for expensive exotics that prompted Christopher Columbus to sail west in search of India. Of course, Columbus did not reach India, and he did not find black pepper, but he did find red pepper; he and his crew were the first Europeans to do so. This occurred on January 15, 1493, on the island of Haiti. The maritime explorers did not like the hellish hot peppers the Haitian natives called "*ají*," but it is said that on the return trip Columbus did eat dried peppers as treatment for heartburn or chest constriction. On the admiral's second trip, the ship's doctor, Dr. Chanka, took some seeds—which he prescribed for migraine—back to Spain. And under the hot Spanish sun the plant thrived. In this way, "Spanish pepper" began its long world journey, and soon found its way into African kitchens, where the sharpest and spiciest kinds are cultivated, and into Indian and Indonesian cooking, where it is used in curries and sambals. Interestingly, India, the country of black pepper, is today the biggest producer of red pepper, specifically extremely sharp capsicum.[1]

Archeological finds indicate that peppers have been cultivated for at least seven thousand years in tropical America. In Mexico alone over seventy kinds are still cultivated—about one-third milder varieties and two-thirds hotter. It's the spicier strains that give such dishes as chili con carne, tamales, and other Mexican culinary delights their typical flavor. ("*Chili*" is the Aztec's Nahuatl word for pepper.) Indeed, the Aztecs peppered all their

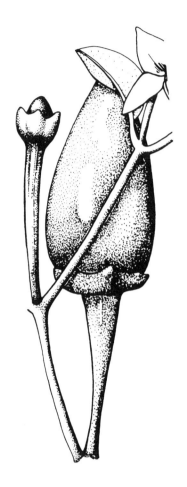

Illustration 15. Chili pepper

meat with the fiery seasoning—such as Chihuahua meat (the maize-fed dogs were raised as we raise chickens), turkey, and other game. Some scholars claim that the upper classes also cannibalized the enemies captured in the "flower wars," who were sacrificed in rituals performed atop the temple-pyramids. With obsidian knives they cut out the victim's beating heart, offering it to the sun god Huitzilopochtli as food; later the victim's head was placed in the temple. Some contend the victims' torsos were served to the elite in a spicy pepper and tomato stew garnished with squash leaves; other scholars consider incidents of Aztec cannibalism to be much more the exception than the rule.

Another misappropriated origin tale of the pepper concerns Tabasco sauce, named after a river in Mexico. But the hot sauce was actually the discovery of Edmund McIlhenny (1815–1890), a New Orleans banker who fled the Yankees during the Civil War. After the war he came back to what little remained of his sugar cane plantation and villa. With nothing left to harvest but a crop of Mexican pepper pods, McIlhenny mixed the chili peppers with vinegar and salt and steeped the brew in oak barrels. He later sold perfume jars filled with the devilish-smelling brew to a large distributor, whereafter it became a culinary hit. And the name *Tabasco?* The entrepreneur simply loved the sound of the name (Panati 1987, 404–405).

Traditional Medical Use

Peppers play a significant role in the cuisines of tropical countries because they have a bacteria-killing quality that keeps foods from spoiling too quickly. The spicy ingredient capsaicin simultaneously discourages intestinal parasites and stimulates digestive juices in the stomach, which helps in the digestion of carbohydrate-rich foods commonly found in developing countries. The hot spices also induce sweating, which vaporizes on the skin and cools the body.

But there is another reason that people love this vegetable, whose biting sharpness nearly burns the mouth and draws tears to the eyes. In 1992 Australian scientists at the Commonwealth Scientific and Industrial Research Organisation (CSIRO), reported that our reaction to extreme spice is in reality an impression of pain, which triggers the body's opiates—essentially feel-good endorphins. Some people in fact become addicted to hot spices (Dayton, 1992). (This knowledge is, however, not really as new as it may seem: the 1741 edition of *Württemberger Pharmacopeia* cites: "Spanish pepper has a caustic effect and therefore lessens pain in inner organs").

For thousands of years Native Americans have discovered many medicinal properties of this nightshade plant. Aztecs found peppers to energize the body, strengthen the stomach, and encourage flatulence—as well as to serve as a diuretic, laxative, and sexual stimulant. They made an expectorant tea of the leaves for asthma and breast pain. From the roots they made a tonic for stomach pain and colic. Rashes were treated with hot urine and paprika powder. Incas and other Peruvian Indians drank corn beer (*chicha*) seasoned with hot peppers for constipation and as a diuretic and aphrodisiac. For the Mayans hot pepper was known as a heal-all used in different preparations for tuberculosis, sore throat, diarrhea, cramps, blood in the stool or in the urine, coughing blood, delayed afterbirth, black widow bites, rheumatism, hemorrhoids, dizziness, skin ailments, and toothache. For earaches the blossom was rubbed between the fingers and wrapped in cotton blossoms and then put into the ear. For bone pain and cramps paprika leaves were cooked and added to a bath. Hot peppers were also rubbed into wounds or onto boils: though the ensuing pain was so strong that the patient often fainted, it was claimed that the bad "magic" that had caused the disease could be killed in this way.

Everywhere Native Americans used chili pepper for fevers—not so much to lessen the fever but to support the fire of life, to energize and to bring the strength of the sun back into the body. During sweat baths cayenne pepper tea supported the effects of the heat. For flu South American aboriginals drink spicy corn beer to increase sweating—which we know today is a sensible cure. The heat, combined with the effect of hot pepper, has a strong stimulating effect on the immune system. This method was the core of the medical reform movement of Samuel Thomson (1769–1843) in the nineteenth century. These patients were given a hot tea with a purgative in it containing cayenne pepper, lobelia, and various herbs for the specific sickness. A portion of the tea was also administered as an enema. After the resulting purge the patient was given a steam bath followed by a cold shower. As these methods often brought about spectacular cures, such approaches are finding their way into modern natural healing as well.

Illustration 16. The Spanish land in Haiti (medieval woodcut)

In Mexico today paprika plants are still used to cleanse (*limpia*) the body of evil spirits or curses by rubbing the body with pepper fruits. (In age-old country practices European grandmothers added so-called "spell plants" to the baths of children who'd been cursed.) The limpia is prescribed for a number of

Illustration 17. A Peruvian woman cooking peppers

conditions: when the evil eye has been cast upon someone; when someone is affected by the *aires*—the cold, sickening wind from the ghosts of
the dead, wicked witches, or from wee men who dwell in caves or near
springs; or when someone has been "shamed" (as in public mortification,
dishonor, or ridicule) or "saddened" (as in depression). As many Mexicans
believe all of these states can lead to vomiting, diarrhea, nervousness, or
sleeplessness. Hot chili peppers are applied to burn the negative energy.

Of course, this ancient vegetable is also a magical and ritual plant. For
the Guayupe Indians in Venezuela, for example, after a couple had their
second child the father would retreat alone, fast, and then wash his entire
body with a pepper brew; it was thought that if he did not perform such
austerities the child would die. This Indio tribe allowed only virginal girls
to sow the pepper seeds; otherwise, they believed, the seeds would not
germinate. The Chibcha tribes in Colombia doused hot chili brew into
the eyes of adulterers. Orinoco Indians rubbed hot chili salve into their
arrow tips. European magicians and witches on the order of Harry Potter
make an amulet out of green pepper seeds to strengthen their own energy.
And, as mentioned earlier, pepper serves as an aphrodisiac; according to

the Magister (Master) Botanicus, a modern school of magical herbalism in Germany, it makes us "hot."

Modern phytotherapy recommends a *capsici* tincture be rubbed into the joints for rheumatism. Cayenne tincture is also used to help alcoholics overcome their addiction. New research shows that pepper also helps lower cholesterol levels, as the spicy seasoning stimulates circulation and dissolves coagulated blood in the arteries. The hot power of chili peppers is also said to combat winter depression (seasonal affective disorder). Some even claim that, used as a flower essence, cayenne stimulates fire; its resulting energy helps to remove blockages so that the soul can develop (McIntyre 2012: 252).

Garden Tips

Cultivation: Pepper seeds should be started in a well-lighted greenhouse or a protected room for about ten weeks before they are transferred outside to a very sunny spot after there is no more danger of frost and the air and soil temperature remains above 50 °F (10 °C). Mulch around the plants to keep the soil moist and the weeds down. (LB)

Soil: All pepper varieties like rich compost in the soil; magnesium and phosphorus are especially important.

Recipe

Bell Peppers Stuffed with Hummus • 4 Servings

Bell Peppers: ¾ cup (175 grams) chickpeas, cooked • 4 tablespoons almond butter • 2 tablespoon sesame oil • 1 teaspoon coriander powder • 1 tablespoon lovage leaves, finely chopped • 2 tablespoons parsley leaves, chopped • 8 tablespoons sunflower seeds, soaked in water • paprika • herbal salt • pepper • 4 bell peppers (preferably green), tops cut off as lids, cored, seeds removed • Chili Garlic Sauce: 1 cup (225 milliliters) olive oil • 2 to 3 garlic cloves • 2 to 3 chili peppers, cored and cut into strips • a few drops of lemon juice

Sᴀᴜᴄᴇ: Put all the ingredients in a small sauce pan and simmer, covered, on lowest heat for about 4 hours. Let cool. Drizzle some sauce on the stuffed peppers. (See also TIP below.)

Bᴇʟʟ Pᴇᴘᴘᴇʀs: Note that the peppers can be eaten raw or baked. If you choose to bake them, preheat the oven to 350 °F (175 °C). In a medium bowl, mash the cooked chickpeas; mix in the almond butter and sesame oil. Add the coriander, lovage, parsley, and sunflower seeds. Season to taste with paprika, herbal salt, and pepper. Fill the prepared bell peppers with this mixture. Bake at 350 °F (175 °C) for 40 minutes or until peppers are tender; alternatively, they can be eaten at room temperature. Serve drizzled with the garlic sauce.

TIP: The sauce is best prepared in a larger quantity, as such produces a more intense flavor. The quantities for 1 quart Chili Garlic Sauce is as follows: 1 quart (945 milliliters) olive oil • 20 garlic cloves • 20 chili peppers, cored and cut into strips • 1 teaspoon lemon juice • Put all the ingredients in a large pan and simmer, covered, on lowest heat for about 4 hours. Once the sauce has cooled, pour it into sterilized jars; store the sealed jars in a cool place. The sauce will keep well for a few months.

Cabbage Family (*Brassica oleracea*)

Plant Family: Brassicaceae or Cruciferae: mustard family

Other Names and Varieties: chou, cole, colewort, green cabbage, kale, karam kala, purple cabbage, red cabbage, repollo, vitamin U (S-Methylmethionine), white cabbage

Family Includes: broccoli, Brussels sprouts, cauliflower, Chinese cabbage, pointed cabbage, Savoy cabbage, collard greens, kale

Healing Properties: taken externally: fresh leaf poultices help heal abscesses, burns, neuralgia, onychia, phlegmon, rubella/German measles, shingles/herpes zoster, tumors, uterus infection, persistent wounds taken internally: cabbage juice soothes stomach and duodenal ulcers, prevents gall bladder infection; sauerkraut juice reduces arteriosclerosis, cleanses blood, detoxifies body, strengthens immune system, regulates intestinal flora

Symbolic Meaning: dullness; excessive vitality, Jupiter-like abundance; opponent of drunken Dionysus; St. Bartholomew

Planetary affiliation: moon and Jupiter; sharp-tasting seeds and red cabbage: Mars; Savoy cabbage: Mercury

The wild form of cabbage still grows as a thick-leafed plant along the coasts of the Mediterranean and the North Sea. On the island Helgoland in the North Sea, which was a sacred place for the Vikings, wild cabbage especially displays its natural beauty. A wax-like layer protects the fleshy leaves from salty fog, and biting frosts. The cold-resistant mustard oil glycosides prevent winter ocean winds from harming the plant. The beautiful flowers are as yellow as sulfur.

Stone Age hunters cherished the nourishing leaves as a vegetable and the seeds for oil. It's an "anthropochore" vegetable—meaning it is distributed by humans, whether deliberately or accidentally. Wild cabbage found a perfect niche growing as a weed on the trampled and bare soils near human settlements fertilized with nitrogenous waste, such as food leftovers and the urine and feces of humans and animals. Gardeners gradually experimented with the plant until there were many variations—from pot-bellied kohlrabi to tree cabbage, which can grow up to seven feet tall. Pointed cabbage, Savoy cabbage, red cabbage, white cabbage, Brussels sprouts, broccoli, cauliflower, and kale all belong to the same species: *Brassica oleracea.* Mild, pale Chinese cabbage (*B. pekinensis*), the robust bok choy or pak choi (*B. chiniensis*), and turnips (*B. rapa*) are closely related, as they belong to the same genus.

Cabbage is, so to speak, the dog amidst the vegetables. Like no other animal, dogs have let themselves be tamed, trained, and bred into various shapes and sizes—from the Chihuahua to the Great Dane—by meddling humans; the same can be said of cabbage. Celtic peasants in central Europe took special care to cultivate the wild plant into a vegetable staple. As such, almost all the names for this plant are of Celtic origin: *kol, kal, kap,* or *bresic*—which became the Latin word "*brassica.*" The Celtic names later traveled all the way to Asia; the Tatars call cabbage "*kapsta*"; in Hindu lands, it's called "*kopi*" or "*ghobi.*" Jacques Cartier (1491–1557) first brought cabbage to the Americas circa 1541. Though there is no written record until the mid-seventeenth century, it can be assumed that both the settlers and Native Americans planted cabbage, as eighteenth

Illustration 18. The many forms of cabbage (John Parkinson, Paradisi in Sole Paradisus Terrestris, 1629)

century records indicate its cultivation in both cultures. Cabbage seeds came to Australia in 1788, where they were planted on Norfolk Island. By the 1830s it had become an Australian favorite.

Cabbage was a sacred plant to the ancient Greeks. According to Greek myth, when Zeus heard an ambiguous oracle he'd start to perspire; cabbage was formed from his beads of sweat. Given this nature, oaths could be sworn on cabbage, and keeping cabbage in bed kept bad spirits from children and birthing mothers.

Another legend from antiquity tells that the vegetable emerged from the tears cried by King Lycurgus. As the king disdained Dionysus, the god of wine and ecstasy, he chased ecstatic wine drinkers off his land and had the vineyards chopped down. In retaliation, Dionysus struck him with a madness that brought the king to a miserable plight; seeing grape vines everywhere, he cut the head off his own son and the foot off his own leg. The myth illustrates that, though cabbage makes the head dull, it also helps sober indulgence in wine; indeed, the Romans believed that cabbage can prevent drunkenness.

Cato the Elder (234–149 BC), who deemed cabbage the best medicinal plant there is, wrote: "Whoever wants to eat and drink a lot at a festival should eat raw cabbage with some vinegar first—then he can drink as much as he wants." Cato's fellow countryman, Pliny the Elder (23–79 AD) claims that, thanks to cabbage, the Romans did not need doctors for six hundred years, as during this period people healed everything with cabbage—a tradition that lasted until Rome became decadent and people got soft, a situation clever Greek doctors, with expensive medications, took advantage of.

Although the German Benedictine abbess and plant enthusiast Hildegard von Bingen (1098–1179) wrote of both red and white cabbage, modern cabbage varieties did not appear in Europe until the Middle Ages when the round head cabbage was cultivated in northern Europe. Slavic peoples in central Europe invented sauerkraut, which involves the lactic acid fermentation of the shredded leaves; previously the Romans had preserved the whole leaves in vinegar without shredding them. Crinkly Savoy

Illustration 19. Cabbage head cut in half (illustration by Molly Conner-Ogorzaly, from B. B. Simpson and M. Conner-Ogorzaly, Economic Botany, *1986, 225)*

cabbage was cultivated in the seventeenth century in Savoy, France; through plant breeding northern Italian gardeners created cauliflower and broccoli; and in eighteenth-century Belgium, Brussels sprouts made their first appearance.

Though today cabbage is grown across the globe, it thrives especially well in the cool, moist northern Atlantic climate of central and northern Europe—indeed, where cabbage first appeared in its wild form. For many in central and eastern Europe—including the Dutch, Alsatians, Polish, Russians, and Germans—cabbage, next to porridge and bread, is a daily necessity, whether eaten fresh in the summer and fall or as sauerkraut in winter. As a result, cabbage came to be known as food for the simple peasants, as well as for simpletons. To this day English speakers call Germans "Krauts" because they eat so much cabbage. (The name of the rather overweight German chancellor Helmut Kohl could be translated as "Chancellor Cabbage.") The pejorative French term for Germans, "*les boches,*" is a shortened version of the old French word "*caboche,*" which means knucklehead—though in Middle French *caboche* was simply a head of cabbage. (Indeed, the word "cabbage" derives from *caboche.*) Interestingly, though, the French also have a term of endearment concerning the popular vegetable: "*mon petit chou*" (my little cabbage).

Traditional and Modern Healing Use of Cabbage

The first time I had anything to do with the healing aspect of cabbage, I was working in a biodynamic garden near Geneva, Switzerland. Every day a family came to get fresh organic Savoy cabbage leaves for their grandfather who suffered from skin cancer. They assured me there was not a better healing plant. The fresh cabbage leaves are bruised with a rolling pin until they are malleable like cloth and then applied to the skin. This is done for abscesses, abrasions, burns, gout, herpes zoster (shingles), necrosis, onychia, pox, neuralgia, scabs, tumors—

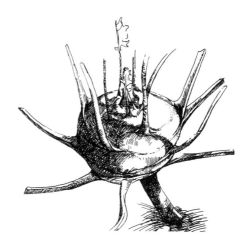

Illustration 20. Kohlrabi, one of the many kinds of cabbage

even just wounds that are not healing well. The wounds are freshly wrapped twice a day with the crushed leaves, cleansed in between with chamomile tea. And though this is, indeed, an ancient cure, modern naturopaths assure us it's very sound treatment. The well-known Swiss medical doctor, Dr. Jürg Reinhard, still prescribes cabbage poultices to draw pus out of wounds, as well as cabbage leaves put on the abdomen for infertility or to counter the effects of long-term use of birth control pills. Famous herbal healer Maurice Mességué calls cabbage a "big, generous king" (*roi du jardin potager*), and "the apothecary for the poor." With a chuckle he says, "Cabbage soup can (almost) resurrect the dead." He also recommends crushed cabbage leaves for all kinds of ailments, such as hot crushed-leaf poultices for rheumatism and aching muscles, and cabbage juice for blood cleansing and liver and intestinal complaints. In traditional folk medicine, even the urine produced after eating cabbage is considered to have healing power. Renaissance doctor Hieronymus Bock (1498–1554) wrote that abscesses heal if they are bathed in the urine produced after eating red cabbage. For a hangover he recommends breathing in the steam from cooked cabbage.

In earlier times, scurvy was an awful winter plague, and one of the main benefits of eating cabbage or sauerkraut was how it kept scurvy at bay; the wonderful vegetable has even more vitamin C than do oranges. (Vitamin C is also an excellent antioxidant.) For this reason cabbage was a favorite winter food, and Christmas and New Year meals included it in ceremonial contexts. In the seventeenth and eighteenth centuries, as Dutch seafarers always had barrels of sauerkraut on their ships, they didn't lose sailors due to scurvy as other sea powers did. The British, in particular, lost many sailors to scurvy; it was considered a miracle that Captain Cook lost no men on his three-year voyage. This was because the respected German scientist and explorer Georg Forster (1754–1794), who accompanied Cook, recommended he bring sixty kegs of sauerkraut for the crew. Any sailor who did not want to eat it could reckon with a flogging.

Though its various active ingredients contribute to the healthful effect of the cabbage, it's also the incredible vitality of the plant that makes this heal-all vegetable such a potent medicine. According to Rudolf Steiner (1861–1925) cabbage leaves, especially when crushed, radiate vital energies or "etheric formative forces" (*Bildekräfte*), which are taken up by ailing tissue in a way similar to fresh cell therapy. This corresponds to the folkloric belief held in France, Belgium, and parts of Germany that mothers receive their babies from the cabbage patch, for the plant is a wellspring of vitality and energy.

Cabbage Magic

In Europe, this important food and medicinal plant is surrounded by more magical folklore and taboos than most other plants. Many gardeners sow or plant on main Christian holidays, such as either Good Friday, Maundy (Holy) Thursday, or the day of a major saint—for example, March 17, the day of St. Gertrude, patroness of gardeners, better known as St. Patrick's Day. Gardeners believe they should sow when the church bells are ringing so the heads grow as big as the bells; or when the moon is waxing so the "heads will grow big and round." A sizable boulder was sometimes placed in the garden bed to inspire the cabbages to "become this large and firm." And as she planted cabbage seedlings the farmer's wife should say, "Heads like mine! Leaves like my apron! Stalks like the top of my thighs!" It was also seen as auspicious if a pregnant woman planted the seedlings, so the cabbage would grow fecund and round by her example.

Similarly, some days are not good for planting, such as April Fool's Day (April 1), because—"they will turn into fools" (meaning the crop will be worthless). Days when the moon was in an inauspicious zodiac sign were also avoided. With a moon in Sagittarius "the growing energy will shoot into the leaves"; in Capricorn the cabbage "will be hard and woody"; in Cancer "worms will gnaw away the roots." One was also careful about which day one made sauerkraut: if the moon was in the sign of Pisces, the kraut would become slimy, like fish.

The seeds themselves were put in holy water before sowing, or in the ashes from Ash Wednesday fires. And as they planted the seedlings men and women would joke, throw sod at each other, or try to bowl each other over—all behaviors remnant of the ancient sympathetic magic practice of performing coitus in the fields in order to increase fertility in nature.

To keep worms out of the cabbage patch, words of blessing would be spoken while sprinkling on the plants holy water from springs named after St. Peter. (Following Christianization, St. Peter took the place of Donar/Thor, the weather god, who fought lindworms and dragons with his hammer.) If caterpillars were devastating the crop, the peasant wife walked naked around the patch at midnight chanting sayings like: "There's a fair in town, young ladies; off to the fair!"

St. Bartholomew, the beheaded saint, was the patron of the cabbage. On St. Bartholomew's Day (August 24), no one was allowed to go into the cabbage patch because they would chase off "old Barthel," who on that blessed day was busy making the heads solid and big. No one was allowed in the cabbage patch on the day of St. Gall (October 16) either, because that would make the cabbage as bitter as bile from the gall bladder. By contrast, walking through the garden on St. John's Day would encourage the cabbages to grow big. On St. Jacob's Day (July 25), the gardeners called out to the cabbages, "Jacob, you bull head, let the cabbages be as big as my head!" *(Jakob, du Dickkopp, Häupter wie mein Kopp!)* And on St. Stephan's Day (December 26), instead of being eaten, cabbage was

Illustration 21. Making sauerkraut (illustration/woodcut by K. Paessler, Gärtner Pötschkes Großes Gartenbuch. 1945)

honored—because the saint had hidden in a cabbage patch in order to escape capture.

With the decline of country ways in the last century, unfortunately, these magical customs died out—and with them the healing virtues of cabbage were mostly forgotten. New research, however, confirms traditional old healing knowledge regarding cabbage. Modern medicine recognizes cabbage, freshly juiced or eaten raw, as a helpful treatment for stomach and duodenal ulcers. Sauerkraut—best eaten raw—is ideal nourishment to counter ailments caused by overly acidic foods containing too much protein and sugar. And sauerkraut juice is one of the best drinks for health; it detoxifies, improves bowl movement, strengthens the immune system, lessens arteriosclerosis, balances out the intestinal flora, and provides ample quantities of vitamin C.

Garden Tips

Cultivation: Start seeds indoors six weeks before transplanting time, which is after the danger of heavy frost is past. Early varieties must be picked while they are firm so be sure to harvest before midsummer heat forces a seed head to form. Late varieties require much longer to mature and will benefit from a light fall frost, which enhances the flavor. (LB)

Soil: Few plants feed more heavily than those in the cabbage family. For best results, work aged compost at least eight inches into the ground, as the roots can grow down to three feet or more. In sandy soil they also need plenty of water, so soak the ground around them thoroughly. During the growing season give the plants a few applications of compost tea.

Recipes

Amaranth on Grated White Cabbage with Thyme • 4 Servings

2 ounces (60 grams) amaranth seeds • 2 cups (455 milliliters) vegetable broth • 1 tablespoon paprika (or to taste) • 1 teaspoon thyme leaves • 4 teaspoons olive oil • 1¼ cup (285 grams) white cabbage, finely chopped or grated • 4 tablespoons mayonnaise • 1 tablespoon honey • 3 tablespoons raisins • 1 teaspoon apple vinegar • 1 pinch cinnamon • herbal salt • white pepper • 2 tablespoons alfalfa sprouts

Pour the vegetable broth into a medium sauce pan. Add the amaranth seeds and simmer gently, covered, over medium heat for about 15 minutes or until the grains are fluffy and the water is absorbed. Add paprika to taste. In a separate pan, sauté the thyme in 1 teaspoon of the olive oil until crispy; mix into the broth. Place the cabbage in a medium bowl. Stir in the mayonnaise, honey, raisins, remaining tablespoon of olive oil, and apple vinegar and mix well. Add the cinnamon; add the herbal salt and pepper to taste. Serve the cabbage salad garnished with the alfalfa sprouts, with the amaranth (it should be lukewarm) on the side.

Barley Soup with Sauerkraut and Yogurt • 4 Servings

5 tablespoons whole wheat barley, soaked overnight • 5 tablespoons sauerkraut, finely chopped • 2 bay leaves • 2 tablespoons olive oil • 5 cups (1¼ liters) vegetable broth • ground coriander seeds • herbal salt • black pepper • 4 tablespoons plain yogurt • a bit of fresh lovage, finely chopped

Sauté the barley, sauerkraut, and bay leaves in olive oil in a large pan. Add the vegetable broth and simmer until barley is tender. Add the coriander seeds; add herbal salt and pepper to taste. Transfer to a serving bowl. Stir the lovage into the yogurt; serve it with the soup.

Baked Red Cabbage with Whipped
Rosemary-Sesame Sauce • 4 Servings

Cabbage: 2 pounds (905 grams) red cabbage, finely chopped • 1 bay leaf • 1 clove • 1 small cinnamon stick • 1 quart (945 milliliters) vegetable broth • 1 egg, plus 2 egg yolks, whisked together • a splash of cream • Sauce: 2 twigs of fresh rosemary • 3 tablespoons sesame seeds • 1 tablespoon olive oil • 2 heaping tablespoons cottage cheese (pressed through a sieve); or cream cheese • freshly ground horseradish, to taste • herbal salt • pepper

CABBAGE: In a large pan simmer the cabbage with the bay leaf, clove, and cinnamon stick in the vegetable broth until the cabbage is tender and the pan is dry. Let cool for 15 minutes Mix in whisked egg mixture and cream. Transfer into an ovenproof form and bake at 300 °F (~150 °C) for 30 minutes or until firm and golden on top. done.

SAUCE: Sauté rosemary and sesame seeds in olive oil. Season to taste with herbal salt and pepper. Let cool. Mix in cottage cheese and horseradish. Serve with the red cabbage.

White Cabbage (or Collard Greens)
with Mustard and Caraway • 4 Servings

4 tablespoons butter • 1 tablespoon caraway • 2 tablespoons black peppercorns • 1 pound (455 grams) white cabbage (or collard greens), finely chopped • 1 cup (225 grams) potatoes, peeled or unpeeled, cubed • ¾ cup (175 milliliters) white wine • 1 cup vegetable broth • 1 table-spoon honey • sea salt • black pepper • 4 tablespoons sour cream

Sauté the caraway and peppercorns in the butter in a medium pan. Add the collard greens and potatoes and continue to cook. Once the ingredients are well sautéed, add the white wine and vegetable broth; simmer until the greens and potatoes are tender. Add honey; add sea salt and pepper to taste. Let stand covered for 2 hours. When ready to serve, reheat and serve with sour cream.

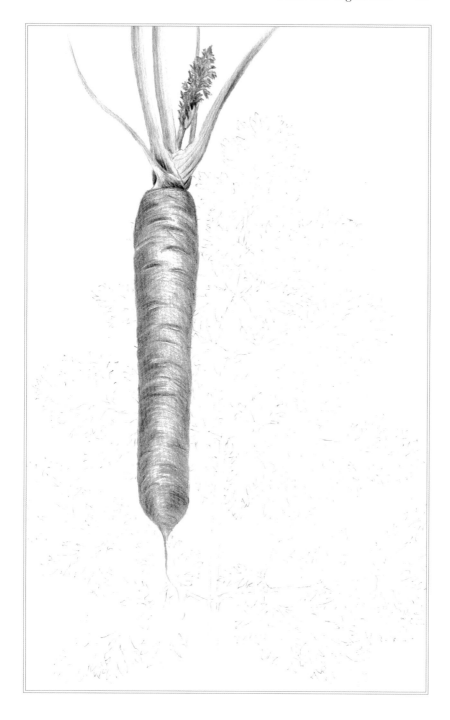

Carrot (*Daucus carota*)

Family: *Apiaceae or Umbelliferae:* umbellifer family

Other Names: Queen Anne's lace, bird's nest, devil's plague (as an invasive alien plant)

Healing Properties

Root: provides antioxidants, aids digestion, strengthens immune system, expels parasitic worms, improves vision

Leaf: externally: heals wounds; internally: tea soothes rashes

Seeds: cleanses blood, alleviates edema, increases female fertility, boosts milk production, stimulates menstruation, promotes urination (diuretic)

Symbolic Meaning: bringer of light; signature of the divine lovers, Mars and Venus; Queen Anne (England) or Ana, the Earth Goddess

Planetary Affiliation: Mercury and Venus; root: Mars

Whether we're talking about its folkloric history, its agricultural development—and by extension its color—or its individual growth in the ground, there is much more to the carrot than at first meets the eye. Let's begin with its journey from soil to sun. In its first year, the carrot has a tap root and green rosette; in its second year, the plant shoots up to form a finely structured, radiant white umbel that offers abundant nectar for all kinds of bugs, especially those with short proboscises. An interesting characteristic of the wild carrot in particular is, usually, a dark purple single flower in the middle of the umbel. Darwinian science finds no explanation for the purpose of this singular, remarkable dark blossom other than that it might signal a good landing place for flying insects.

The folklore of various regions has its own explanations for the striking purple bloom. In England, since the umbel of the wild carrot looks like lace, it's called "Queen Anne's lace." It is considered that the dark blossom appeared when the good queen pricked her finger as she was embroidering, from which a drop of blood fell to the middle of the flower head. In eastern European countries, the dark blossom is called "girl's shame" or "girl's honor," as it is seen as a signature concerning the plant's connection with menstruation, fertility, and desires of the flesh. In Transylvania, it is said that if the purple blossom is missing, or especially large, it tells something about the honor of the young women in the surrounding area. Continuing along this vein, the dark bloom is said to have been bigger in the olden days but, as nowadays there is no modesty among young people, it is smaller, or even nonexistent. This could be considered a concern, as it is also said that if, one day, all the carrot flowers bloom without the purple blossom the end of the world is near.

Illustration 22. Old drawing of flowering carrot plant

While the seeds ripen, the flowering umbel pulls together until it looks like a bird's nest—which is also one of the plant's names. The resulting small bristled fruits easily cling to animal fur or clothing, which then spreads the plant's reach.

Researchers cannot agree about where carrots were first cultivated, whether in Central Asia, in the Mediterranean area, or in northern Europe. The earliest record of the carrot dates from the Stone Age; carrot seeds were found in the debris of lake dwellings on Lake Constance, but they were surely from wild carrots. (The seeds of wild carrots cannot be distinguished from cultivated carrot seeds.) The oldest report regarding carrots goes back to Greece, where the fibrous, finger-sized, whitish roots were sometimes cooked and eaten. Herbal doctor Pedanius Dioscorides (~40–90 AD) noted that "the leaves crushed and mixed with honey can be applied to cancerous abscesses; a decoction of the seeds has a warming quality and it facilitates urination, menstruation, and birth; it helps drive out chronic coughs and severe stomach cramps; and conclusively, the cooked root helps [as a poultice for bites of] vipers and other poisonous animals." Other possible references to the carrot—including the *carvitas* that Charlemagne (742–814) grew on his estates, or the *morkrud* of Hildegard von Bingen (1098–1179)—cannot be confirmed. As the Slavic-Germanic word "*mohra*" merely means "edible root," von Bingen could just as easily have been referring to parsnip or skirret. (We discuss skirret in the Forgotten and Rare Vegetables section to come.)

The carrot first expanded its global reach when Spaniards brought it to Central America in the fifteenth century, very shortly after the discovery of the New World. The Dutch transported the vegetable to France, England, and other countries in their flight from the ravaging Spanish conquerors under the leadership of notorious Duke Alba (1507–1582). The carrot first reached North America with the arrival of the first English settlers in 1607. Soon the carrot broke out of its garden confinements and spread to fallow land, where it quickly mutated back to its original wild form. As the common garden carrot and the wild carrot (endemic from Siberia to Europe and Northern Africa) belong to the same species, they easily cross-pollinate. Wild carrots are currently regarded as pesky invasive plants.

The orange strain was intentionally developed in the sixteenth or seventeenth century in the Netherlands, possibly in honor of their national color.[1]

The carrot became a very popular vegetable wherever it was introduced. Fashionable ladies of Europe were so impressed with it that they adorned their hats with the fine-leaved fronds. Soon older root vegetables—such as parsnips, rampion root, or skirret, which had been eaten prior to the introduction of orange carrots—were no longer cultivated, essentially forgotten until the modern day. In the meantime, the carrot rose to impressive heights in the vegetable world; it is now considered a worldwide economic agricultural product.[2]

Carrot Magic

The carrot took from other root vegetables more than just popularity; traditional European practical and magical lore surrounding root vegetables transferred to the new orange carrots as well. For example, carrot seeds were stored in round-bellied pots so that the roots would grow big like the pots, and Maundy (Holy) Thursday or St. Benedict's Day (March 21) was a favorite day for sowing carrots. Silesians and other Central Europeans chose the latter holy day, since a play on words in German makes the saint's name mean "thick legs" (*bene* = legs, *dikt* = thick), it was thought that planting on Benedict's day would make the carrots grow thick.

In most areas, the astrological sign also played an important role on growing practices. Root crops were sown when the moon was in an earth sign (Taurus, Virgo, Capricorn), a convention biodynamic gardeners maintain today. It was thought that if carrots were sown with the moon of Cancer, the roots would become "thread-like," like crab legs; if sown in Scorpio, they'd become wormy; in Gemini they would split—but in the sign of Pisces they would become nice and smooth. In another auspicious practice, in various rural areas peasant women would discreetly roll around naked in the carrot patch early in the morning on Pentecost to aid the carrots in growing well.

Biodynamic gardeners regard the carrot as a plant receptive of and saturated with light. It absorbs cosmic light energy to the point that the succulence of the leaves melts away and practically "vanishes," leaving behind fine, filigree fronds. Light energy, which materializes as fragrance, essential oil, vibrant color, and sugar content, permeates the entire plant, even down into the orange-colored root. This "light energy" is also responsible for the healing nature of the plant.

The Healing Qualities of Carrots

One of the carrot's primary benefits is its work as a gentle vermifuge countering the effects of parasitic worms. Worms, considered creatures of a moist, dark, "moony" and dank milieu, are more likely to colonize human intestines when a person's energy is low and the body is weak.

As raw carrots are too "sunny" for the parasites, they effectively expel the worms from the intestines. The essential oils of the carrot are also antibacterial. There is hardly a better means to cure bacterial diarrhea in infants than perfectly cooked and mashed carrots.

Inspired plant enthusiast and German poet Johann Wolfgang von Goethe (1749–1832) once wrote: "If the eye were not sun-like, how could we ever see light?" Our eyes, thus, were "created by light for light." As such, it is not surprising that carrots and their strong affiliation to the sunlight are so beneficial to our vision—a quality prominent in the folklore of the vegetable. A precursor of vitamin A, carotene, which is responsible for the bright orange color of the root, strengthens and protects the retina, which improves night vision. Carotene is also an antioxidant—a magnet for free radicals—and as such renders harmless cancer-inducing, free-roaming, aggressive oxygen radicals. Research has shown that people with high carotene levels in their blood are less likely to suffer from stomach or lung cancer than those with low carotene levels. This provitamin also strengthens the immune system, feeding that system's macrophages, the "killer cells." Excess carotene is stored in the skin, thus protecting against harmful ultraviolet rays.[3] And the carrot is potent as well: just fifty grams (less than two ounces) is sufficient to cover the daily needs of the human organism.

While carrots are always a good food choice, this is especially true in the winter—in northern climates—when our bodies suffer from sunlight deficit. (Luckily, the fact that fresh young carrot leaves are good in soups can be extended throughout the year: the leaves can also be dried for tea or winter soups.) This was clearly shown by a study done in Norway, where it had been observed that school performance dropped off drastically during the dark winter months. To counter the phenomenon, the schools launched the "Oslo breakfast" program, which consisted of milk-soaked whole wheat bread (Kneippbrød) and freshly grated apple and carrot. The effort was a startling success, as the pupils became much more lively and alert (Andresen/Elvbakken 2007, 374–377).

Many consider it is the light quality of the carrot that "radiates" into the lower body chakras (Muladhara, Svadhisthana, Manipurna) of the digestive and the sexual organs. As to the former, traditional herbal lore prescribes tea made of the blossoming flowers in cases of edema, chronic kidney ailments, urinary passage ailments, and—because the plant is both diuretic and blood cleansing—for gout. As to the latter, carrots have always been associated with sexual drive and conception, though this has less to do with the obvious phallus-like signature of the taproot than with the cosmic light energies the plant transmits. According to veritable seers, we are beings of light; before we are conceived, we are attracted to the passionate fire generated by our parents so that we can incarnate in a physical body. Thus, given its high light "content," the carrot—especially the wild carrot, which is much more aromatic and has very thin, rather woody roots—was traditionally used as an aphrodisiac and a tonic for the regenerative organs. Up until very recently, young women in the Hebrides gathered wild carrot roots to give to their partners

to chew at dance festivals—or on the weekends. The Greeks also chewed wild carrot roots in the springtime, when the milder weather supported the rush of hormones. Renaissance botanist Hieronymus Bock (1498–1554) reported: "The wild carrot root gives fertility, and also helps all who merely dribble when they try to urinate, as well as helping against impotence in marriage."

This advice gives an entirely new twist to Bugs Bunny's cheeky question addressed to that irate old fuddy-duddy, Elmer Fudd: "What's up, Doc?" What is

Illustration 23. Bugs Bunny

implied by the taunt is an ancient archetypal association: both rabbits (hares) and carrot roots have long symbolized both sexual penchant and potency. Or, as modern phytochemists would phrase it: the plant contains porphyrin, which triggers the releases of gonadal hormones through the pituitary gland.

But it's not just the roots that affect sexuality; carrot seeds also share in the reputation. The ancient Greeks made a drink of carrot seeds, or a suppository made from powdered seeds, to encourage menstruation or conception. In the Islamic Unani healing tradition, carrot seeds are used in love potions to increase the flow of semen (*ma'jun pumba dana*) and for relaxation (*ma'jun rah-ul-mominin*). To this day Egyptians cook the seeds in honey for aphrodisiacal purposes. The Renaissance herb doctor Pietro Andrea Mattioli (1501–1577) concurred: "The seeds generate unchaste desires." It must also be mentioned that they can have an abortive effect, and thus should be avoided by pregnant women. Other effects are that they reduce flatulence, increase the milk flow of nursing mothers, and are diuretic.

As carrot fronds are also known as an antiseptic diuretic, they are often made into a tea for bladder and prostate infections and as a prophylactic against stone ailments. The leaves can also be crushed and used as a poultice for burns, frostbite, or wounds that aren't healing well.

Local Color

Our discussion of carrots closes in sharing how the root vegetable has inspired some fantastic stories. One legend tells of a carrot seed that fell out of a seed merchant's bag when he was crossing the Rhine. The seed grew into a carrot so gigantic the farmer who found it was able to feed two oxen all winter with it. In turn, the oxen's horns grew to be so big that when they were blown (cattle horns are still used as horns today) the sound traveled from St. Martin's Day (November 11) until St. George's Day (April 23).

The King's Bride—by E. T. A. Hoffmann (1776–1822), the German Edgar Allan Poe—tells in of a girl, Anne von Zabeltau, who worked in a vegetable garden. A wicked gnome, Daucus Carota the First, was the king of all the vegetables. Upon seeing the beautiful maiden, he was possessed by desire for her and proceeded to abduct her into his musky underworld realm of roots and worms. But then one day the carrot king perceived the wailing of his subjects—the carrots, celeriacs, and turnips—as they were being chopped up and cast into a boiling pot. Trying to save them, the gnome himself fell into the soup kettle and perished. Only then could the maiden escape the dark underworld.

Garden Tips

Cultivation: Although carrots require far more personal attention than do most garden vegetables, many gardeners know that the results are worth the extra effort; grown well, their sweet goodness will turn your garden into a candy store. Carrots can be sown directly into the ground as soon as the soil can be worked in spring. As the seeds are slow to germinate, the rows must be kept weed free and, after sprouting, thinned out; for the initial thinning leave each plant one to two inches apart, depending on the variety. When the young seedlings are about two inches tall, the plants may be further thinned throughout the season to a maximum of four inches apart. In order to avoid having all the carrots mature at once, successive sowings can be done up until midsummer. For ease of hoeing and for weed control, carrot seeds are best sown in rows across a raised bed; for ease of sowing one can also make seed tape. For best texture and taste, carrots should be harvested as soon as they have reached full size.

Illustration 24. Proud carrot gardener (illustration by K. Paessler, Gärtner Pötschkes Großes Gartenbuch. 1945)

Soil: As taproots, carrots prefer loose, sandy loam free of obstructions. Long varieties need at least one foot of well-prepared soil of fine texture, so work in plenty of compost. If your soil is heavy, it is better to choose one of the shorter carrot varieties.

Of Special Note: Try inter-sowing radishes with carrots. Sow the radishes very thinly (use about 30 percent radish seed) right in with the carrot seeds. As the radishes will germinate first, you can pick them before they start to crowd the carrots. The early-germinating radishes serve another purpose in that they will mark the rows in which you planted the slow-to-awaken carrot seed. (LB)

Recipe

Carrot Salad on Alfalfa • 4 Servings

6 tablespoons vegetable broth • ginger powder, to taste • splash lemon juice • sea salt • black pepper • 1 pound (455 grams) fresh carrots, grated • 1 tablespoon cold-pressed olive oil • 2 tablespoons cream (18% fat) • 1 cup sprouted alfalfa or cress • radishes (for garnish)

In a medium pan, slightly warm the vegetable broth. Add the ginger powder, lemon juice, and salt and pepper, all to taste. Add the grated carrots and let stand for 2 minutes. Mix in the olive oil and cream. Serve on the alfalfa, or cress. Garnish with radishes.

Celery (*Apium graveolens*)

Family: Apiaceae or Umbelliferae: umbellifer family

Other Names and Varieties: smallage (the original wild plant), celeriac

Healing Properties: stimulates menstruation (emmenagogue), increases male potency, calms nervous system, promotes urination (diuretic), facilitates vomiting; excessive base properties make ideal for diabetes, gout, and rheumatism

Symbolic Meaning: connects to chthonic earth forces, simultaneously helping to overcome them; death and sexual desire; heroism

Planetary Affiliation: Mercury

Like carrot and parsnip, celery is a biennial Apiaceae. The second part of its botanical name, "*graviolens*" (strong smelling), derives from the fact that all parts of the plant have aromatic essential oils. These oils (mainly phthalide), have a diuretic effect; celery also has flavonoids, furanocoumarins, plant hormones, the glycoside apiin, and lots of vitamins and minerals, including especially high sodium chloride (salt) content.

Today there are three varieties of celery available:

- Green celery or smallage, whose aromatic leaves are used, fresh or dried, as herbal seasoning or as celery salt.
- Celery root or celeriac (*Apium graveolens* var. *rapaceum*), which is especially popular as a soup vegetable in France and central Europe.
- Celery stalks, with typically swollen, crispy, mild leaf stems, were first cultivated by Italian master gardeners in the seventeenth century. Until then the plant had been used mainly as seasoning (leaves) or as a medicine (all parts).

Wild celery, or "smallage," grows endemically on all the coasts of Europe, western Asia, and Africa, as well as inland wherever there is moist, somewhat salty soil. The Latin name "*apium*" does not mean "bee plant" as is often claimed, but comes from the Celtic *apon* (water). The wild plant has become nearly extinct on the northern coast in Europe due to drainage trenches, intensive agriculture, and the building of dykes.

The modern name "celery" comes from Greek *selinon*. It was ascribed to Silenus (or Seilenus), the son of a nymph and lustful Pan (or, according to other depictions, Hermes, the messenger of the gods who transgresses all borders). Silenus, constantly drunk and lecherous, is depicted as pot-bellied with a beefy bald head and often with the ears, tail, and legs of a horse. He was the leader of the lustful horde of satyrs as well as the teacher and companion of Dionysus, the god of inebriation. Half human, half horse, Dionysus symbolizes, among other things, the powerful animal drive. The association of this satyr with celery, emphasizes the plant's use as an effective agent of sexual potency.

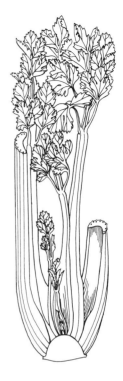

Illustration 25. Celery stalks (illustration by Molly Conner-Ogorzaly, from B. B. Simpson and M. Conner-Ogorzaly, Economic Botany, *1986, 230)*

Celery is presented as signifying both death and sensual pleasures in Homer's epic *The Odyssey*: celery grows among violets in the meadows on Calypso's magical island. (The Hellenes classified violets as "erotic plants," which they dedicated to Priapus, the little deity with the big phallus; Aphrodite, the goddess of love; and Persephone, the goddess of the underworld and the dead.) The enchantress Calypso took in shipwrecked Odysseus and held him enraptured for seven years; she also turned his men into "swine." Comparative religion studies indicate that Calypso was a goddess of death, as the name suggests (*kalypto* = to enshroud) and that pigs were sacred to the earth and death goddess of antiquity. That Odysseus ultimately freed himself from her magic is seen as a victory over death, as in all mythologies the hero, having come dangerously close to

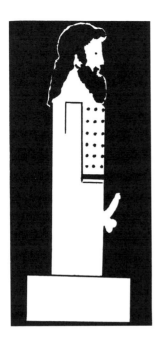

Illustration 26. Stele of Hermes

death, succeeds in wresting new life from the dark forces. This interpretation lends meaning to the ancient Greek practice of crowning winners of riding and gymnastic games with celery leaves.

Celery has a long association with death. Ancient Egyptian mummies were often decorated with celery and blue lotus blossoms. Ancient Greeks planted it on graves and used it to season funeral feasts. The Roman Virgil (70–19 BC) described much the same: "Godly Linus decorated his head with flowers and bitter celery [as a sign of mourning]"; "It is not right to put celery in common dishes because it belongs to funeral feasts." (Nonetheless, celery, next to dill and coriander, was a favorite condiment in the Roman cuisine.) The Romans also dedicated celery, as part of the death rites, to Orcus, the god of the underworld, as told by Plutarch (45–120 AD): "We decorate our gravesites with celery." Given such practices, it was considered a bad omen to see a cart loaded with celery first thing in the morning. And for someone who was marked by death, the Romans said: "There is only celery left for him." This is an interesting angle given the fact that, like the ancient Greeks, Romans also crowned their victors with celery leaves.

Celery's association with death lasted well into our own times. Wend (Slavic) tradition in northern German Spreewald claims that *merek* (celery) protects against being haunted by the dead. And the Italian fairy tale "Marianne and the Celery King" tells of a maiden who, attempting to pull a celery bulb from the soil is instead pulled into the ground; "the ground closed over them like water over a stone." Below the earth, she finds a golden castle and an old, long-bearded hunchbacked man who resembles a celery root: the Celery King, who marries and impregnates her. But he is also an enchanted prince. After the heroine surmounts numerous tasks and challenges she is able to redeem the prince and bring him back to the world above the ground.

Nowadays such stories are given anecdotic value at most. However, traditional customs, folklore, and imaginative perception teach us much about the essence of the plant. In such imaginative terms, let us consider the celery.

Celery is a biennial; its "incarnation" lasts two years. In the first year, it concentrates on absorbing salty, moist earth forces, during which time it swells and becomes lush. During this year there is a clear pull to the dark, cool earth realm, to downward-moving elements and, figuratively speaking, to the grave, bitter death, and the mourning that causes salty tears to flow—but also to the fertile, ever-bearing primal source. In the second year the plant ascends to the light, shooting up into bloom, opening and branching out as it bathes in cosmic light. The plant now sets a counterpoint to the earthy, moist, salty forces with its "light and fiery" essential oils. Thus it becomes a plant for victors and heroes, one that overcomes the dark forces, that wards off the evil eye (in Spain), that thwarts the scheming of wicked witches. Even in modern Greece celery blossoms—together with garlic and onion—are hung for good luck. They protect the area where silk worms are being raised; small children are given amulets of celery to keep them from harm. In Prussia and Pomerania the leaves were stuffed into cracks in floors and walls in pigsties to protect the animals from evil magic—and young married couples were given a piece of root to put in a pocket or a shoe for good luck.

The Healing Virtues of Celery

Nicholas Culpeper (1616–1654) recognized the ambivalent nature of celery. He ascribed the plant to the hermaphroditic god, Mercury—the Roman Hermes, who can as easily fly up to the light-filled world of the gods as he can descend to the underworld. Indeed, Mercury-Hermes is the ruler of rising and sinking energy flow. He loosens, cleanses, opens, splits, and removes blockages by bringing everything back into flow. Culpeper, just as other doctors before and after him, used this mercurial plant to heal "water

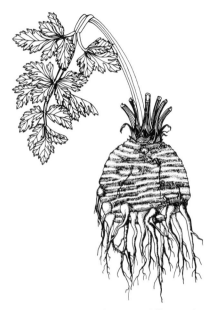

Illustration 27. Celery root (illustration by Molly Conner-Ogorzaly, from B. B. Simpson and M. Conner-Ogorzaly, Economic Botany, 1986, 230)

diseases," "obstructions" while urinating, and stone ailments, and to activate the liver and the spleen.

Celery works in the microcosm of the human body true to character. It affects the root chakra, the Muladhara, down into the sexual organs and the "salty, watery" urinary organs. Celery can reduce the milk flow for nursing mothers—a compress can actually temporarily reduce the breast size—but can also stimulate the uterus and bring on menstruation. As "maiden's smallage" it belonged to the herbs that women took in case of a "belated period," when they feared they'd been impregnated. German scholar and bishop Albertus Magnus (~1200–1280) described the downward pull of the plant: "Celery causes sensual desire to descend from the breasts of wet nurses to the genital area and bring about menstruation."

It is often the case that emmenagogues work for men as aphrodisiacs, as indicated in such names as "stand-up herb" (Lausitz, Germany), "stand-up wort," "stud wort" and "buck's wort." A fifteenth-century medical book tells us: "So that your wife stays faithful forever mix celery juice and honey and rub your genitals with the mixture. This way she will be satisfied and will want no one else but you." Consider too this German saying:

> *Fry me eggs, sweetheart,*
> *with celery and lettuce,*
> *on Sunday we will go courting,*
> *my mother told me this.*

This aspect of celery is also well known in France, the country of *savoir vivre* and *l'amour,* as in the following: "If a woman knew what celery does to a man, she would be willing to go from Paris to Rome to find it." And, "If a man knew what celery does for him, he would plant his garden full of it."[1]

Illustration 28. Albertus Magnus (1193–1280)

Modern-day French master of herbs Maurice Mességué claimed to know the ingredients of Tristan and Isolde's love potion. The brew was supposedly made of mandrake blossoms, truffles, the testicles of a young rooster, river crabs, pepper, thyme, caraway, allspice, bay leaf, and, of course, celery. He otherwise prescribed celery for diabetes, gout, and rheumatism (because it purges the blood), to stimulate the glands, and for shattered nerves (Mességué 1972, 98).

Medieval cloister medicine, as represented by Benedictine abbess Hildegard von Bingen (1098–1179), was well aware of the effect of celery on glands. *Apium* was mainly known as a diuretic, as an emmenagogue (meaning it stimulates blood flow in the pelvic area and uterus), as an abortive, and as a cure for kidney, bladder, spleen, and liver ailments. Hildegard also prescribed a compress of celery and fennel juice for weepy eyes (Müller 1993, 35).

Celery is still known as a healing plant today. Like many umbellifers, it stimulates the glands, particularly the adrenal glands. Both celery juice and the vegetable itself has an alkaline effect in that it inhibits uric acid accumulation and keeps the blood from becoming too acidic. It also helps flush poisons and wastes out of the system. As such it's an excellent treatment for gout and rheumatism; it also helps relieve the liver and the spleen. As a diuretic, it increases the excretion of water and salts, which in turn helps lower blood pressure. However, a cautionary note to those with kidney ailments: the diuretic effect of celery, which is even stronger than that of asparagus, can irritate ailing kidneys. Nursing mothers should also be aware that celery reduces milk flow.

Celery is well known for its calming effects. In India celery seeds are used as an expectorant cough treatment; in English folk medicine celery seeds serve as a carminative against flatulence. Since celery lessens cramps in the chest, it also eases the constrictions caused by asthma. It's also an excellent tonic for anxiety, as told by Hippocrates (460–370 BC): "Celery is nourishing and healing for spent nerves." Paracelsus (1493–1541) advises: "Whoever is beginning to be consumed by fear should eat a stalk of (wild) celery every other day." (Today celery is used in herb therapy for men's fear of failure.) Celery seeds are also thought to help against hysterical reactions and compulsive thinking. As such, the heroic plant not only helps relax the glands, but also the functions related to them.

Garden Tips

Cultivation: As the seeds are slow to germinate and grow, indoor sowings should be made a full nine weeks before the last average frost date of spring. If using a cold frame, seeds may be started indoors even earlier and then transplanted to a cold frame to harden the seedlings. This approach provides larger plants with which to start off the outdoor growing season. But be careful not to break the taproot when transplanting, as such could prove fatal. (To avoid this it's wise to start the seeds in biodegradable peat pots that you later plant directly in the ground.) Once you've transplanted the celery, keep light mulch around the plants, and don't let the soil dry out.

Soil: The forerunners of modern garden celery come from the marshes of western Europe and northern Africa; not surprisingly, celery still grows best in marshy, fertile soil, rich in all elements, plus plenty of water. A generous supply of well-rotted manure will assure a good harvest.

Of Special Note: Though celery is a heavy potash user it will react badly to excessive nitrogen supplies. Instead, supply potash by sprinkling hardwood ashes along the plants several times during the growing season. (LB)

Recipes

Celery Bulb (Celeriac) with Prunes and Potatoes • 4 Servings

1 celery bulb • 1 quart (945 milliliters) coconut milk • 2 tablespoons fresh herbs (thyme, sage, rosemary, sour dock) • 1 small chili pepper • 2 bay leaves • ground cardamom • 8 dried plums without pits • 1 tablespoon honey • ½ cup (115 milliliters) vegetable broth • 1 tablespoon fresh ginger • 1 tablespoon turmeric • 2 pounds (905 grams) potatoes, peeled or unpeeled, cut into fine rods (like for fries) • 4 tablespoons olive oil • garlic, chopped (to taste) • herbal salt

Put the celery bulb into an ovenproof dish. Add the coconut milk, herbs, chili pepper, bay leaves, cardamom, dried plums, honey, vegetable broth, ginger, and turmeric; blending the ingredients evenly. Cover and bake at 375 °F (190 °C) for 1 hour or until the celery bulb is tender.

Once the bulb has been baking for about 40 minutes, fry the potato rods in the olive oil. When they are nicely browned, season them with the garlic and herbal salt.

When the baking is done, set the celery bulb on a serving dish and cut it like a roast. Purée the remainder of the baked ingredients and pour over the sliced celery. Serve with the fried potatoes.

Celery Bulb (Celeriac) Fritters • 4 Servings

1 celery bulb • ¾ cup (175 grams) bread crumbs • salt and pepper • 1 egg • ¼ cup (60 milliliters) cream (18% fat) or milk • light-tasting oil for frying

Cut the celery bulb into ¼-inch-thick slices. Steam them in a steamer until cooked but not yet completely tender. In a small bowl, whisk the cream or milk with the egg. Dredge both sides of each slice of celery bulb, first in the egg batter and then in the bread crumbs. Sauté in oil over medium heat until golden brown.

Chicory (*Cichorium intybus*)

Family: Compositae or Asteraceae: composite, daisy, or sunflower family

Other Names: blue sailors, succory, and coffeeweed; also called cornflower, although that name is more commonly applied to *Centaurea cyanus*. Common names for *foliosum* varieties of chicory include endive, Belgian endive, French endive, red endive, radicchio, sugarloaf, witloof (white endive)

Healing Properties: lowers blood lipids, soothes inflamed eyes, detoxifies intestines, promotes urination (diuretic); ideal for liver and gall bladder

Symbolic Meaning: faithfulness in love, bitter longing, the vegetation goddess's love for the sun god, the soul's love for the higher self

Planetary Affiliation: Jupiter, Saturn

Chicory lettuce is one of the few vegetables—next to leeks and lamb's lettuce—that is robust enough to defy cold wind and the first frosts when all of the other vegetables have long since been harvested. Common chicory relatives in the northern climates are endive lettuce, white endive, radicchio, and sugar loaf. Sugar loaf—an interesting name, given that it's rather bitter—makes a very large head, similar to cabbage in size and compactness; and though its leaves are relatively tender, it can withstand quite a strong frost. Sugar loaf can be eaten raw in salads or stewed as a vegetable, and nicely complements beef. Less bitter endive lettuce is also hardier than regular lettuce; in northern climates it can be planted in August for tasty fall salads. Radicchio, originally from Italy, is closely related to sugar loaf and makes for a colorful addition to any salad with its red, white-ribbed leaves. White endive or witloof is a crisp, yellow-white, torpedo-shaped salad plant whose cultivation is very work-intensive; fortunately, it's available in most supermarkets nowadays.

Most people do not know that the endive plant is none other than beautiful blue-flowering chicory that grows wild along roadsides and pathways, found over the entire northern half of the globe. And it blooms readily: if a gardener leaves chicory lettuce in the garden over the winter,

Illustration 29. Chicory (Joachim Camerarius, Neuw Kreütterbuch, *1586)*

the next year it will blossom back into this typical divaricating flowery shrub. Chicory flowers from midsummer and on into the fall, but the blossoms only open on sunny days. Historically, each blossom blooms for only one day—from exactly 5:00 until 11:00 AM. This cosmic rhythm is so exact that the Swedish botanist Carl Linnaeus (1707–1778) planted chicory in his famous flower clock in the botanical garden in Uppsala. (Nowadays this rhythm seems to have been disturbed, with the flowers blossoming into the afternoon without necessarily following the sun as they used to. It is surmised that electromagnetic disturbances such as microwave radiation and WiFi may be responsible for this.)

Toward the end of the eighteenth century in northern Europe, when coffee was exorbitantly expensive, roasted chicory root was added to coffee beans as a stand-in. Indeed, the Prussian king Fredrick the Great (1712–1786), ever ready to reduce the outflow of capital spent on luxury imports like coffee, encouraged the extensive cultivation of chicory. The addition of chicory makes coffee stronger and darker; the French acquired a taste for this *mocca faux* (false coffee) and brought it to their colonies in America. (The lasting Southern preference for bitter, dark coffee later got a boost during the Civil War, when the Yankee blockade cut Louisiana off from oversea coffee imports; to this day one can still find roasted chicory root brewed with coffee in New Orleans. Indeed, the French, too, like roasted chicory root in their coffee today.)

As is often the case with culture, one practice begets another. In 1830, Flemish gardeners began planting chicory roots in boxes and letting them bud underneath a clean layer of turf and sand to keep them blanched while sprouting. They marketed the harvested product as Brussels *chicorée* or witloof. But they can't be credited with the inspiration; in earlier times the shoots of wild chicory were covered with a basket or a pot to bleach them for milder taste.

Chicory Lore and Magic

Many would be surprised to learn that chicory was once a highly esteemed, even sacred plant. In pre-Celtic times the plant was seen as an embodiment of the goddess of vegetation, the lovely daughter of Mother Earth. As her lover and husband is none other than the radiant sun god, son of the highest heavens, the chicory goddess always watches for him with her comely blue eyes. For the Greeks the plant was the enchanted nymph Cynthia, the lover of radiant Phoebus (the sun god Apollo). It's not surprising, then, that an old name for chicory common in the Middle Ages was *sponsa solis:* sun's bride.

The chicory-maiden lived on in the folklore of later eras. One tale concerns a young knight who pledged his love to a blue-eyed girl before riding eastward to join the crusade aiming to free the holy city of Jerusalem. Faithfully, she awaited his return, standing by the roadside every morning, looking with tearful eyes to the east. When her parents urged her to take another man, she answered defiantly: "I would rather turn into a common flower in the field"—at which point God turned her into a chicory flower.

As such, in traditional flower lore chicory stands for true love. When a damsel handed her knight a chicory flower, she without words told him:

> *The chicory flower so heavenly blue*
> *always turns its face to the sun;*
> *In the same way my heart turns to you*
> *and promises to be true.*

In the Judeo-Christian worldview, however, chicory found its place among the other bitter herbs, symbolizing either the suffering of the Lord or Passover herbs that the Children of Israel ate while in bondage in Egypt. In Catholic regions the faithful bride of the sun was turned into a cursed maiden, and the flower of unremittent love into a symbol of sinful pride. One clerical legend tells of a maiden drawing water from a well on a hot summer day when Jesus and his disciples passed by. Tired and thirsty, the holy men asked for a drink. But the hard-hearted girl refused, saying: "What am I, your maid? Get your own water!" Thereupon the Lord cursed her to stand as a chicory flower on the wayside, to do penance until Judgment Day.

Despite these exceptions, the lore of the sun bride's immense love of the sun lived on throughout the Middle Ages. Chicory was often included in love charms or used as an oracle in matters of love. Maidens plucked the flower buds before sunrise and placed them in their corsets, murmured magical words such as, "O chicory, growing on the wayside / My hand has plucked you now for luck / Now please send to me my own dearest one / do not make me wait in vain like you have had to."[1] If the flower bud later opened, it was seen as a sign of good luck, promising good fortune in love. Married women added the blossom to their cooking so that their husbands remained faithful.

The magic of the chicory was considered to be especially potent if the root was dug up when the moon was in the sign of Leo or, more specifically, at two o'clock on the day of St. Peter and St. Paul (June 29). For digging it was best to use a stag's antler, or a piece of wood from a tree struck by lightning. The reward of such pains was great: any person touched with this chicory root would instantly fall in love with the holder. But not all shared in such beliefs. Indignant over such heathen customs, abbess Hildegard von Bingen (1098–1179) claimed that, quite to the contrary, anyone who had such a root would be hated. It was also believed that such a root could be worn as a protective amulet, as it could break any magical fetter, even if fettered while sleeping. And placed under the pillow, the root could make thieves visible in dreams.

The specification of digging a chicory root with a stag's antler is not an arbitrary custom. In pre-Christian Europe the stag or hart (male elk) was considered the sun god in animal form. The Celts called him "Cernunnos," the companion of the White Goddess. By using a hart's antler to dig the root, the magician or herb gatherer identifies with the sun god, for it is only he who dares touch the exalted plant goddess. (As gold is also attributed to the sun, the plant could also be dug up with a golden blade.) Extending the hart antler theme, the German and Dutch terms "*hintläufe*" and "*hintloop*" (doe's legs) and "*hirschsprung*" (stag's jump) are other names for wild chicory, implying that the plant, whose flowers constantly turn toward the sun, is a doe following her stag. The medieval legend of the St. Hubertus stag is a later Christian interpretation of the Celtic myth of the dark god of the underworld, who hunts and kills the sun stag in the dark, nebulous days of November (Samhain). In the Christian version the huntsman Hubert perceived Christ as an apparition of radiant heavenly light between the antlers of the hart he was about to shoot. (This image appears on the label of the herbal digestif Jägermeister, which means "master huntsman.")

Occasionally chicory has white blossoms; these are considered to be especially powerful. If dug at the right time and with the proper incantation, whoever is in possession of white chicory will never be harmed by arrow or sword—and can become invisible at will. The best time to gather white chicory is on the early morning of Mary's Ascension Day/Assumption of Mary (August 15). Heading out before sunrise, the herb gatherer must be careful to neither speak a word nor be spoken to by anyone, as such would be a bad omen. He could only speak upon reaching the plant, when, facing east, he should recite:

> *I greet you in God's name, dear chicories, all of you.*
> *Greetings to you in front of me and to those behind me:*
> *Staunch the blood and heal the wounds.*
> *And keep the power lent to you*
> *by God and the holy Mary.[2]*

Then, after blessing the plant three times with the sign of the cross, the gatherer would dig out a root with an antler, a wooden stick, or a gold coin. (He must not use iron, which is believed to drive off healing spirits.) Then the root was quickly fastened to a stave so that its power would not flee, for it was "as swift as a deer or stag."

And, finally, it was believed that demons could be driven off with chicory. A traditional saying tells us:

> Wild marjoram, chicory, and St. John's wort
> Cause the devil pain and hurt.

As such, it's not surprising that chicory root was traditionally given to women to hold in their hand during childbirth.

The Healing Virtues of Chicory

Adding to its rich list of assets, chicory is also a valuable healing plant, especially for liver and gall bladder ailments. I myself was able to cure a bad case of hepatitis in India with the help of tea made of the stems. In India chicory is cultivated in rather large fields, with mainly the seeds used as a condiment. Ground seeds are used in a refreshing drink (*thandai*) enjoyed during hot summer days in the Ganges River Valley in Uttar Pradesh.

In European folk medicine, a tea is brewed from the root that is harvested in the fall. As the tea has a detoxifying, "blood cleansing" effect, it is helpful for those suffering from kidney problems, rheumatism, gout, or a weak spleen. In the Galenic theory of the four humors *chicorium* is classified as "bitter, rarified, earthy, cold to the second degree, and dry to the second degree." According to Galenic physicians the plant has the signature of Saturn, and so therefore it's effective for flushing excessive "bitter, black gall" (*melancholia*) out of the body, simultaneously freeing the soul from the poison of bitter, melancholy thoughts. British Herbal astrologist Nicholas Culpeper (1616–1654), who classified chicory as a plant belonging to Jupiter, wrote: "It drives forth choleric and phlegmatic humours [and] opens obstruction of the liver, gall, and spleen." To this day phytotherapists recognize chicory as a detoxifying agent for the liver and pancreas.

In Indian Ayurvedic medicine chicory, called "*kasni*," is also a highly valued plant. Tea made from crushed chicory seeds is used as a tonic for the liver, spleen, and gall bladder. Root powder is prescribed for lack of appetite, upset stomach, and fever. Drinking the juice of the root along with carrot and celery juice is recommended for eye troubles. As Hieronymus Bock (1498–1554) noted, Europeans also knew of distilled chicory blossom water as "noble medicine for inflamed eyes with no luster." An old folk saying adds to the respected lore: "The noble plant chicory makes eyes healthy and strong."

Indeed, chicory's tonic effect on the liver and gall bladder has been scientifically proven in clinical studies. The plant has also proved valuable in chelation therapy. Due to its cations (positively charged ions), it is able to bind to toxic heavy metals (cadmium, lead, mercury) and flush them out of the body, thereby preventing them from entering the blood stream. And endive lettuces are known to help lower blood pressure and reduce cholesterol in the blood, thus improving cardiac health; they also have a detoxifying effect and help stabilize intestinal flora.

One last modern psychosomatic treatment can be mentioned in relation to this marvelous plant. Edward Bach (1886–1936) used chicory in his Bach Flower Remedies. With a mind to sparing a sufferer from self-pity, he prescribed a chicory flower essence for personalities that are possessive and clinging or who crave love, compassion, and attention. (This kind of personality, by the way, often suffers from digestive and intestinal problems.) As such, the chicory flower essence helps such personalities learn selfless love, the love for the higher self.

Garden Tips

Cultivation: Witloof chicory (white or Belgian endive), which has an unusual and delightful flavor, makes a delicious salad. Sow seeds outdoors in late spring. In the fall, very carefully dig out the taproots. Trim their lush green tops and add them to your compost pile, which will welcome the nitrogen of the leaves. Trim the roots to be six to eight inches long. To grow shoots, pack the roots, root end down, in boxes or metal pails. Fill in the space between the roots with one of the following, noted in preferred order: sand, loose sandy soil, soil with good humus, or peat. Top with about ten inches (twenty-five centimeters) of sand, and store at about 60 °F (15 °C). The roots will produce large, tender white sprouts, which have an unusual and delightful flavor; they can be harvested as soon as they come up. When growing varieties used as a coffee substitute, dig the hard roots before the last hard frost. (LB)

Soil: Any deeply prepared, reasonably fertile, loose garden soil is fine for chicory.

Recipe

Autumn Salad • 4 Servings

Salad: 4 chicory lettuces, such as endive • 1 apple, cubed • ½ cup walnuts (115 grams) • 1 small onion or 3 green onions, chopped • ½ cup (115 grams) cheddar or Feta cheese, cubed • 2 medium carrots, sliced or grated • Dressing: cup (80 milliliters) oil • 2 tablespoons vinegar • sea salt • pepper • ¼ cup (60 grams) plain yogurt or cream (optional)

Mix all the salad ingredients in a serving bowl. Mix all dressing ingredients until combined. Toss the salad with the dressing.

TIP: To reduce the bitterness of chicory, you can first gently—but only briefly—sauté the chicory lettuces before mixing with the other ingredients.

Corn (*Zea mays*)

Family: Gramineae: sweet grass family

Other Names: baby corn, Indian corn, sweet corn, corn on the cob, maize, popcorn

Healing Properties: pure corn oil lowers cholesterol; corn silk aids urinary ailments and promotes urination (diuretic)

Symbolic Meaning: mother goddess (Native American), life energy, wholeness, material wealth, Americanism

Planetary Affiliation: Saturn, Sun

Cereal grains are the pillars of the great civilizations. The cultures of East Asia are hardly imaginable without the delicate, semi-aquatic grass: the rice plant. The rice farmers of Burma, Thailand, and Cambodia see rice as an emanation of the benevolent Buddha. In western Europe and western Asia wheat is the "staff of life," the "body of the Lord," which constitutes, thus, the "communion with God." In America, corn plays a similar role as the divine creator of civilization. "Our life," "life giver," and "sustainer of life" are some of the typical names various Native Americans have given to corn. The Aztecs called it "*tonácatl*," (our flesh). For the Mayans corn is the "first father." The Ojibwa called it "*mondamin*," (miracle corn).

Botanists have not yet been able to find the original wild forerunner of the first cultivated corn, which is believed to have grown in Mexico some ten thousand years ago. Its origin most likely goes back to a sudden mutation of *teosinte*, a grass native to Central America. Or perhaps it was as the Native Americans claim: that corn came down from heaven to earth as a goddess. Or, as the Ojibwa tell the story, corn came from other worlds as a green-clad stranger with yellow hair. When a young man on a vision quest wrestled the stranger and killed and buried him, the magical being came back to life as a corn plant.

Like a mighty deity, the corn plant conquered one tribe of people after the other. Its realm expanded to the north into Canada and south as far as Argentina; and wherever the corn deva appeared, people's lives changed. Hunters and gatherers became sedentary; villages and even cities sprang up; elaborate irrigation systems, stately warehouses, and temples were built—solely for corn. Priests told myths surrounding corn and celebrated elaborate ceremonies. Even humans were sacrificed to the maize deity. Amerindians fattened turkeys with corn; Mexicans did the same with the Chihuahuas they bred for meat.

According to the *Popul Vuh*, in the Mayan tradition the first human beings were made from corn mush. Primeval, divine male and female ancestor spirits created these "shining children of light" by grinding yellow and white ears of corn, which became their flesh and

Illustration 30. Oldest European drawing of corn (Leonhart Fuchs, De Historia Stirpium Commentarii Insignes, *1543)*

blood. Even the gods themselves got their strength from corn. Nahuatl lore tells how *azcatl*, the ant, once went on a pilgrimage to the mythical mountain of food. On the way, the ant met up with Quetzalcoatl, the feathered serpent, who also took on ant shape. Together they carried corn from the mountain to give to the gods; that is how the gods got too be so strong.

The Arikara tell that in the beginning of time humans lived miserable lives in the dark depths underneath the surface of the earth. But the Corn Mother, who lived with the Great Spirit in the heavens, took pity on their misery. With the help of badgers and moles she dug into the earth's surface and led the humans into the light of day. She then gave the first people corn to grow and then returned to the heavens. Unfortunately, humans turned out to be lazy, and constantly fought with each other. So the Corn Mother had to come down to earth again to teach them rituals and ceremonies so that they could live in harmony.

The Zuni tell that the Corn Mother planted a piece of her heart into the earth and that the sacred plant developed out of it. The goddess then explained, "This corn is my heart and shall be like milk from my breasts that you may not go hungry."

The Cherokee and other forest peoples tell how in the beginning of time the corn goddess lived with her children, who were the first humans, in the forest. In order to feed her family she brought a basket of corn every day from an isolated hut. One day her curious children followed her to see where the delicious corn came from. They were shocked to find her turning into corncobs dirt that she rubbed from her belly and private parts. Convinced that she was a wicked witch, they killed and buried her. Out of her grave grew a reed-like plant that soon produced ears of corn. And so the children were able to eat their daily corn again, but now they had to work hard for it.

Over thousands of years Native American gardeners developed hundreds of different varieties of corn: varieties with white, yellow, red, and blue kernels; flint maize; starchy kernels or soft corn; dent corn, today used for feeding livestock; pearl corn, with delicate kernels; and the giant white corn of Cusco. Native women ground the corn and mixed in a bit of wood ash in order to make porridge, grits (hominy), or tortillas. Adding some ash is important because its alkaline nature helps the body make maximal use of the nutrients, especially niacin, calcium, and protein. (Since corn lacks the important amino acids tryptophan and lycine, it's best eaten in combination with beans in order to avoid protein deficiency.)[1]

Native Americans have known popcorn for at least five thousand years. One of the gifts they gave to the pilgrims newly arrived in New England was popcorn in deer leather pouches. One of the favorite delicacies of the forest Indians was spoonfuls of corn mush cooked in sizzling bear fat and eaten with maple syrup; the white settlers named these fritters "hush puppies."

Illustration 31. Native Americans cooking soup with corn and fish (copper engraving from a painting by John White, "Indians Round a Fire," *1590)*

Central American natives make an inebriating and healthful corn beer, *chicha*. It's made from women chewing corn kernels and spitting the resulting mash into a vat to let it ferment. Because corn has no malt in it like barley does, the amylase in saliva is needed to turn the starch to sugar.

Native Americans have always eaten corn on the cob, either boiled or roasted in the husk over a fire, but their original corn was not the sweet corn that we know today. Sweet corn seems to have originated about two hundred years ago from a mutation in the raised beds of the Iroquois. Due to the loss of a gene responsible for turning sugar into starch, the kernels remain sweet; but because they have so little starch, the kernels shrivel soon after ripening.

In a strange twist, the corn of today is completely dependent on human care in order to survive; the seeds are so tightly fixed that it could never sow itself out.

Healing Aspects of Maize

As one might expect, the sacred corn is also a healing plant. Similar to our European ancestors, who baked healing herbs into bread, Native Americans often administered their medicinal plants in corn mush. The Mayans said that a very sick person should eat nothing but pure corn mush, as this was the best way to create healthy flesh to replace the sick flesh. The patient would be literally recreated, much like the first human originally created from corn. Native American healers generally used hot corn mush poultices for swelling, abscesses, and infections. For slowly healing abscesses and heavy bleeding after birth, as well as for a bleeding uterus, corn kernels infected with corn smut (*Ustilago maydis*) were ground to a powder; this was used—very carefully dosed—as a vasoconstrictive means to stop bleeding.[2] (In Europe midwives also very carefully used *Claviceps purpurea*, the ergot fungus that grows on rye, for similar purposes.) Native healers also made a very effective diuretic tea out of corn silk that they used for dropsy and genital and urinary diseases. Today corn silk tea is still used in Mexico for cleansing the urinary tract.

The Cultural Impact of Maize

Columbus brought "Indian wheat"—or "*mahis*," as it is called in the language of the Caribbean Indians—to Europe. It spread from Andalusia over southern Europe, Turkey, and the Balkans. The Portuguese brought it to Java in as early as 1496. In the following century, corn was raised in China, India, and Africa on hillsides that were otherwise not well suited for conventional crops. Wherever it was cultivated, the novel plant triggered a population explosion, which in turn changed local lifestyle and culture. For example, after its introduction, the populations in Africa, Asia, and southern Europe doubled within a short time.[3]

The deva of the corn plant has proven to be a power house. With the help of advanced agricultural technology and an intensive energy input, the annual production of corn worldwide amounts to some 600 million tons (over 50 percent of that in the United States alone). As such, corn is well on its way to replacing wheat and rice as the most cultivated staple. *El maíz* is the "daily bread" in both Mexico and, indirectly, the United States, where it is the main feed for cattle, pigs, turkeys, and chickens. In America, both beer and bourbon are made primarily of corn. Starch, glucose, and cellulose from genetically engineered corn make up an important factor in

Illustration 32. Kachina doll—one of the Pueblo guardians of the cornfields

chemical, pharmaceutical, and cosmetic industries. Cornbread and a gargantuan corn-fed turkey are a must at every Thanksgiving feast. Even George Washington preferred cornbread to wheat bread.

In contrast to the grain grasses of the old world—rice, rye, millet, wheat, barley, or oats—corn is much heavier and much more massive. The heavy spikes, or ears, are not poised gracefully on top of the stalk, but seem to slide down the stem as though pulled by gravity. It follows logically that corn is an appropriate symbol of material abundance or wealth. Because of this heaviness, and because corn comes from the West, the land of the setting sun, traditional European herbal astrologers attributed the vegetable to Saturn.[4]

Extensive monocultures of corn have changed our landscape; it's also allowed us to wallow in mountains of meat, butter, and eggs. Popcorn, corn chips, corn oil, corn syrup, and canned corn have also transformed traditional European eating habits and way of life. It's been a long time since Europeans wrinkled their noses at the corn in post-WWII American care packages, considering such "animal fodder." Cornflakes—developed toward the end of the nineteenth century by Dr. John Harvey Kellogg as a "wellness food"; indeed, as part of an antisexuality campaign—have ousted most other breakfast flakes. It would appear the crispy, often sugarcoated flakes, next to Coca-Cola and hamburgers, make the most significant American contribution to "our daily bread" (Pollmer 1994, 111). In the wake of the Americanization of the globe, people worldwide are getting ever more used to enjoying Hollywood films with popcorn and corn syrup–sweetened soft drinks.

Lest you think I dislike this mighty American, know that corn has established itself firmly in my garden here in the foothills of the Alps. I sow this vital wind pollinator in a block instead of in single rows and fertilize it with good compost, as it is a heavy feeder. (The Iroquois stilled its hunger by putting a fish in each mound as fertilizer.) The corn patch thanks me for this good care by producing plenty of delicious sweet corn in the fall. The rule of the house is to not pick the corn for the meal until the water is already boiling—because the sugar turns to starch so quickly.

Despite the short summers in northern climates, corn can still thrive due to its accelerated photosynthesis, the so-called "turbo photosynthesis" or C4 carbon fixation, which utilizes carbon more efficiently than most plants do.

Garden Tips

Cultivation: Sweet corn can be planted about the time of the last killing frost. For pollination to occur, which provides a full ear of corn, seeds should be planted in blocks rather than in rows. As soon as the plants are a few inches tall put on a good mulch to keep weeds at bay and protect the shallow roots from drying out or injury. If you do not want your corn to come in all at once, plant one-fourth of it every week for four weeks. (LB)

Soil: Corn needs a lot of nitrogen, so work plenty of compost into the soil before planting.

Recipe

Corn Soup à la Paul Silas Pfyl • 4 Servings

1½ pounds (680 grams) fresh corn kernels • 2 tablespoons butter
• 3 tablespoons paprika powder • 1 tablespoon honey • 1 quart
(945 milliliters) vegetable broth • ½ cup (115 milliliters) cream
(18% fat) • black pepper • chili pepper (optional)

Sauté corn kernels in butter in a medium pan. Add paprika powder and honey and mix well. Add broth and simmer for 20 minutes. Purée the soup with a blender. Add the cream and pepper to taste. Serve hot.

TIP: This soup pairs nicely with flat bread.

Cucumber (*Cucumis sativus*)

Family: *Cucurbitaceae*: gourd family

Other Names or Varieties: Armenian cucumber, cuke, English cucumber, gherkin, Kirby cucumber, lemon cucumber, Persian cucumber

Healing Properties: taken externally: smooths skin, heals blemishes and rashes taken internally: cleanses blood, promotes urination (diuretic)

Seeds: expel parasitic worms (vermifuge)

Symbolic Meaning: fertility, reincarnation, pleasant coolness, merriment

Planetary Affiliation: moon

The cucumber is a creeping vine from the melon and pumpkin family. Its preference for ripe old compost, moisture, and a fair amount of shade and warmth tells us it's a jungle plant. Its original home was the steamy hot jungle of India, where it has been cultivated for over four thousand years. The presumed wild form still grows in subtropical valleys on the southern slopes of the Himalayas. As this variety is very bitter, Dravidian natives probably first used it as medicine before milder cultivated forms were selected over time. To the dismay of gardeners even the cultivated cucumber will sometimes turn out tasting bitter, especially if it is too dry or if the stems get accidentally bent.

Cucumbers of many different kinds (Sanskrit *chirbhita*, *urvaruka*, or *sukasa*; Hindi *khira*) are cherished in their native India, especially in the premonsoon season when the temperatures can climb to 113 °F (45 °C). Cucumber is just about the only garden plant that can thrive in that kind of heat; even flies and mosquitos can't take it. Like all cucumbers, the Poona Kheerā variety, which looks like a cross between a cucumber and a gourd, is cooling and refreshing. It is cooked as a vegetable and served with rice and lentils. When eaten raw it is cut lengthwise and sprinkled with some sugar or spicy salt (*masala*). Indians also love to drink seasoned

Illustration 33. Krishna, the god of loving devotion

cucumber water; like the sour pickle juice that eastern Europeans and Turks drank before the advent of Coke, it is very thirst quenching. Another popular refreshment during India's hot season is raita, yogurt with grated or pickled cucumbers.

The cucumber plant has been treasured in traditional Indian medicine since pre-Vedic times. According to Ayurvedic teachings, the enjoyment of cucumbers affects the bodily fluids or humors (*dosa*) by lessening dry, fiery heat (*pitta*) while simultaneously increasing moisture or phlegm (*kapha*) and the cool air element (*vata*). The taste of cucumber is described as sweet, earthy, and moist, and its effect on the body as cooling, calming, and refreshing—which in turn can affect our mood, making us "as cool as a cucumber."

Ayurvedic medicine has so many uses for the cucumber that it would be impossible to list them all. Cucumber seeds—often cooked into syrup with chicory seeds and sugar—are prescribed as a diuretic. An emulsion of seeds and sugar has proven useful for kidney insufficiency, urinary tract inflammation, and inflammation of the bladder. Drinking fresh cucumber juice is good for urinary gravel. Individuals with stomach and intestinal ulcers, constipation, or stomach acidity benefit from cucumber juice and cucumber soup. Cholera patients are given a glass of cucumber juice mixed with coconut juice every two hours to maintain electrolyte balance and to avoid dehydration. Cucumber juice is used internally and externally for rashes and bad skin (Bakhru 1995, 105).

When a culture has such a long tradition with a plant species as India has with the cucumber, it is inevitable that all kinds of symbolism, tradition, and custom will envelop it. As we have seen with other vegetables, the "deva" or archetype of a plant species doesn't just express its nature in the form of its leaves, flowers, and fruits; its preferred environment; or its chemistry—its nature is also expressed in the images, dreams, imaginations, and rituals it inspires. A plant is, thus, more than its botany; it has also a cultural dimension.

In India the cucumber is associated with Vishnu, the preserver of the universe, especially in his form as Krishna. (On Krishna's birthday in August, households are decorated in his honor with flowers, lights, and ripe cucumbers.) It is believed that, as a youth, the dark-skinned god was so attractive that he melted women's hearts. When the moon was full and the glimmering heat of the day gave way to the cooling night, he played softly on his shepherd's flute. On hearing his music the women left their abodes and their sleeping husbands, hurrying to join the true lover of their souls. Each of them believed that the handsome youth, with whom they shared the tender joys of love, was there for her alone. But this myth doesn't depict a story of ordinary adultery—it speaks of divine love. It is *bhakti,* the selfless abandonment and love of human souls who have relinquished worldly life and given themselves to their higher Being.

In all of Southeast Asia, even for the Buddhists, the cucumber is a symbol of fertility. Legend tells of a famous king named Sagara who, though he had two queens, had no heir. A wise man, convinced that Sagara was a virtuous king, blessed the two queens, deeming one of them would bear him one son and the other sixty thousand sons. Soon thereafter, the queens were expecting. As predicted, one bore a healthy son. The other? She bore a cucumber. But the cucumber had sixty thousand seeds, which the father soaked in milk. They turned into sixty thousand strong boys.

Even today Indian women whose wish for children remains unfulfilled believe in the magic of cucumbers. They fast on an especially sacred day and swear to never again eat their favorite vegetable or fruit, hoping the gods will have pity on them; or they pilgrim to sacred wells and cliff crevices where it is believed that children's souls can be found. There they pray, take off their old clothes in exchange for new ones, and offer a cucumber. One of these sacred wells is Lolark Kund in the city of Varanasi. According to legend, once upon a time the sun stood still directly above the well, creating a break in the ever-rotating wheel of life. This break in the circle is a loophole through which the spirits of children can enter the material world and incarnate. Each August, on "the day the sun stood still,"[1] one can witness hundreds of barbers cutting the hair of thousands of small children. Parents offer hair offerings to express their thankfulness to the gods for blessing them with children.

Cucumber Travels

The cucumber started its voyage to nearly all the countries of the world quite early in agricultural history. In the seventh century BC it crossed Mesopotamia to reach Greece, where it became known as *siküos*. The Greeks learned to appreciate its cooling nature and cultivated cucumbers on a large scale; former "opium poppy city" Mekone near Corinth became "cucumber city" Sikyon (or Sicyon). The Romans also appreciated the cooling vegetable. Emperor Tiberius (42 BC–37 AD), who had greenhouses built for growing cucumbers, ate them year-round. The Romans called the plant "*cucumis*," from which comes *cucumber* in English and *concombre* in French. But, interestingly, the cucumber didn't enchant everyone; though the vegetable was brought north by the Roman legionaries, it failed to enthuse the Celts and Germanics. Although Charlemagne (742–814) ordered that *cucumeres* be planted on his landholdings, scholars don't know if such meant cucumbers or melons. By the Middle Ages in western Europe the plant seemingly was lost in oblivion; in any case, the twelfth-century abbess and polymath Hildegard von Bingen did not seem to know it.

The cucumber debuted in North America in the Jamestown colony in 1607, having arrived among the seeds brought by English settlers.

The watery green fruit found its way to the Far East in the fifth century AD. The Chinese called it the *hugua* ("melon of the Barbarians"). Though fully ripe, yellow cucumbers are occasionally mixed with other vegetables in the wok, but the Chinese never really showed much enthusiasm for them. They regarding them as "poisonous." This isn't to say that one could die from poisoning oneself with them, but they are seen as having too much *yin* (moist, dark, female energy)—so much so that they can disrupt an individual's yin-yang balance, thus encouraging disease. Despite this belief, however, in Chinese herbal lore the plant is used as a cooling, diuretic, laxative, and detoxifying medicine. Leaves and roots are used for dysentery and diarrhea, and the shoots for dysentery

Illustration 34. Cucumber plant (Joachim Camerarius, Neuw Kreütterbuch, *1586)*

and urinary disease. Even today the shoots are cooked and the decoction of cooked shoots is given for high blood pressure. The fresh juice of cucumber leaves is supposed to help reduce sudden flatulence with infants. Freshly mashed roots are used for swelling. Unfortunately, here in the West, we have no experience with these treatments.

The Indian enthusiasm for the cucumber was shared by the Slavs: Poles, Czechs, Wends and Sorbs in eastern Germany, and other Slavic folk groups love cucumbers. The German word for cucumber, "*Gurke*," as well as the English word "*gherkin*," both come from the old Polish term "*ogurek*."[2] According to archeological records, the first verifiable cucumber seeds were found in eastern Europe and eastern Germany, including seeds in Cracow dating between 650 and 950 AD, in Breslau from the eleventh century, and in the Czech Republic from the fourteenth century. In western Europe they did not appear until the sixteenth century, and then only in the commerce metropolis of Amsterdam.

Gustav Hegi (1876–1932), master of central European plant lore, described the Slavs as passionate admirers of cucumbers, noting how the Wends, who settled southeast of Berlin on the river Spree some two thousand years ago, grew fantastic cucumbers—even without hotbeds. He wrote:

> Even today the Spree forest is the cucumber basket for Berlin. Indeed, cucumbers pickled according to Slavic custom in salt with or without vinegar, or in vinegar with horseradish, dill, mustard, and pepper, are inexpensive foods for the hot summer months. The fairly slow months of July and August—due to the summer heat—are even called in common parlance "pickle time." Pickles taste sour due to lactic acid fermentation; the lactic acid bacteria that develop in the salty water create lactic acid from the sugar in the cucumbers, even without any vinegar in the brine (Hegi 1918, 331).

Cucumbers fermented with lactic acid are very good for the health, aiding, for example, the beneficial intestinal bacteria in repopulating after a treatment of antibiotics.

Sociologists tell us that emigrants' own traditional food is the most important part of their identity. Even after leaving behind customary clothing, customs, even language, newcomers cling to the culinary inheritance of their ancestors. For example, consider Italian pasta and pizza; Irish corned beef with cabbage; German beer, sausage, and hamburgers; the kosher food of the Jewish. The third-generation-Polish neighbors I knew as a child in Ohio were no different. For them, pickles (*ogórki kiszone*) and kielbasa sausage had an almost sacred status; no festivity was complete without them, as they stood for communion with the "spirit of the tribe." The mother of a friend of mine, Mrs. Kostecki, made especially good pickles, which "demanded" ritual care. In providing that care, first the cucumber bed was generously fertilized with composted cow dung. The seeds were sown according to the moon and astrological signs:

sowing when the moon was in a water sign, Pisces or Scorpio, made the resulting cucumbers juicy and smooth. (There were additional secret rules, I'm sure, but I missed a lot of them because Mrs. Kostecki spoke to her plants in Polish.) The harvest and pickling process was also performed according to astrological signs. Mrs. Kosteki let some get very ripe and yellow; these were then peeled and made into what she called "mustard pickles." The others were picked before they were ripe. Though Anglo Americans pickled their cucumbers in a hot brine of vinegar, sugar, and spices, Mrs. Kosteki soaked hers in salt brine with or without herbs, letting lactic acid fermentation do its work. This was never to be done in the sign of Pisces; since Pisces is connected to feet, they would go bad and smell like unwashed feet. For a similar reason she would not make pickles when the moon was in Scorpio, as it's connected to the genital area.

In all of eastern Germany and the bordering areas, the folklore involving "sympathetic magic" is similar. Everywhere cucumbers are sown in the garden when the moon is in either the water signs of Scorpio and Pisces; the water sign of Cancer is not ideal because such creates too many tendrils but few or crooked fruits. If the seeds are sown when the moon is in Gemini, there will be a big harvest but of a lower quality. And if one sows or plants in the fire and air signs, or in the earth sign of "virgin" Virgo, one will get a lot of blossoms but few cucumbers.

Country people used to choose especially sacred days for sowing cucumbers, such as Walpurgis Night (April 30), St. Sophia's Day ("Cold Sophie," May 15), or Corpus Christi (sixty days after Easter Sunday). In the German state of Brandenburg the gardeners hoped the cucumbers would grow as fast as the witches ride their brooms up the "Bocksberg" on Walpurgis Night. In Mecklenburg it was considered best to sow when the church bells chimed on Christ's Ascension Day (Holy Thursday). Country folk reckoned that male patron saints' days were better than those of the female saints for tending this obviously phallic vegetable. As such, cucumbers were traditionally cared for by the menfolk. In eastern Europe it is often the grandfather of the household who takes care of the cucumber bed; it is thought the plants thrive best if fertilized and watered with his urine. And were a menstruating woman to go into

Illustration 35. French cartoon, "The Masked Cucumber" ("Le Concombre Masqué") (illustration by Nikita Mandryka)

a cucumber garden, or even look at the garden, the plants might shrivel. (A menstruating woman should not touch a man's member for the same reason.)

There is something comical about cucumbers. In German there is an expression "to cucumber one's way through the countryside," which means driving around aimlessly, having nothing else to do. In Saxony a comical person is called "a cute cucumber." There was a popular comic in France in the 1980s, *The Masked Cucumber* (*Le Concombre Masqué*); its main character was a clever cucumber that, as "the enlightened master of the universe," had subsumed all the power of his garden fellows. Like sect leader Bhagwan Rajneesh, he was depicted wearing a flowing robe and a knitted cap. In Berlin those who, like the "Masked Cucumber," allow themselves indecencies and impertinence may hear: "They have the nerve of a cucumber! (*Wat nimmt sich der Mensch für 'ne Jurke raus!*)" And, finally, rumor has it that Mick Jagger owes some of his erotic charisma to cucumbers: he is said to have stuffed a good-sized cucumber in his tight jeans before performances.

In Jonathan Swift's *Gulliver's Travels* the Lilliputians tried to extract sunrays from cucumbers and save them in jars, as they wanted to warm the air on unfriendly and rainy days with the stored light. What the Lilliputians could not achieve in the realm of fantasy a German scientist did achieve in our own history. In 1975, biophysicist Fritz-Albert Popp examined germinating cucumber seeds with a photomultiplier—an apparatus that picks up and intensifies light emissions (bioluminescence) produced from living organisms. In so doing he proved that living cells radiate light (photons). As such, the cucumber is actually the godfather of modern biophotonic research.

Nowadays, the popular cucumber is readily available at all times of the year, as they are considered essential to many diets. In stimulating intestinal and kidney activity they give hope to those working to maintain a healthy weight. Contemporary research also shows that cucumbers are ideal for diabetics because they have a hormone that optimizes pancreatic function and supports insulin production. Both cucumber juice and grated cucumbers are good for smoothing the skin. Many film stars and models prefer cucumbers to beauty creams for their valuable "outer coating." As such, these modern women maintain practices derived from the wisdom of their ancient grandmothers, as old herbal books note the cucumber combats off all kinds of spots and flaws.

Garden Tips

Cultivation: The tropical cucumber is very frost-sensitive in spring and fall, so seeds shouldn't be sown until nighttime temperatures remain above 50 °F (10 °C). To speed the germination process one can soak the seeds in milk the night before sowing, they will germinate faster. To strengthen the plants themselves cucumbers like fermented stinging nettle tea and rock flour. Should mildew threaten the plants, one can spray them with a tea made of horsetail.

Soil: Cucumbers succeed in a well-drained sandy loam that is well supplied with compost, lime, and moisture.

Of Special Note: Bees play an essential role in cucumber production by carrying the pollen from the male flower to the female. For perfect fruits to form, the female flower must be pollinated on the first day it is ready; otherwise, the cucumber will be misshapen—or won't form at all. In addition, it is vital that cucumbers are harvested every day; otherwise they may stop producing. (LB)

Recipe

Cucumber Soup with Sour Cream and Sour Dock • 4 Servings

2 medium cucumbers, cubed • 2 tablespoons sunflower oil
• ¾ quart (175 milliliters) vegetable broth • herbal salt
• 20 small sour dock leaves, whole • 4 tablespoons sour cream

In a medium pan, sauté the cubed cucumbers in the sunflower oil. Add the broth and simmer for 10 minutes. Blend and let cool. Add herbal salt to taste. Stir in the sour dock leaves. Transfer soup to bowls; garnish each with a spoonful of sour cream.

Eggplant or Aubergine *(Solanum melongena)*

Plant Family: Solanaceae: nightshade family

Other Names: brinjal, garden egg, Guinea squash, melanzani, melongene

Healing Properties: stimulates appetite; facilitates bowel movement; lowers cholesterol; smooths skin (emollient)

Symbolic Meaning: mysteries of the night, passion, dedicated to Shiva

Planetary Affiliation: moon

Eggplant—or aubergine, as the Brits know it from its French name—is a member of the nightshade family, along with the tomato, potato, and pepper. Unlike these, however, it does not have its origin in tropical or subtropical America; like the cucumber, it hails from India. Dravidian gardeners and other indigenous peoples cultivated this vegetable many thousands of years ago, long before the Vedic-Aryan shepherd nomads made their appearance on the subcontinent. Originally it was a very thorny plant; its fruits were small and bitter, and its gray leaves felt-like on the underside. Today the ripe fruit can grow as heavy as two pounds, and it has since become treasured all over the world.

During the so-called Ghaznavid Incursions in the tenth century, Muslim armies invaded the Indian subcontinent. Not only did they enrich themselves with gold, precious jewels, and spices but—fortunately for us—they also took with them many healing and garden plants previously unknown outside India (Basham 1982, 73). Before long the eggplant established its place in the gardens and eating habits of the entire Islamic Realm from Persia to Andalusia. By the thirteenth century the plant had reached Italy and France; the widely educated scholar Albertus Magnus (~1200–1280) referred to it as "melogena."

The plant's long journey is mirrored in its French name. *Aubergine* derives from the Catalan word "*albergina*," which is from the Arabic term "*al-badingan*," which in turn is from the Persian *batinghan*, which itself came from one of the old Indian-Dravidian languages. Today the plant is known in India as "*baingan*," and in most of Southeast Asia as "*brinjal*."[1]

The first northern Europeans who encountered eggplant didn't trust the strange-looking plant with its white to black-violet egg-shaped fruits any more than they did the Moors then occupying Spain. Besides, it did not escape their attention that eggplant is a nightshade, similar to belladonna or other bittersweet nightshades with which witches and other enemies of Christianity reportedly made diabolical salves. They called this member of the notorious nightshade family "*mala insana*" or "*melzano*," meaning "apple of craziness"—anyone who ate it would surely go insane. In fact, except for the

Illustration 36. Eggplant blossom (illustration by Molly Conner-Ogorzaly, from B. B. Simpson and M. Conner-Ogorzaly, Economic Botany, *1986, 121)*

shiny, deep purple fruits—which are almost too beautiful to eat—all of the other parts of the plant are indeed poisonous. The leaves and roots contain solanine alkaloids, which cause nausea, upset stomach, and other ills. North of the Alps only scholars, druggists, and the clergy at first planted eggplant as an oddity, an exotic ornamental plant. But southern Europeans took to it more readily as a vegetable, especially since their climate suits it. European settlers introduced the plant to the Western Hemisphere when they came to America.

Today there exist many mouth-watering "aubergine" dishes in the Mediterranean countries. In Greece the eggplant is cut into sticks (*militzanes*) like French fries, put in the sun, and dried, to be eventually deep-fried in batter until golden brown. The southern French dish ratatouille—a stew of ripe tomatoes, zucchini, green peppers, onions, garlic,

Illustration 37. A young eggplant fruit

sweet basil, and parsley—would not be complete without eggplant. In Italy eggplant is popular sautéed in oil with garlic and parsley, called "*al funghetto.*" Another tasty Italian dish is *alla pizzaiola:* eggplant baked with tomatoes and bread crumbs. Japanese eggplant, *nasu,* is marinated in the salty soy paste miso.

Having originated in India, eggplant is an important ingredient in various regional Indian cuisines. In eastern India it is marinated in a mixture of bitter neem leaves and turmeric and then deep-fried in mustard oil. In central India, eggplant is slowly cooked at low temperature generously covered with yogurt. And in northern India a whole vegetable is held over an open flame until the skin is scorched, at which point it's easily removed; the flesh is then mashed with ginger, green chili pepper, and fresh coriander leaves.

Ayurvedic medicine has recognized many healing aspects of the plant. The unripe fruit is considered both a tonic for the heart and for reducing cholesterol, both ideal for diabetics. It is even considered to be an anticarcinogen. In any case, Charaka, the Hippocrates of Indian medicine, prescribed hot poultices of eggplant for infections, swelling, and tumors. The vegetable is otherwise recommended as an appetizer and a digestive.

Eggplant is as common a vegetable in India as potatoes are in the West. It is found in every garden, rich or poor. Its deep color indicates its dark, heavy nature, the *tamasic* category in the Indian system of foods; as such it suits the stodgy, earthy, country population, and is thus attributed to the dark, unpredictable Shiva. Just like the simple folk, the god Shiva himself is not considered worthy of the fine foods the Brahmins (priests) eat—even though Shiva is recognized by all as the god of gods, the origin of all being! Indeed, the long, dark vegetable fits well to the *linga*, the phallic symbol of Shiva, the divine member representing the masculine side of the universe. When the dark god unites in bliss with his Shakti (the universal female energy), the two generate the entire universe; as such the tamasic nightshade plant belongs to the mysterious night, the deep, dark world of sensuality and passion.

In Bengali poetry the deep purple aubergine symbolizes the summer sky at the moment, shortly after the sunset, when night comes. The white eggplant symbolizes, in contrast, the hazy morning sky just before the summer sun rises.

Garden Tips

Cultivation: Eggplant can be cultivated under the same conditions as its cousin the tomato. Above all, the plant needs warmth and should be planted in the garden and covered to protect it from the cold for the first week or two. Put down a thick mulch to both preserve moisture and even soil temperatures. The plant needs four warm months of summer in order to become full sized (three feet), blossom, and produce fruit. In cold regions one must, just like with tomatoes, sow the seeds in a greenhouse in late February or early March— about ten weeks before planting time. The plant needs rich soil with plentiful good compost and water. It takes well to phosphates and can be fertilized several times during the season with watered-down liquid manure from chickens or doves. The vegetable should be harvested before the seeds are fully ripe; otherwise it will become bitter. Potato bugs like the plant almost better than they like potatoes, but otherwise there are few insects that find the plant attractive.

Soil: Eggplant likes well-drained loam (between medium and sandy) that is rich in nutrients, as it is a heavy feeder.

Recipes

Eggplant with Pear Mustard • 4 Servings

Eggplant: 4 small eggplants • 2 tablespoons sesame seeds • 2 tablespoons olive oil • herbal salt • ground nutmeg • black pepper • 1 cup alfalfa sprouts • Pear Mustard: 1 ripe pear • 4 tablespoons mustard

EGGPLANT: Poke the eggplants with a fork a few times on both sides. Bake in a pan in the oven at 350 °F (175 °C) until the skins are wrinkled and easily peeled off. (Alternatively, roast the eggplants over hot embers: holding them over the heat by the stems, rotate them to roast evenly until the skin turns black and is easily peeled off; the flesh should be soft.) Remove the charcoaled eggplant skin. Put the remaining flesh in a bowl. Add the sesame seeds and olive oil and mash with a fork until well mixed. Add herbal salt, pepper, and nutmeg to taste.

PEAR MUSTARD: Cube the pear. In a blender, purée the pear and the mustard.

Arrange the alfalfa sprouts on a serving dish. Put the eggplant mixture on alfalfa sprouts and serve with the pear mustard.

Fried Eggplant with Herbal Yogurt • 4 Servings

Eggplant: 4 eggplants • 2 garlic cloves, chopped • 1 teaspoon lemon juice • herbal salt • pepper • 4 tablespoons flour • 4 tablespoons olive oil • Yogurt sauce: ¼ cup fresh herbs (such as rosemary, thyme, parsley), finely chopped • 1 tablespoon olive oil • 1 cup plain yogurt • garlic cloves to taste • herbal salt

Cut the eggplants into slices (about ½-inch thick). Place them in a pan. Add the garlic and lemon juice and let rest in the refrigerator for 1 hour.

Sauté the herbs in the olive oil until crisp. Let them cool. Put the yogurt in a bowl; mix in the herbs. Add garlic and herbal salt to taste.

Put the flour in a small bowl. Dredge the eggplant slices on both sides in the flour; season with herbal salt and pepper. Fry in olive oil until golden brown. Serve with the yogurt sauce.

Evening Primrose (*Oenothera biennis*)

Family: Oenothera: evening primrose family

Other Names: fever plant, German rampion, night willow herb, sun-cups, sundrops

Healing Properties: helps alleviate stomach and intestinal cramps, coughing, and bronchial spasms

Root: eases coughing and hemorrhoids

Oil (seeds): eases effects of hangover, heals endogenous eczema, eases eye and mouth dryness (Sjögren's syndrome), aids healing of liver; eases menopause symptoms, multiple sclerosis, PMS, polyarthritis

Symbolic Meaning: transience, inconstancy (in the Victorian language of flowers), secret love, reincarnation

Planetary Affiliation: Sun

Very few people know that evening primrose is a very tasty edible root. For that reason it "should" appear here in the category of forgotten and rare vegetables, but I present it here because it deserves a central place in a modern vegetable garden. Why? Because it is an outstanding source of nourishment that also ranks among the best healing plants.

The great Swedish botanist Carl Linnaeus (1707–1778) named the flower *Oenothera biennis*, but, interestingly, etymologists aren't sure what he intended. *Oenothera* could mean something along the lines of "smelling of wine" (*oinos*), or "catcher of donkeys" (*ono-théras*). Another puzzle as to his choice: in ancient Greece there was another plant with this name, a kind of fireweed (*Epilobium*) that also belongs to the evening primrose family. The second name, "*biennis*," is clearer, as it concerns a plant with a two-year life span.

Given how many tales about the evening primrose there are to be found in European plant lore, one might assume it to be a native of the region. But, as it came originally from the eastern forest area of Northern America, it is actually an invasive alien plant (neophyte) to the Old World. Curious botanists sowed the evening primrose for the first time in Europe in 1612—in a seedbed in the famous botanical garden of Padua, Italy. How astounded the gardeners must have been to see the tall flowering plant for the first time! The amazing spectacle of the opening of the flower bud occurs about half an hour after sunset. Within a few minutes four brilliant yellow flower petals burst open, much like a butterfly emerging from its cocoon. A pleasant vanilla scent soon fills the air and in no time moths swarm in, seeking the sweet nectar. The Renaissance spectators found it so fascinating they might have even postponed heading to the theater until after this flower's performance. Every European aristocrat of the Baroque era grew evening primroses. Not long afterward members of the bourgeoisie, proud of their exquisite gardens, could not resist following suit. And, of course, the pattern continues to the common folk. Thus the evening primrose—this lazy maiden, who does not get up until after sunset—also took her place in peasant gardens.

Europeans had numerous names for the unusual alien plant: "key to the night sky," "nightlights," "lazy girls," "dim candle," "sleeping virgins." These all relate to the fact that the post-sunset blooms last only one night and day before wilting. The references to light derive from scientists puzzling as to whether the petals of this flower are luminescent or whether they simply reflect the last evening light.

Poets were readily inspired by this unusual flower, seeing in it a symbol of the transient nature of life, or a sign of heavenly love. Upon seeing the evening primrose one such lovelorn poet, C. F. Bürger, was inspired to write this verse:

> When the night has rewarded
> all who are tired with sweet slumber,
> I stealth off to the cottage
> where my sweetheart lives.

For about a hundred years the evening primrose remained just the object of aesthetic admiration. Then the peasants, simple tillers of the soil, discovered that the plant can be eaten as food; soon thereafter it was regularly cultivated in vegetable gardens for its tasty, fleshy taproot, which

Illustration 38. Roots and seedpods of the evening primrose

develops at the end of this biennial's first year. (In the second year the root becomes woody and tasteless.) The light pink color of the root looks like tender cooked ham; the flavor is comparable to the delicate taste of salsify, which we'll discuss later on.

Though health advocates of the day believed the root provided more nutrition than oxen meat, it was its likeness to ham that prevailed in this enigmatic plant's mystique. In Catholic countries the evening primrose was dedicated to the patron saint of pigs, St. Anthony. For that reason a French evening primrose dish is called "*jambon de St. Antoine*" (St. Anthony's ham). Soon enough, the vegetable became known as "ham root," "edible root," "wild stalk," "Spanish rampion," or "Rapunzel celery"—depending on regional delicacies that developed out of the fashionable garden vegetable. Then, in 1863 a cultivated variety developed by German gardeners arrived in the land of its origin. This novel root vegetable, ironically called "German rampion," became a success in North America.

Unfortunately, the use of evening primrose as a vegetable has for the most part been completely forgotten in the West. But in Russia—and of course in my garden—this vitamin-rich appetizing root still has a place of honor. The young leaves are also very good eaten as a green vegetable or added to soups. The yellow blossoms can also join other edible flowers—nasturtiums, the heavenly blue borage, the delicate pink radish, and the daisy—in garnishing a summer salad.

The Healing Potential of the Evening Primrose

According to biodynamic gardeners following the teachings of Rudolf Steiner, in the evening primrose's first year—as is the case with most biennials—lunar forces (using the ponderous elements of water and earth) are at work building the root and rosette. In the second year, the influence of the sun and the distant planets (using the imponderous—lacking weight—elements of air and fire) brings the plant to shoot into flower and seed.

In the twentieth century practitioners of "flower remedies"—the therapy originally developed by the English physician Edward Bach in the 1930s—discovered the evening primrose. The Californian Flower Remedies prescribe the essence of evening primrose as therapy for those traumatized in the womb because they were unwanted, that is, those whose mothers considered aborting them. Therapists claim that "evening primrose helps the soul be literally reborn by providing the emotional nourishment that was missing in the beginning of the incarnation" (Kaminski and Katz 1996, 294).

In the 1980s medical science turned its attention to the evening primrose, but neither for its flower or its root, but its seeds—specifically the seeds' oil. Massaging this oil into the skin is said to help for PMS (premenstrual syndrome) and endogenous eczema; it can also be ingested for polyarthritis, burns, dry eyes and skin, and brittle nails; it is even said to help with scleroderma, Sjögren's syndrome, and multiple sclerosis. It's also considered to help lower high blood pressure, and improve digestion, circulation, and function of the endocrine glands. There are also reports that it has a general strengthening effect on the immune system, helps wounds heal, improves skin turgor, and helps rejuvenate livers damaged by alcohol. To add to the bounty: it's not known to have any side effects.

How is it possible that this plant oil indicates such a wide spectrum of beneficial effects—especially since the above-named effects were hitherto unknown in traditional healing lore? Is evening primrose oil just another "snake oil"? Well, let us consider its earliest-known beneficial effects. Country folk knew it had certain healing properties: tea made from the blossoms was used for coughs, bronchial spasms, and stomach and intestinal cramps. In American folk medicine practice the leaves were cooked with honey to make a cough elixir. The North American natives used the plant to calm the lungs and stomach. The Ojibwa made a poultice out of stamped leaves for major bruises and sprains. The Cherokees made tea from the roots for obesity, or applied the hot roots topically to hemorrhoids. Johann David Schoepf (1752–1800), who wrote the first *Materia Medica Americana Potissimum Regni Vegetabilis* (*Medical Material of America—Especially of the Vegetable Kingdom*), which included four hundred native plants, mentioned the plant as ideal for healing wounds.

The list continues. The Iroquois chewed the seeds "against laziness;" players of the sacred Lacrosse ball game would chew the seeds and then rub the pulp into their arms and leg muscles to keep them strong throughout the game. The southwestern Navaho cooked the roots of this "life medicine" and rubbed their limbs with the brew when carrying heavy loads. Young maidens waiting to be married wore the blossoms in their hair at festivals. Zuni sun priests gave the young ladies evening primrose blossoms to chew and then rub on their breasts, arms, neck, and hands to help them do the ritual dance intended to guarantee plenty of rain and a good corn harvest. Other Native Americans such as the Payute rubbed their bodies and moccasins with chewed blossoms and seeds when they went deer hunting, for double benefit: attracting the deer while also repelling snakes (Moerman 1999, 361).

But somehow much of that knowledge was lost. It wasn't until modern day that British researchers took recent interest in the oil from the seeds. They discovered that the oil is mainly made up of essential fatty acids, of which a large portion (around 10 percent) is gamma linolenic acid (GLS). GLS is a fatty acid from which the body can produce the tissue hormone prostaglandin (PG), which is found plentifully in the human organism in mother's milk and in semen. A deficiency of prostaglandins implicates a diversity of health issues, including dermatological, cardiovascular, and gynecological problems. Indeed, premature babies who spend their first days in an incubator are in danger of not developing the capacity of producing enough PG; such runs the risk of these symptoms developing in adulthood. Alcoholism, a diet of junk food, old age, or the effects of radiation can also hamper the organism's ability to produce enough of its own prostaglandin (Mabey 1993, 89).

Thanks to these clinically tested discoveries, today evening primrose is grown commercially on a wide scale and the wonderful oil is available in health stores everywhere. An industrial variety has even been bred that has stronger seed pods that won't break open when harvested by machines—however the question remains whether or not other qualities were also bred out in the process.[1]

Those up for an adventure can seek out wild evening primrose seeds. Besides getting seeds in wild plant nurseries, one can find this pioneer plant growing profusely in the wild, along waysides, in bushy overgrown areas, and around gravel pits and abandoned fields. In autumn many seedpods ripen on the top half of nearly one-yard-high stalks. Each pod contains about half a teaspoon of the tasty seeds, which are easily harvested by shaking the ripe capsules upside down into a bag. If one doesn't have an oil press, the seeds can be ground in a mortar and pestle or even chewed directly. The poppy-like seeds can also be strewn into cereals or salads, baked into bread, added to soups, or used to garnish the tops of buns.

Both in the garden and in the wild evening primrose prefers full sunlight—the seeds need light to germinate—and a relatively dry location. In Europe the wild plant likes to settle on railroad embankments—giving it the name "railroad flower." It's also known as the "Swiss freeway flower": in recent years Switzerland has used fewer herbicides on freeway shoulders; as a result, the evening primrose found a new spot in which to flourish.

Garden Tips

Cultivation: Evening primrose is frost-hardy and long lasting; once established in a garden it will come back year after year. The seeds can be sown directly into the garden bed from late spring into early summer. The bed should be dug over, the seeds sown thinly and covered only lightly, then left to germinate. Weeds must be kept out of the bed, especially during the growth period. The seeds develop after the plant blossoms and ripen during late summer and fall. Interestingly, in the wild the plants thrive in quiet places with meager soil and need hardly any care. (LB)

Soil: Evening primrose likes fertile and porous soils. And though it prefers a sunny location, it can also thrive well in less-sunny spots.

Recipes

Evening Primrose Roots with Walnuts • 2 Servings

4 evening primrose roots, finely grated • turmeric • 1 pinch ground coriander seeds • chives, finely chopped • 1 teaspoon mustard • 1 teaspoon lemon juice • 2 tablespoons tahini • sea salt • black pepper • walnuts (for garnish)

In a medium bowl mix the evening primrose roots with the turmeric, ground coriander, and chives. Add the mustard, lemon juice, and tahini and stir well. Season with sea salt and pepper to taste. Transfer to a serving dish, garnished with walnuts.

Evening Primrose Stew with Stinging Nettle Pesto • 4 Servings

Stew: 2 yellow onions, cubed • 2 carrots, cubed • 1 small celery root, cubed • 1 small savoy cabbage, finely chopped • 6 potatoes, peeled or unpeeled, cubed • 8 evening primrose roots, cubed • small quantities of sage, bay leaves, clove, thyme, and lovage (about ¼ cup total) • 2 tablespoons olive oil • 1½ quarts (1½ liters) vegetable broth

Pesto: 2 handfuls baby spinach (or orache) • 1 cup (225 grams) bread, cubed • ¼ cup (60 grams) olive oil • sea salt

In a large pan, sauté the vegetables with the seasoning and herbs in the olive oil for about 20 minutes. Add the vegetable broth and simmer until tender, about 15 minutes. Transfer to a serving bowl. In a blender, blend pesto ingredients until smooth. Serve with the stew.

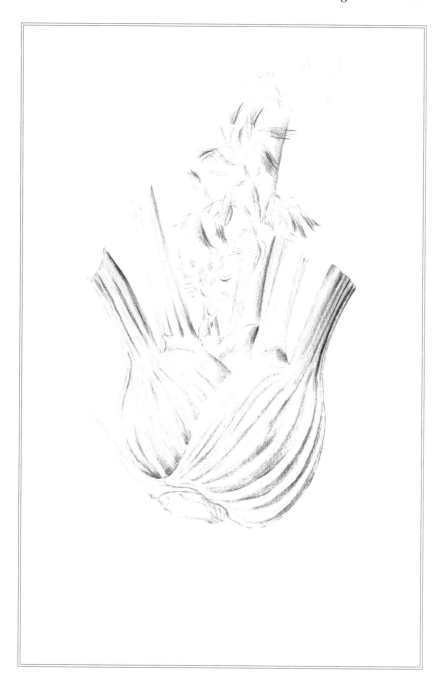

Fennel (*Foeniculum vulgare*)

Family: Apiaceae, Umbelliferae: umbellifer or carrot family

Other Names: finocchio, Florence fennel (the bulb used as a vegetable), spignel, sweet fennel

Healing Properties: detoxifies body, prevents convulsions (anticonvulsant), reduces flatulence, inhibits fungi and bacteria, stimulates menstruation (emmenagogue), increases milk production, clears mucus (expectorant), reduces phlegm, calms stomach; beneficial for spleen

Symbolic Meaning: clairvoyance, spiritual clarity; success, victory; transmits cosmic fire, expelling demons. In ancient world attributed to Prometheus and Dionysus; in Christianity associated with St. John and St. Giles

Planetary Affiliation: Mercury

Though fennel was not known until fairly recently as a comestible, this fine, aromatic vegetable is becoming ever more popular. It has a lot of roughage, it improves cellular metabolism, and it's a diuretic, an expectorant, and a detoxifier. It soothes the intestines and calms the nerves. Eaten raw in salads finocchio (Florence fennel) is a veritable health elixir, one particularly ideal for those working to lose weight. Indeed, the seventeenth-century English doctor William Cole (1626–1662), wrote: "Those who have become fat and indolent use the seeds, leaves, and roots in drinks and soups in order to lose weight and become slim and trim." When scientists recently tested the effects of fennel oil on mice they discovered that those consuming higher doses lost more weight. Fennel does this by binding lipid substances in the intestines so that the body absorbs fewer triglycerides, which are associated with obesity. Aromatic, yellowish fennel oil has an antiflatulent, antifermentative, antispasmodic effect: it relaxes smooth musculature and also stimulates the flow of bile. Small doses of fennel oil increase discharge in the mucous membranes in the stomach, intestines, and lungs (fennel is often an ingredient in cough medicine). The roots of this biennial, harvested in March of the second year, are regarded by folk medicine—next to parsley, celery, and asparagus—as "cleansing, healing roots." Anthroposophic doctors emphasize that these effects are typical of the entire *apiaceae-*, or *umbelliferae*, family, as they all seem to have either a boosting or an inhibitive effect on the gland system. Warming and relaxing, fennel stimulates the glands.

In western Asia and the Mediterranean region—where fennel originated—there are different kinds of wild fennel. They are

Illustration 39. Prometheus and the eagle (detail from a drinking vessel, ~540 BC, Greece)

all characterized by light green, fine filigree, aromatic leaves and yellow umbrella-shaped blossoms, and everywhere they grow they are regarded as sacred and healing. In ancient Greece wild fennel played a central role in the mystery cults. Giant fennel, which grows up to nine feet (three meters) high, was dedicated to Prometheus, the god of fire. This Titan, whose name means "forethinker," hid the fire he stole from heaven in the stalk of such a fennel plant when he brought it to humankind. (This could be a remnant from primeval memory: archeologists assume that Stone Age foragers of the Mediterranean area carried glowing embers from camp to camp inside dried fennel stalks.) The Greeks believed fennel, a member of the carrot family, improved eyesight. Roman natural historian Pliny the Elder (23–79 AD) claimed that snakes eat fennel after shedding their skin and rub themselves on the stalk so as to renew their eyesight with its juice. Medieval doctors prescribed eye baths with fennel tea, an ophthalmological treatment known to modern-day Egyptian Copts.

The *thyros*—a wand or scepter that the Greek god of inebriation, Dionysius, used to rule over his enraptured maenads (female followers),

Illustration 40. Dionysus on a donkey with a scepter (thyros) (copy of an ancient Greek illustration reproduced in Lexikon abendländischer Mythologie, 1993)

satyrs, and sileni—is said to have been made of a fennel stalk decorated with ivy and pine cones. Scholars report that the actors in the Dionysian mystery dramas wore wreaths made of fennel foliage.

In the ancient Greek language fennel is called "*marathón.*" Marathon, or "fennel field," was the name of the location where in 409 BC the Greeks defeated the far more powerful Persian invaders. A messenger then ran forty-two kilometers nonstop to bring the joyous news to Athens, where he shouted before he collapsed and fell dead to the ground, "Victory is ours!" Due to this dramatic incident fennel came to symbolize courage, victory, and success. A marathon-race is still carried out ritually in the Olympic games. Warriors—and later also gladiators—ate fennel or rubbed themselves down with fennel juice in order to succeed in battle and the victors were crowned with aromatic fennel foliage.

The ancients were convinced that evil, disease-causing spirits could be conquered with this strong plant. The physician Dioscorides (~40–90 AD), who was well versed in plant lore, prescribed the marathon plant for bladder and kidney ailments, for nausea and heartburn, for the bites of poisonous animals, as an eye medicine, as a remedy for menstruation irregularities, and "to fill women's breasts with milk"—all uses that have lasted through to modern day.

For the Romans fennel was of no less importance. The seeds, herbage, and roots of the umbellifer were valued for their healing virtues. Galen (129–~216 AD), founder of humoral pathology, assigned the medicinal properties of fennel as "warm to the third degree" and "dry to the first degree." The effects were described as warming, diuretic, diluting, widening (for blockage in the glands), dissipating, and loosening. In other words, fennel purifies or purges "bad fluids." Galen also noted that it increased milk flow and facilitated menstruation.

The Romans valued the plant as a spice and raw vegetable as well. They seasoned vinegar, bread, meat broth, and pickled olives with the seeds, and added the foliage to salads and soups. But even so, though Roman legionaries cultivated fennel as one of their favorite plants in the colonies north of the Alps, it was the Christian monks who established it as a spice and medicinal herb in their cloister gardens. This is partly because fennel was a genuine monk's medicine, considered an ally in heralding a Christian "spin" on established, "pagan" beliefs; it could stand its ground in the face of the traditional healing plants used by heathen wise women and "wortcunners": knowers of herbs. It is listed in the St. Gall Cloister Garden layout plans in Switzerland; it appears as well in the ninth-century poem *Hortulus,* in which monk Walafrid Strabo described the garden he tended. Charlemagne (742–814), untiring conqueror of the heathens, decreed it be planted on all of the royal estates.

Fennel was considered one of the best means of driving off devils and demons; just as it cleanses the body fluids, it also cleanses the astral atmosphere. Like other aromatic herbs—dill, lovage, oregano, thyme, sage, rue—it repels the invisible, swirling astral bodies of wicked witches. Indeed, religious legend claims fennel was one of the herbs that relieved the Savior's pain as he hung upon the cross. As stated in the tenth-century "Nine Herb Charm (*Lacnunga*)" of the Anglo-Saxons:

Chervil and fennel, fearsome pair,
These herbs were wrought by the wise lord,
holy in heaven, there did he hang;
He set and sent them in seven worlds
To remedy all, the rich and the needy.

Such a powerful plant soon found a place of honor in Christian folk culture. Fennel became obligatory for seasoning fish in the time of fasting; the poor ate the fasting herb even without fish. Anglo-Saxon *laece* (leeches, shamanistic healers) brewed a healing potion out of fennel and other herbs as protection against harassment by the devil—which, after Christianization, meant either a figure of a furry, horn-bearing nature spirit or the shaman god Wōdan (Odin). A German folktale claims that the fennel plant is as effective as holy water in driving off nasty dwarves and elves: dangerous figures that not only spook human beings but also inflict pain and disease with their "elf-shots." In England children wore a sachet with fennel seeds as a necklace to protect them from the evil eye. At the birth of Till Eulenspiegel, a German prankster and magician, the midwife supposedly said: "I bring the lucky child angelica, which protects people from lust; and fennel, which drives the devil away."

Fennel played also a role in the St. John's Day celebrations, which were a continuation of old heathen midsummer festivities. Before going to the festival on the village greens, French peasants stuffed fennel foliage into the keyholes of their doors, saying: "In case a magician wants to enter the room through this keyhole, fennel, let him feel your presence and power, so he will be afraid to enter." Then they could dance and drink with no concern. In the olden days the French also believed that a fennel stalk that's been drawn nine times through the St. John's Day fire would protect from magical spells. In England, fennel foliage was hung on doors and windows at the time of St. John. This effective preventative meant witches trying to enter buildings would be forced to count the countless pointed leaves; but as they constantly lost count and had to start over again, their efforts for evil magic proved futile. In East Prussia it was customary to brush the udders and horns of the cows with fennel foliage on the St.

John's Eve (June 23); in Italy the cows' horns were decorated with it to protect them from the bad spirits that cause disease.

On September 1, the patron day of St. Giles, the Spanish celebrate a regular fennel benediction. In the seventh century St. Giles lived as a pious hermit in a forest hermitage in Provence. There he took into his protection a female deer that had been wounded by hunters. From that day on he became the patron of nursing mothers and milk cows. (Again, fennel, an effective galactagogue, increases the flow of mothers' milk.) In France, where he is called "St. Gilles," he replaced the old Celtic god Cernunnos as the "patron of the animals." For the Germans, too, he became the "patron of fennel"; depending on the region, he is known as Till, Gild, Gill, or Ilg, and is considered one of the "Fourteen Holy Helpers."

Naturally Benedictine abbess Hildegard von Bingen (1098–1179) was also delighted by such a truly "Christian" healing plant that aids both humans and animals. "*Feniculum*," she declared, "enlivens people, helps with digestion, gets rid of bad breath, helps as a collyrium (eye-cleansing water) for inflamed-eye conjunctiva, helps as a compress for bad eyesight and headaches, as a smudging plant along with dill for a painful runny nose, as a body rub against melancholy, as a salve for inflamed swelling of the male member, as a warm poultice to ease in giving birth; besides it is also good for lung ailments, strong coughing, heart pain, stomach and intestinal colic, and as a healing means for alcoholism." She also advised, "An alcoholic should eat fennel foliage or

Illustration 41. Cernunnos (etching copied from an ancient Roman relief, Manfred Lurker, Lexikon der Götter und Dämonen, 1984)

fennel seeds. He will feel better afterward because fennel's mild warmth and moderate power will tame the madness that the wine has caused." She might have intended these wise words for monks, often confirmed drunkards. Indeed anethole (anise camphor), one of the main active ingredients in fennel, is thought to detoxify the liver of alcohol poisoning and reduce the effects of snakebites, poisonous plants, and mushrooms.

The "*feniculum*" Hildegard knew, the "ordinary" Mediterranean healing herb and spice plant, was not the fennel we grow today as a vegetable delicacy. It was not until the Renaissance that Italian master gardeners bred the delicate and popular Florence fennel, or finocchio, with its whitish green, thick, onion-shaped leaf sheaths. Fennel stalks, *carosella* (*F. vulgaris* var. *azonicum*), a popular vegetable in southern Italy, were also developed at this time. The Renaissance was, in fact, a time of glory for this aromatic plant. Nicholas Culpeper (1616–1654), who put fennel under the rule of the planet Mercury and the zodiac sign Virgo, was completely taken by fennel, as was the German herbal doctor Jacobus Theodorus Tabernaemontanus (1525–1590), who filled twelve pages of his 1588 publication *Neuw Kreuterbuch* describing fennel's healing properties.

Since that time this "sacred plant of Italy" has spread across the globe, as it prospers in any climate where grapes do well. Today it can be found as an invasive plant growing wild in South Africa, in Argentina, or in California. Presumably European settlers brought the seeds to the Americas, where wild fennel is considered an aggressive invasive plant. In the world of culinary delights, it has become a regular cosmopolitan, serving as seasoning in fish soups and in salads.

Garden Tips

Cultivation: The biggest mistake a home gardener can make is to sow a whole row of fennel at once, as the plants will become woody if not harvested quickly. It is best to sow in short intervals, starting in early spring through to early summer—skipping any periods of summer that exceed temperatures of 70° F (24° C), when fennel can bolt to seed. (LB)

Soil: Fennel prefers neutral soil. If planting in strongly acidic soil, it's best to mix some limestone into the compost.

Recipe

Fennel Soup with Pesto • 4 Servings

Soup: 4 fennel bulbs, cut into square cubes • 2 onions, cubed
• 3 tablespoons olive oil • ¼ cup (115 milliliters) white wine
• 1 quart (945 milliliters) vegetable broth • 2 tablespoons
fennel seeds • sea salt • white pepper

Pesto: 5 garlic cloves • 1 tomato, cubed • 1 bunch of sweet basil,
leaves picked from the stems • 3 ounces (80 grams) Parmesan cheese,
grated • 2 tablespoons olive oil • black pepper

In a medium pan, sauté the fennel and onions in the olive oil. Add the white wine, then the vegetable broth. In a separate pan, roast the fennel seeds without oil on medium heat, constantly stirring or shaking the pan, until they become fragrant but before turning brown. Remove the seeds from the heat and grind them with a mortar and pestle. Stir them into the soup. Season the soup with salt and pepper, to taste. Simmer for about 30 minutes. Transfer to a serving dish.

PESTO: In a blender, mix the garlic, tomato, cheese, and olive oil until smooth. Add pepper to taste. Serve the pesto with the soup.

Jerusalem Artichoke (*Helianthus tuberosus*)

Family: Compositae: composite, daisy, or sunflower family

Other Names: Canada or French potato, earth apple, girasole, pig's potatoes, sunchoke, tuberous sunflower, topinambour

Healing Properties: curbs the appetite, improves intestinal flora; ideal for diabetes diet

Symbolic Meaning: the sun god Helios imparts the strength of the higher self; exoticism, luxury; but also hunger and need

Planetary Affiliation: Sun

Many today have no idea what a Jerusalem artichoke, or sunchoke, is, especially as the information about it found in cookbooks or garden literature is often both minimal and incorrect. Occasionally one may find the reddish purple, beige, or pale brown tubers in stores—alongside exotic vegetables such as ginger, Inca berries, mangos, and okra—and some gourmands are willing to pay a pretty penny for them. Sometimes they're assumed to be sweet potatoes, although the latter belongs to the morning glory family. (In the seventeenth and eighteenth centuries, merchants and common people alike were confused about the various exotic tubers from the New World.) For the French or Germans, who call it *tobinambour,* Jerusalem artichokes conjure up images of the jungle and the Amazon.

The root tuber is tasty when prepared correctly. Sliced raw into salads, seasoned with oil and lemon, it's similar to the refreshing, crunchy Chinese water chestnut.[2] When roasted, steamed, or boiled it has a slightly sweet flavor, somewhere between artichoke hearts and salsify. It's a delicacy when pickled like cucumbers. For the Europeans who survived the Second World War, however, the Jerusalem artichoke is considered anything but exotic; for them the mild, sweetish vegetable awakens memories of hardship, deprivation, and hunger. This was because it was grown everywhere in Europe at the time, and for good reason: the plant produces three to four times as much edible bulk as would potatoes on the same amount of land, it requires minimal tending, and it doesn't leech the soil. After the economic boom in the 1960s the tuber mostly sank into oblivion. Hunters planted

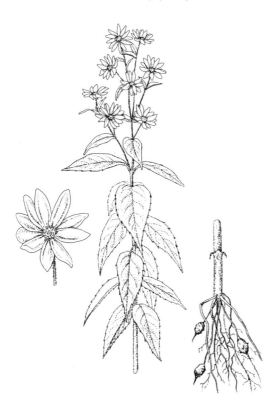

Illustration 42. Jerusalem artichoke: leaves and roots

it to feed the deer and other wild animals in the European forests. Only anthroposophists remained faithful to the plant. They saw it as an "astrally sunny" alternative to the—in their opinion—more dubious, dark, "materialistic and Ahrimanic" potato of the nightshade family.

The Jerusalem artichoke is actually a kind of sunflower with storage roots and flowers that are three to five inches in diameter. Like its sister, the much larger common sunflower (*H. annuus*), its blossoms rotate in following the sun's daily movement across the sky. A native of the North America prairie, it grows from Saskatchewan to the Mississippi Delta. Jerusalem artichokes and other kinds of sunflowers grew in the endless expanse of six-foot-high prairie grass that once fed the huge population of freely roaming bison. The sunchokes lifted their yellow floral disks above the waving ocean of grass much like dandelions or daisies do in our mowed lawns. But the Jerusalem artichoke differs from its annual sunflower cousins in that it keeps its life force concentrated in its tuber rather than expending its energy on a huge blossom with many heavy, oil-bearing seeds before dying off. As a short-day plant, the sunchoke blossoms only after the fall equinox, when the days become noticeably shorter than the nights. In Canada and Norway the plant is often surprised by the sudden onset of winter and cannot even make seeds—thus highlighting the value of its storage roots energy source. Not only does the plant send out vital offshoots in all directions, which take on mass as they expand, but the tubers are also carried off and widely distributed by rats, prairie dogs, gophers, and voles. Each small piece that rodents drop sprouts and becomes a new plant.

The Prairie Indians considered Jerusalem artichoke—"*pangi*" or "*panhi*," as they called it—an important edible plant. In the dearth of springtime, when winter provisions were running out, the freshly dug tubers made survival possible. All the same, some of the Native Americans didn't value the plant as much. For the Omahas it was "nourishment for orphaned boys who have no relatives to feed them." The Sioux did not like it because it causes flatulence—which complicates life inside a tepee. (In Europe the cooked tubers are often seasoned with caraway, which counters their flatulent effect.)

The Huron and other eastern forest tribes both gathered the tubers and cultivated them in round raised beds. Samuel de Champlain (1574–1635), the founding father of French Canada, discovered the plant—the "sun root" to the Algonquian—in Native American gardens near Cape Cod. When he later brought some back to France, these "Canadian potatoes (*batatas de Canada*)"—"as thick as a fist, with an artichoke taste and incredibly fertile" (*Histoire de la Nouvelle France*, 1609)—became a sensation in the French court, a delicacy in high demand.

A side story explains how the plant got its modern exotic name. Around the same time (1613), a French nobleman returning from Brazil brought with him some Indians from the tribe of the "Tupinambous" as a living present to his queen. The abducted Amerindians—already known to the French—belonged to a larger ethnic group, Tupí-Guaraní, that lived near the Amazon region in palisaded villages. They were previously known in Europe because the Hessian adventurer Hans Staden (1525–1576), who'd been captured by this warrior-like tribe, wrote a book about his adventures, *True Story and Description of a Country of Wild, Naked, Grim, Man-Eating People in the New World, America* (1557).[3] In addition, French

Illustration 43. South American Tupí-Guarani Indians, "exhibited" in France in 1619; the tuber is named after them (from Le Voyage au Brésil de Jean de Léry, 1556–1558)

seafarers had traded with them, winning them as allies against the Portuguese. And now these native people, celebrated as "*Allies of La Grande Nation*," stood in the flesh for everyone to gawk at and paw over—after having first been baptized and anatomically examined by scientists before being passed around, not least of all for erotic amusement, in French society. As such, the "*Tupinambá*" were a grand sensation. Their name became a fashionable word for everything that was exotic, strange, and fantastic. And so, the new tuber was sold as "the vegetable of the marvelous Topinambous," despite the sheer lack of connection these South American Natives had with the North American prairie plant. All the same, it soon joined Parisian haute cuisine under the name "*topinambur.*"

Soon thereafter the "Canadian potato" also became known in England. Botanist John Parkinson (1567–1650) described it as "a delicacy fit for a queen." Benjamin Townsend, gardener of a British lord, wrote in his 1726 *The Complete Seedsman,* "The cooked tuber is most appropriate for Christmas dinner." Given the vegetable's burgeoning popularity, it inspired many venturesome recipes. The tuber was baked, peeled, and sautéed in butter, wine, and expensive spices; or it was baked with bone marrow, dates, ginger, and raisins in a sherry sauce. It was also cooked in milk and served with roast beef.

The Italians also made friends with the "sunflower that tastes like artichoke." It was first cultivated in the famous Farnese Gardens near Rome, and known as *girasole articiocco*. (English gardeners later distorted the name into "Jerusalem artichoke.") But the simple folk didn't glorify the vegetable as others had done, and considered these tubers much as they did potatoes. They were both grown in the ground and were both called "earth apples"—*pommes de terre*. Like ordinary potatoes, they were also often distilled to make homemade liquor.

But the Jerusalem artichoke's popularity wasn't to last. For one thing, it grows prolifically—once planted it can hardly be removed. This makes it a poor candidate for the age-old practice of rotating crops and leaving fallow fields. Instead, the summer crops of broad beans, millet, and lentils were cultivated instead. Then, in the nineteenth century, with the development of modern agriculture, those time-worn crop-rotation practices were abandoned as well, and potatoes (*Solanum tuberosum*) were planted in every field. Soon boiled potatoes and fried potatoes became the mainstay of both industrial workers and the soldiers of modern draft armies. Already pushed out of the field, and difficult to harvest with machines, the Jerusalem artichoke could not compete with the ordinary spud. With the increasing mechanization of agriculture the sunchoke sank slowly into near oblivion, serving only as emergency food in times of hunger and as fodder for hogs. Indeed, they proved very useful with pigs, who in grubbing them out of the ground with their snouts simultaneously ploughed and manured the soil. And so the once-proud vegetable of lordly banquets became "pig's bread" or "pig's potatoes."

Fortunately for us, modern organic gardeners and nutritional researchers have rediscovered the Jerusalem artichoke. More popularly called "sunchokes," they are praised as highly nutritional and healthful. They have far more mineral nutrients than potatoes, more blood-building iron than spinach, and six times more potassium as bananas. (Potassium has a strong flushing, cleansing effect.) Sunchokes are very rich in calcium carbonates and silica, good for teeth and bones, as well as vitamins and protein. They're also a good source of fructooligosaccharides (FOS), which trigger an increase of bifid bacteria in the lower intestines—thus contributing to intestinal health and, by extension, the immune system.

They are also regarded as appetite suppressants. The tuber does not contain starch, but inulin; in the liver the inulin gets converted into glycogen, a polysaccharide that stabilizes blood sugar levels and, by extension, reduces hunger. It's no wonder, then, that so many Jerusalem artichoke products—juice, pills and supplements—abound in the health food stores. In addition, sunchokes' fructose compound inulin makes it a delicate potato for diabetics. As inulin stimulates insulin production in the pancreas, it's ideal for early stages of diabetes and adult-onset diabetes. In fact, in as early as 1878 the "sleeping prophet," Edgar Cayce (1877–1945), brought out of the spiritual realm a message declaring that the Jerusalem artichoke was capable of waking "God's forces" in diabetics. (Cayce was an interesting character; while in a trance he was able to diagnose and prescribe cures and medication—considered accurate today—knowledge he did not possess in his waking consciousness.)

Anthroposophical medicine also recognizes Jerusalem artichoke for healing diabetes. According to Rudolf Steiner (1861–1925), sugar is mineralized sunlight. If the "Self"—our spiritual essence—is not strong enough to support the processes of sugar digestion in the organism, then help from nature becomes necessary. That is when this sunny tuber comes into consideration. In imparting (or conveying) macrocosmic sun/sugar power, the sunchoke helps the internal "true being," the "spiritual sun," bring order into one's metabolism.

Garden Tips

Cultivation: This tuber is best planted in a sunny, sectioned-off spot; since they spread out very fast, they can easily overtake a garden if left to do so. They should be planted much like potatoes in rows or hills, set about a foot apart. Plant either a whole tuber or a tuber cut into pieces with at least one eye per piece. Planting should be done around the same time as potatoes. Harvest the tubers after the first frost in the fall and continue to harvest as needed until the ground becomes too frozen; they will survive the winter and continue to grow in the spring. They can be stored as one would potatoes. Another benefit: because the plant grows so tall (up to six feet), it makes an attractive screen against prying eyes. (LB)

Soil: Jerusalem artichokes/sunchokes grow in any soil except heavy clay. Contrary to most vegetables, the plant even prospers in poor soil. Too much nitrogen forces greater top growth and the tubers remain small.

Recipes

Sunchoke Soup with Nutmeg • 4 Servings

1 pound (455 grams) sunchokes or potatoes, peeled or unpeeled, finely chopped • 3 ounces (85 grams) leeks, cubed • 2 ounces (60 grams) pumpkin, cubed • 1½ quarts (1½ liters) vegetable broth • ground nutmeg • 1 ounce (30 grams) brown lentils, ground • herbal salt • pepper • 2 ounces (60 grams) cream cheese • 1 tablespoon hazelnut oil • chervil, finely chopped

In a large pot boil sunchokes (or potatoes), leeks, and pumpkin in the vegetable broth until tender. Season with nutmeg to taste. Stir in the ground lentils. Bring the soup to a boil again. Season with herbal salt and pepper to taste. Add the cream cheese. Transfer the soup to individual bowls. Garnish each with a few drops of hazelnut oil and a pinch of chervil.

Sunchoke Gratin with Plums • 4 Servings

Butter for greasing • ground nutmeg • cinnamon • 1 pound (455 grams) sunchokes, sliced ½ inch thick • 2 pitted, tart plums (~100 grams), halved • ¾ cup (175 milliliters) vegetable broth • ¾ cup (175 milliliters) cream (18% fat) • 2 eggs, whisked • 1½ ounces (40 grams) ground hazelnuts • 3 ounces (85 grams) cheddar cheese, grated • herbal salt

Preheat the oven to 350 °F (175 °C). Butter the casserole dish; sprinkle with nutmeg and cinnamon. Put a layer of sunchokes in the dish. Add the plums in a layer. Top with the remaining sunchokes. In a separate bowl, combine vegetable broth, cream, and eggs; season with herbal salt. Pour the mixture over the sunchokes and plums. Sprinkle the hazelnuts and cheese on top. Bake at 350 °F (175 °C) for 1 hour or until firm and golden.

TIP: This dish pairs nicely with a delicate salad.

Lamb's Lettuce (*Valerianella locusta, Valerianella olitoria*)

Family: Valerianaceae: valerian family

Other Names: corn salad, field lettuce, little valerian, mâche, vineyard lettuce

Healing Properties: cleanses blood, regulates bowel movements, prevents infection; prevents spring fatigue

Symbolic Meaning: green life energy that withstands winter and death, a light bringer, an attribute of the goddesses Persephone, Brigit, and Freya

Planetary Affiliation: Saturn

Lamb's lettuce is surprisingly new as a garden vegetable. John Gerard (~1545–1612), an English herbal doctor who lived in Shakespeare's time, wrote in his 1597 *Herball, or Generall Historie of Plantes* of his astonishment at seeing foreigners—Dutch and French living temporarily in England—sow "lamb's lettuce" in their gardens and harvest it during the time of fasting. His was the first official mention of the plant being cultivated. He was astonished because to him lamb's lettuce was a prevalent wild plant; though the shiny, lush little rosettes were valued in soups and salads, it was nonetheless just one of countless field weeds. It grew in fallow fields, between stubbles in grain fields, and especially in vineyards or grape orchards. It was even called "vineyard lettuce" in many regions, and was gathered by the basket. It didn't need to be sown any more than one would sow dandelion, sour dock, or watercress. It was a gift of goodly nature. (Today, except for in the dry, western states it can be found growing wild all over the United States.)

Though it was a latecomer to the cultivated garden, lamb's lettuce has been eaten for thousands of years. Prehistorians found seeds of the small plant in excavation sites of Neolithic and Bronze Age lake dwellings on Lake Constance, Lake Zurich, and other Alpine lakes. Botanists assume that the plant was originally native to the entire Mediterranean region and Caucasia, and that when Neolithic swidden farmers crossed the Alps to settle in the North they carried their seed and livestock with them. Incidentally they also brought the seeds of agricultural weed species, including the nut-like seeds of corn lettuce.

Returning to John Gerard's observation: lamb's lettuce was first taken into garden cultivation toward the end of the seventeenth century in central and western Europe. French settlers later brought the plant to North America; in the early 1800s Thomas Jefferson cultivated it in his garden in Virginia. Its mildly nutty tasting leaves were especially valued as a winter lettuce, when other lettuces are rare. A spot in a president's garden was certainly a step up for what others had deemed mere weeds.

Of course, the concept of "weed" is a rather modern category; for most shifting cultivators and simple planters the wild companion plants in the fields played an important role as healing plants, psychedelics, spices, and as nutritional supplements in soups and salads. It was usually believed that they were under the protection of certain gods, spirits, or totems, and that they had a prominent place in the rituals and cult practices of the cultivators. Now, lamb's lettuce is neither a healing or psychedelic plant, but it has a significant asset—even in cooler climates, it grows abundantly in the winter. As a lettuce that could withstand frost it had an important

Illustration 44. Lamb's lettuce was once sacred to the goddess Persephone (motif from a Greek vase in Gerhard Bellinger, Knaurs Lexikon der Mythologie, 1989)

task: when the days were lacking in sunlight, it helped to keep the winter demon scurvy at bay. This wretched disease saps the life energy out of the body, loosens teeth, causes gums to bleed, and makes the skin saggy and scabby. The tender yet ever-so-hardy dark leaves can drive off scurvy because they contain large amounts of ascorbic acid. (*Ascorbin* is a Greek coinage joining *a-* [not] and *scorbin* [scurvy].) Ascorbin is better known as vitamin C.

There is much evidence that lamb's lettuce was dedicated to the White Goddess, the virginal goddess of light that returns from the underworld and brings light and joy to the beings on earth as the days become longer. This radiant, divine maiden, dressed in white, was the muse of the poets, prophets, and healers. The Greeks knew her as Persephone, the Celts as Brigit, and the Germanics as Ostera ("the one who comes radiantly from the East"). Candlemas Day (Groundhog Day) in the beginning of February was originally her holyday. Lamb's lettuce is sacred to this goddess, as are the first green of springtime, the primroses, the lesser figwort, and cress. She made her appearance in the season that the lambs are born, and one of her attributes is indeed the gentle lamb. European names of the plant suggest the connection: such as the French *laitue brebis*, or, in parts of Germany, "sheep's mouth" (*Schaufmäule*) or "little lambs." In the Middle Ages it was called "lamb's pasture," or *pastus agnorum*, known as an herb that "lambs like to eat and is fine fodder for them," as Tabernaemontanus wrote in 1588.

When it first appears in spring the lamb's lettuce leaves form a shiny, lush rosette. In time a shoot with many branches grows up out of the rosette. Soon after, small, pale whitish-blue blossoms appear, out of which egg-shaped seeds develop. In midsummer the annual plant dies off. Once the plant reaches the flowering stage it's recognizable as a member of the valerian family—especially recognizable to cats. Many a gardeners has encountered a wrecked bed of lamb's lettuce after a cat has delightedly wallowed in it. Ethologists believe that the essential oils in valerian-type plants—specifically the iridoid actinidin—affect felines similarly to how natural hormonal attractants do.

As the anthroposophist Rudolf Steiner (1861–1925) emphasizes,

Illustration 45. Lamb's lettuce

valerian plants are light and warmth plants. They have a special relationship to "phosphor processes" in nature. Steiner claims that phosphorus (Greek for "light bearer") is materialized etheric light and etheric warmth, and categorized valerian as "phosphorus in plant form." An inherent "phosphorus" effect, the warmth and light radiation, in lamb's lettuce keeps the rosettes fresh and green despite snow and cold. On a subtle material-energy level it is this same radiation that makes the plant so attractive to warmth-loving cats. (According to Steiner, cats are "phosphorus animals.")

Just as the cat is especially fond of valerian, the goddess is especially fond of cats—whether that be the goddess Diana of ancient Greece, Durga of India, Isis of Egypt, or Freya of northern Europe. Lovely Freya, who incorporates love and joy, rides across the countryside in a carriage drawn by wild cats. Like the Celtic goddess, Brigit, she was associated with the fresh green of spring. In northern Europe in the spring, in honor of Freya women used to gather fresh green wild plants ("the nine green worts") and prepare a ritual food out of them in order to reconnect with the rebounding spirit of life and help rid the body of its winter slack. Lush green lamb's lettuce was always one of these gathered wild plants.

There are many interpretations of the Latin name of lamb's lettuce. Some linguists believe that *Valerianella* (little valerian) refers to a rather mystical Roman doctor named Valerius. Others think it refers to the sun god Baldur, or the Roman province Valeria. But it is most likely that the name comes from *valere*, Latin for "healthy, fit." This name is very appropriate! Even though lamb's lettuce is not classified as a medicinal herb, it is extremely healthful. The shiny green leaves are antibacterial, blood cleansing, and "softening"; as such the plant can help regulate bowel movements, as it can soften stool. Lamb's lettuce contains a lot of bioavailable (absorbable) iron, which serves to build red blood corpuscles, as well as calcium, phosphoric acids, and magnesium. As it contains relatively large amounts of vitamin A, the "little valerian" is beneficial for infections, helping to regenerate dermal tissue and accelerating the building of scar tissue. The previously mentioned ascorbic acid (vitamin C) in the small plant helps prevent spring fatigue, its riboflavin (vitamin B2) provides important digestive enzymes, and its thiamin (vitamin B1) calms nerves and aids in carbohydrate metabolism.

All in all, there's a lot to be found within this little plant!

Garden Tips

Cultivation and Soil: Lamb's lettuce grows well in just about any kind of soil and can be sown from spring to early fall. (Potato farmers, for example, often sow it in the fields after the potatoes are harvested.) In milder climates it can be easily grown all winter long. (LB)

Recipe

Lamb's Lettuce Salad with Saffron and Strawberries • 2 Servings

Salad: 4 ounces (115 grams) lamb's lettuce • 4 ounces (115 grams) fresh green onions • 12 strawberries, halved • Sauce: 4 tablespoons vegetable broth, cold • 1 tablespoon apple vinegar • 2 tablespoons olive oil • 1 tablespoon parsley, chopped • 1 pinch saffron • cayenne pepper • herbal salt • pepper

Mix the lamb's lettuce and onions in a salad bowl. In a separate small bowl, mix the vegetable broth with the vinegar and olive oil. Add the parsley. Season to taste with saffron, cayenne, herbal salt, and pepper. Add the strawberries to the sauce; let marinade for about 5 minutes. Gently stir the berry sauce into the salad and serve.

TIP: This dish pairs nicely with freshly baked dark (whole wheat or rye) bread.

Leek (*Allium porrum*)

Family: Amaryllidaceae: daffodil family; formerly Liliaceae: lily family

Other Names and Varieties: overwintering leeks, summer leeks

Healing Properties: lowers cholesterol and blood fat levels; hinders fungi and putrefactive agents in the intestines; helps to prevent constipation, gout, hemorrhoids, lumbago, urinary tract ailments, and varicose veins

Symbolic Meaning: health, protection against wounds; heroic courage, manly virtue, victory; national emblem of Wales

Planetary Affiliation: Mars, moon

While the Swiss, especially the French Swiss, have long treasured leeks as a gourmet garden vegetable, in America they are a relatively new among the vegetable selection; in Germany they are basically only used to give soups and sauces more flavor. But this robust member of the Liliaceae family, a relative of onion and garlic, deserves a closer look. Leeks are easy to care for, take up little room, and can be left in the garden over the winter. The leek's sulfuric essential oils, which also provide its healing properties, allow it to resist frost even in the coldest weather, making it, and the lamb's lettuce discussed above, an important winter and spring vegetable. It has a whole palette of vitamins—A, B, and C, and fertility vitamin E—as well as rare minerals such as zinc (good for connective tissue and the body's natural hormones), manganese (important for metabolism and sex drive), and selenium (which supports the immune system). It is thought that one can overcome leaden spring fatigue with a dish of leeks with spring herbs and eggs. One disadvantage: leeks cause flatulence, but preparing them with caraway seeds counters the effect; indeed, a popular cheese-scalloped Swiss dish pairs sautéed leeks and carrots with caraway seeds.

The leek has been cultivated in the eastern Mediterranean region for at least four thousand years. In ancient Egypt it was not only a common vegetable but, like the onion, it was regarded as a symbol of the universe—each layer of leaves standing for a stage of the demonic or divine other

Illustration 46. Drawing of a leek

worlds. In the Fourth Book of Moses (Numbers) we read that the children of Israel, before reaching the Promised Land, implored Moses about their bland manna diet: "We remember the fish, which we did eat in Egypt freely; the cucumbers, and the melons, and the leeks, and the onions, and the garlic . . ." (Numbers 11:5).

The Greeks and Romans dedicated the leek to Apollo. Indeed, at the Delphic festival of the sun god Apollo, whoever brought the biggest leek as a gift to Leto, the mother of the gods, was given the honor of eating a portion at the god's banquet. But nowhere were more leeks (*porrum*) eaten than in old Rome. It was Nero's favorite food. He considered himself to be a great musician, and is said to have eaten a bit of raw leek dipped in olive oil every day in order to preserve his sonorous singing voice. This habit earned him the nickname "*Porrophagus*," (leek eater). While it is more common to eat it cooked or baked, small amounts from the tender inside can also be eaten raw.

It is questionable whether the Germanic tribes knew of the leek before the Roman army and settlers introduced the "Welsh leeks"—"welsh" referring to foreign—to the countries north of the Alps. The plant joined company with the many other various kinds of "leeks"—all of which were considered to be sacred, curative, and magical plants. Almost every edible fresh, green shoot or leaf that popped out of the ground after the long winter that was capable of reviving the spirits used to be called "leek" (from the Old Norse *laukr,* Dutch *look,* and Old English *leac*). Such plants gave the men more virile strength, gave the women cheerful smiles, and restored the children's rosy cheeks. These different kinds of "leeks," considered gifts from vegetation goddess, Freya, embodied the

Illustration 47. In ancient Egypt leek numbered among the foods offered to the dead (Egypt, twelfth dynasty)

virtue and nobility of green vegetation.[1] The various fresh green shoots and leaves were seen as the pointed spear tips, or swords, that drive back obdurate, hostile ice and frost giants—as well as demons of disease and lingering illness. The word "garlic" (Anglo-Saxon *gar* = spear, *laec* = leek) still shows these connotations.

The old Germanics even had a leek rune (*laukr-runa, laguz*). This rune had the magic power to dissolve blockage—to melt what is frozen and bring it into flow again. Rune masters carved the leek rune into wooden beams and colored it with sacrificial blood in order to ensure health to the people, as well as prosperity and abundance in the fields. Just as the plant itself, the leek rune protects life fluids from drying out, and safeguards a man's semen and manly strength. It is also believed to protect mother's milk from illness so that it continues to flow.

Even the word "leek" was believed to have magical power. It was hammered into coins (bracteates) in order to guarantee the wearer—a traveler or a warrior—preservation of health. Leeks were put into drinks whenever one suspected a vile poison had been secretly put into one's mead or beer; the leek would either neutralize the poison or indicate its presence. "Put leek green into the drink," advises the Brunhilde song of the twelfth-century *Nibelung Saga.* Nobles were honored with leek greens:

A prince was born to his people,
they wished for fortune, golden times.
The king himself left the battlefield
to bring noble leek to the newborn nobleman.
        —from Helgi's Song ("Lay of Helgi Hjörvar sson")

The leek is regarded as a noble amidst the vegetation. Gudrún sings: "My Sigurd (Siegfried) was like this, like noble leek rises up high amidst the stalks, like a stag rises up high above foxes and rabbits."

Nordic warriors carried leeks on their bodies to both protect them from getting wounded and help them vanquish their enemies. It is reported from the Middle Ages that knights and their knaves wore the root of alpine leek (*Allium victorialis*), also referred to in German as "victory root," or "any man's armor," as an amulet. Well into the sixteenth century in England it was still a sign of provocation to wear a leek on a hat or helmet.

Historical records indicate that pre-Roman women folk cultivated fenced-in leek gardens (AS *laukagardr*) that were dedicated to the fair goddess Freya. Indeed, four major plants were grown in such old Anglo-Saxon gardens: onions (*ynneleac*), garlic (*gar-leac*), chives, and leeks (*por-leac*). In other areas bear leek (*Allium ursinum*, or bear's garlic, ramson) was also included. The women—responsible for health in the

Illustration 48. The beautiful goddess Freya, who gave leek plants to humanity (illustration by Arthur Rackham from a 1910 post card)

home and the barn—considered the leek, no matter which kind, a veritable ally. The saying "flax and leek" was the traditional formula for wishing health and prosperity—referring to the leek as an antiseptic healer of wounds and the use of crushed leaves with a fresh linen (flax) cloth as a bandage. Malicious worms could also be driven off with leek juice, not only intestinal worms but also the invisible "elfen worms" and "spirit worms" that, once settled into organs, suck out one's life energy. Leek juice was heated in milk and used to dispel so-called "ear worms," the warm liquid carefully trickled into the infected ear. Leek juice together with the smoke of henbane was used against nibbling, red "tooth worms" that hollow out the teeth (Storl 2000, 109). And in a ceremonial spring meal that lasted even into the Christian Middle Ages, communities feasted on pancakes with fresh leek, believing they'd stay healthy for the entire year.

Leek gardens were also sacred places for the Celts. As leeks' sulfuric smell reminded the island Celts of the strike of lighting, they were seen as an attribute of Aed (Aeddon), the Celtic "thunderer" and bearer of the lightning bolt; the plant honored him as one of the progenitors of humankind and as a son of the sun. The god possesses a magic spear and his curse can make water dry up and evaporate, but he is also a great healer who can even bring the dead back to life.

In Celtic Britain the leek is revered to this day. As it is the national symbol of Wales, Welsh farmers still observe the custom of eating a meal of leeks together before the spring plowing begins. Each brings a leek to the meal. The symbolism is obvious: leek not only has a phallic form but it is also furthers physical potency; in archaic imagination, plowing was always regarded as a sort of sexual act, as a penetration into the fertile earth to make it receptive for the seeds.

The leek is also the insignia of the famous Welsh Guard, and today still decorates the caps of the Welsh troops. In Shakespeare's drama *Henry V* we see that the Welsh fighters placed leek stalks on their helmets in the wars between the English and the French. In one scene an English petty officer who had made fun of the custom was forced to go over to the angered Welsh and eat some leeks. To this day the British say "to eat a leek" for those who have to eat their words.

When the Anglo-Saxons tried to occupy Wales in the sixth century the leek became the identification symbol of the free Welsh. Bishop Dafydd (~500–~589), an ascetic in the tradition of the old druids—he ate nothing but dry bread and vegetables, drank nothing but water, and bathed only in ice water—told the men to wear a leek on their helmets to distinguish themselves from the enemy. At the decisive battle, the Welsh were able to drive off the far more powerful Saxons. After that decisive event Dafyyd, known as St. David today, became the patron saint of Wales. On St. David's Day, March 1, Welsh still march in parades wearing leeks on their hats.

The leek remained a popular vegetable throughout the British Islands. In Northumberland in northeast England there is an annual contest among male gardeners prizing the biggest, thickest, and longest leek grown in the community. The men spend so much time on the project that the women are pitied as "leek widows."

In some rural areas in England it is still a custom to let a suitor know whether he is welcomed or not as a son-in-law through the food served to him. If he is served red beets and potatoes, he is not welcome, and might as well leave before eating. Flour pudding and coffee informs him he is desired not as a groom but as a family friend. But if he is served pancakes with leek, then he knows he is welcome.

The Healing Potential of Leeks

In modern times various kinds of these onion-like greens—leek, garlic, or bear's garlic—are still regarded as good weapons against illness, especially when eaten raw (though with leek only a small amount of the tender inside parts is advised). The essential oils (allicin) mildly stimulate the stomach, intestines, liver, gall bladder, and spleen; they also inhibit putrefactive agents that can cause flatulence, cramps, and diarrhea. The oils also help clear the phlegm of congested respiratory organs. Blended leeks cooked in milk with honey is an excellent remedy for coughing and lung disorders. Leeks also rid the intestines of fungi resulting from bad eating habits. In addition, leeks help reduce cholesterol and lipids in the blood, and their blood-thinning (fibrinolytic) quality benefits worn-out varicose veins.

French traditional healing lore recommends leeks with potatoes cooked in milk as a diet for various kidney ailments. A brew of boiled-out leek seeds is prescribed for urinary ailments; many consider leeks in general good for bladder ailments. Crushed leek bulbs and leaves can be applied for lumbago and gout, and leeks cooked in milk can be applied to abscesses.

These recommendations stand in opposition to statements made by some naturopaths who adamantly claim the leek is "poisonous." For example: "There are harmful vegetables that should be banned from our tables or at least be eaten only very rarely. One of them is leek (*Allium porrum*)" (Werdin 1995, 30). Hildegard von Bingen (1098–1179) is supposed to have declared that the leek is as bad as any poisonous plant when eaten raw because it perverts the blood and the other humors. I find this opinion curious, as I have yet to meet someone who would eat bunches of overpowering raw leeks. Great amounts of raw leek can be poisonous indeed, but the same can be said of beans and potatoes if eaten raw, and neither of those vegetables has earned similar scorn. But, in all fairness, I'll close by offering a tale of poison. In ancient Rome, Emperor Tiberius accused Mella, an administrator of one of the provinces, of bad book-keeping and sent for him. Instead of complying, the discredited official committed suicide by drinking a liter of leek juice.

Garden Tips

Cultivation: Leeks are raised from seed instead of sets, but otherwise they are treated the same as onions. If the growing season is short they should be sown in a protected place six weeks before planting out into the garden. As they grow they should be hilled up to blanch them, thus keeping the flavor milder. Occasional composting with ripe compost can increase their size. (LB)

Soil: Leeks flourish in any well-composted garden soil.

Recipes

Leek Pie with Beer Sauce • 4 Servings

Leek Pie: 2 cups water • 1 teaspoon sea salt • 2 leeks, cut in fine strips • 1 pound (455 grams) pie dough • butter for greasing • 2 eggs • ¾ cup (175 milliliters) cream (18% fat) • 7 ounces (210 grams) cottage cheese • 5 ounces (150 grams) hard cheese, grated • sea salt • black pepper • ground nutmeg • Beer sauce: 1 quart (945 milliliters) light or dark beer • 5 ounces (150 grams) arugula (rocket) leaves, finely chopped • 2 bay leaves • some lentil or chickpea flour • sea salt • pepper

LEEK PIE: Preheat the oven to 350 °F (175 °C). Put the water and salt in a medium pan. Add the leeks and simmer for 20 minutes. Drain well and cool. Roll out the pie dough. Grease a cookie sheet. Place the dough on the cookie sheet, poking holes in it with a fork. Spread the leeks evenly over the dough. In a small bowl, mix the eggs, cream, and cottage cheese; season with salt and pepper. Pour this mixture over the leeks. Cover with the grated cheese and bake at 350 °F (175 °C) for about 1 hour. It should be firm and golden brown on top.

SAUCE: In a medium pan, bring the beer to a boil. Add the arugula (rocket) and bay leaves and simmer for about 20 minutes. Add salt and pepper to taste. Mix in flour in small amounts until you reach a nice sauce consistency. Transfer to a dish; serve with the leek pie.

Lettuce (*Lactuca sativa*)

Family: Compositae: composite, daisy, or sunflower family

Other Names and Varieties: salad, greens, leafy greens; butter lettuce, head lettuce, iceberg, leaf lettuce, Romaine

Healing Properties: calms, including sexually calming; increases fertility and milk production; induces sleep

Symbolic Meaning: chasteness, remorse, sleep, fertility; the Virgin Mary; attributes of the phallic gods Min and Adonis

Planetary Affiliation: moon

> *It takes five minds to create a good salad:*
> *A miser who trickles vinegar,*
> *A spendthrift who pours oil,*
> *A wise person who gathers herbs,*
> *A fool who mixes them,*
> *An artist who serves the salad.*
> —Jean Anthelme. Brillat-Saravin, 1755–1826

Given the many reasons we today seek lower-calorie foods—to counteract our sedentary lifestyles, to please our partners and appease our doctors—it's no wonder that vitamin-rich lettuce has earned a prominent role in our diets. Various salad creations complement almost every main meal—or are even the entire meal. And with the many kinds of premixed salads to be found in stores, even the busiest of us have no excuse for not getting our greens.

And there are many varieties to choose from: head lettuce, curly leaf, oak leaf, iceberg, romaine. All belong to the genus lettuce (*Lactuca sativa*). Another in this family is Chinese lettuce (asparagus lettuce, or celtuce). It first appeared in the 1942 Burpee's seed catalog, after a missionary brought the seeds from China to the United States; this variety, however, is usually not eaten raw, but cooked like asparagus.

A contemporary author considers the invention of salad "one of the greatest cultural achievements in gastronomy, . . . a refreshing and healthy side dish to hot dishes" (Mercatante 1976, 195). But such is a contemporary opinion; green lettuce was not always so popular. Even as recently as the pre-World War II era, such "rabbit fodder" was only eaten on Sundays for its cooling effect after a sumptuous roast. Then the lettuce leaves were often soaked for hours in water with vinegar and some sugar producing fairly wilted fare. And the range of salad dressings available to us—balsamic vinaigrette, blue cheese, Caesar, French, honey mustard, Italian, Ranch, Russian, Thousand Island, etcetera—are also relatively modern creations.

It is very likely that Christian monks first brought lettuce from the Mediterranean to the cool northern climates, where they planted it in small cloister gardens. Lettuce is first mentioned in the north in the ninth century when Charlemagne (742–814) decreed it be planted in the land holdings under his rule. Lettuce is also found in the first blueprint of a cloister garden in St. Gallen, Switzerland.

The Health Effects of Lettuce

Lettuce had a reputation for dampening immodest desires, erotic dreams, and consequent nocturnal emissions. As nightly visits from seductive incubi and succubi plagued the poor nuns and monks in the cloisters, there was hardly a cloister without lettuce and some other anaphrodisiac such as dill and chaste tree (monk's pepper). The monks knew the writings of, for example, Dioscorides (~40–90 AD), who wrote: "Lettuce is good for the stomach, cools a little bit, relaxes, softens the stomach, and helps lactation. . . . The seeds made into a decoction help those who suffer from involuntary nightly ejaculation and discourage coitus." Pythagorean philosophers, who

Illustration 49. Drawing of an incubus (Francis Barrett, London, 1801)

tried to avoid dissipating sexual energy but rather to sublimate it, also included lettuce in their diets. In the ancient theory of Humorism, well known to all cloister dwellers, this vegetable plant was categorized as moist and cooling to the third degree: it cools the body as well as the passions.

In Christian symbolism, as exemplified in the Renaissance paintings of the Last Supper, lettuce leaves not only represent abstention but also remorse and penance. Except for the tender young leaves, lettuce is a bitter plant; if let grow and mature into seed the plant becomes ever milkier and ever more bitter. The pale yellow blossom was even once seen as a symbol of the chastity of the Virgin Mary.

"Herbal fathers" of the sixteenth century in Europe who drafted the first printed herbals take up the lettuce theme once again, claiming it "diminishes animal drives": "Lettuce juice spread on the male member reduces immodest desires and blocks [the natural formation of] semen"; also, "All who have vowed to remain chaste should eat nothing but lettuce and rocket" (Piedro Andrea Matthiolus, 1565). Hieronymus Bock (1560) concurred: "Lettuce, eaten regularly, dispels lecherousness." Seemingly sound advice—except it seems the plant didn't always comply. A medieval report tells of a poor nun who ate a leaf lettuce upon which an invisible devil happened to be sitting. Because she forgot to make a cross over the salad bowl, the devil was able to enter her body and arouse her desire. It took some doing to exorcise and drive him out of her.

If it is really the case that this delicate member of the composite family actually dampens animal drives, then it's curious that the ancient Chinese praise it as an aid in fertility: it helps wishes for children to come true. And in the Nile Valley, where leaf lettuce was first cultivated as a garden vegetable, it was even dedicated to Min, the god of sexual fertility and orgiastic rites. Small lettuce gardens in the temples were dedicated to Min: the "bull that satisfies the needs of women and creates seed for gods and goddess," the "stud that inseminates women with its member." The Egyptians carried bowls of fresh lettuce plants during sacred processions in honor of this mighty god. Indeed, Christian Rätsch and other modern-day ethnobotanists presume that the milky, white juice of the lettuce is analogous to the ithyphallic god's milky semen.

In ancient Greece lettuce was dedicated to the phallic, youthful god Adonis. Lettuce seeds were sown ritually into beds called "Adonis gardens." These gardens, which symbolized the ever-dying-and-resurrecting god, were left to dry shortly after the seed sprouted and turned green. And Aphrodite, the goddess of love, in mourning her lover bedded Adonis's corpse upon lettuce leaves.

Now how can this contradiction—anaphrodisiac and fertility plant—be resolved? The modern-day genial herbal healer Maurice Mességué assumes that this "plant of the eunuchs" (*herbe des eunuques*), though it seemingly can dampen sexual desire, simultaneously furthers fertility with its quantity of vitamin E (from the Greek *tocopherol*, bringing birth). In any case, the Ayurvedic tradition advises pregnant women to eat a lot of lettuce. Indian scientists claim that lettuce beneficially influences the

Illustration 50. Min, ancient Egyptian god of fertility; this depiction is from the Fourth Dynasty (2613–2494 BC)

building of pregnancy hormones (progestogens) and helps prevent miscarriages. Ayurvedic teaching also advises nursing mothers to eat plenty of lettuce in order to increase milk flow. Northern Native Americans believed the same; they cooked a tea from the leaves of closely related wild lettuce (*Latuca virosa*) to keep women's milk flowing.

Modern research affirms that the folk medicinal use was correct. The white juice in lettuce activates a discharge of prolactin, the hormone that enables female mammals to produce milk. Prolactin can sedate an organism into a dreamy stupor—it correlates to natural body opiates—while simultaneously dampening sexual desires. So when Native Americans give lettuce juice to crying babies to calm them, they are using the same empirical knowledge as Maurice Mességué when he prescribes eating three heads of lettuce in the evening for his patients suffering from insomnia. Since most stomachs can't hold three heads at once, he suggested cooking them—to lose the watery mass but not the effect. Mességué credits this to the Romans: it was a custom in old Rome to eat cooked and salted lettuce before going to bed. Our word "salad" comes from Italian *insalata:* salted food (*sal* = salt). Roman doctor Galen (129–~216 AD) wrote: "When I grew old and wanted to be sure to sleep enough, I found that I was often not able to sleep, often due to simply lying awake at night and other times due to the fact that old people often sleep very little; it was only by eating a dish of cooked lettuce in the evening that I was able to get enough restoring sleep."

Head lettuce is a milky composite—as are dandelion, chicory, meadow salsify, and sow thistle. It is an annual long-day plant, which means it shoots into blossom when the days become longer than the nights. It has small, pale yellow blossoms, similar to its relatives prickly lettuce (*L. serriola*) and wild lettuce (*L. virosa*), with which it can even be crossed. When blossoming it contains the most milk. The dried milk (*Lactucarium*) was used as a healing means in antiquity. Lactucarium—"cold opium" (*opium frigidum*)—is a calming but not addictive narcotic. Along with opium, hemlock, and henbane juice, it was included in the so-called "sleep sponges" (*spongia somnifera*) that medieval doctors used as anesthesia and that henchmen gave to those about to be executed. Pure opium from opium poppies could also be stretched with lactucarium, and many witches' salves contained sticky, milky lettuce juice. And, not surprisingly, Benedictine abbess Hildegard von Bingen (1098–1179) did not have good words for "the useless juice of this weed," claiming "it makes the brain empty and dull."

Traditional folk medicine knows lactucarium as a cooling, pain-killing, soporific agent, as well as a means for healing infected eyes. Cloth soaked in the juice was placed on the eyes. Legend says that eagles eat lettuce leaves from time to time to keep their eyes sharp. Lettuce leaves, or lettuce juice, were also used in poultices for painful abscesses, as well as for healing the chronic skin infections favus and eczema. Native Americans also used lettuce to alleviate rashes and poison ivy.

Modern medicine has rediscovered lactucarium. Pharmacological research shows that, similar to codeine, it has a calming, inhibitory effect on breathing—but as it is weaker than codeine it is less dangerous. For that reason the juice is used for spasmodic coughs, whooping cough, and asthma. The somewhat inebriating plant was even used as a drug for a time; in the 1970s it was offered in magazines as a legal drug and substitute for hashish. But it soon became clear that the "trip" it induced was boring—in addition to the fact that it tastes awful. The claim that it is a "gateway drug" that "leads to brain damage," as the *FAZ* magazine in Germany fabulated, could not have been further from the truth. Thanks to the bitters found in lettuce that further digestion, raw lettuce is ideal for sluggish digestion. In addition, the greens are part of a good alkaline diet, effective in lessening blood acidity. For that reason it is recommended in diets for heart and kidney troubles.

For occultists, plants with white, milky juice stand for something special. The long-lived Dutch herbalist Mellie Uyldert (1908–2009), as well as theosophists and anthroposophists, see these plants as the last representatives of a long-past evolutionary stage on earth—that of Lemuria, a time when the moon had not yet separated from the earth and the earth itself floated like a cosmic embryo in milky fluid, much like an egg yolk in the egg white. They believe that at that time the highest form of consciousness was a sort of dreaming sleep state, and sexuality did not yet exist. Plants like poppy, spurge, and lettuce contain remnants of this milky primeval atmosphere. Like mother's milk today, this macrocosmic milk helped the young creation to incarnate into the material sphere. For many, such thoughts are surely some kind of "esoteric gobbledygook," but for these occultists it is surely "fact."

Garden Tips

Cultivation: To develop well, lettuce needs warm days and cool nights. All lettuces flourish best in half-shaded areas where the light is filtered during at least part of the day. (LB)

Soil: Though lettuce needs a well-drained soil, it must be kept moist enough for its quick and succulent growth.

Recipe

Head Lettuce Salad with Honey-Mustard Blueberry-Mint Dressing • 4 Servings

Fresh mint leaves • 1 tablespoon apple vinegar • 4 tablespoons fresh blueberries • 3 tablespoons sesame oil • 1 teaspoon mustard • 1 teaspoon honey • sea salt • black pepper • 1 head lettuce

In a small bowl, mix the mint leaves with the vinegar, blueberries, sesame oil, mustard, and honey. Let stand for 10 minutes, then season with salt and pepper to taste. Prepare the lettuce in a serving bowl. Toss with the dressing and serve.

TIP: This salad pairs nicely with hearty bread.

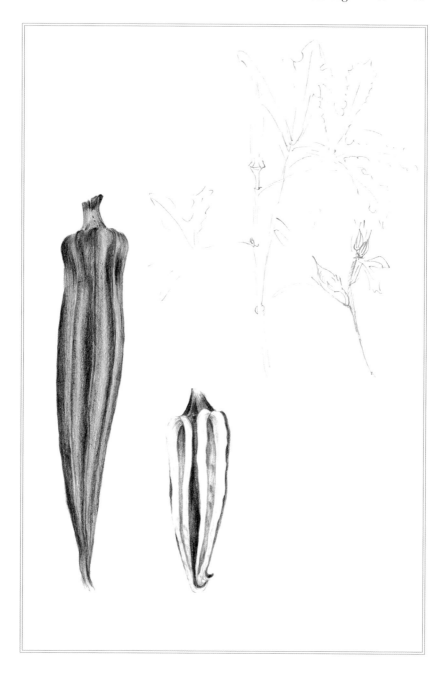

Okra (*Abelmoschus esculentus, Hibiscus esculentus*)

Family: Malvaceae: mallow family

Other Names: abelmosh, bamia, bhindi, bindi, gumbo, ladies' fingers

Healing Properties: taken externally: the plant slime has a softening and soothing effect as a poultice for frostbite, lesions, and skin burns: taken internally: eases gastritis and hoarseness

Symbolic Meaning: male sexual energy, black "soul," *négritude,* relaxed southern lifestyle

Planetary Affiliation: Mercury

The lush okra plant, which can grow up to six feet (nearly two meters) high, is an adornment for any vegetable garden. The beautiful blossoms, with their yellow petals and deep red pharynx that resemble the hibiscus, are excellent bee feeders. The plant constantly produces new pods—the so-called "ladies' fingers"—until frosts come.

This member of the mallow family, a close relative of hibiscus and cotton, is a child of tropical Africa; wild forms of the plant are still found in Nubia, in the area of the White Nile. Anthropologists and paleobotanists have evidence that okra has been cultivated since Neolithic times in sub-Saharan Africa—as far back as six thousand years. Presumably the mild, slimy/gooey leaves and pods were eaten as vegetables; the stem fibers used to make rope, nets and carrying bags; the mucilage used medicinally; and the ripe seeds roasted as "coffee" or used to make cooking or lamp oil.

The mild-tasting vegetable is very healthy: it has a lot of calcium, provitamin A, vitamin C, and folic acid. The seeds are antioxidants—replete with unsaturated fats, such as linoleic acid—and they have as much protein as soybean seeds do. Today, okra seeds—which contain up to 25 percent fatty oil—are used in margarine production. Since okra is so slimy, it's ideal for intestinal ailments.

Like the many plants described in this book, okra has made a long journey, which began when it traveled from Africa to India in Neolithic times. Even then, trade routes existed between pre-Aryan Harappan culture and eastern North Africa. Since that time one cannot imagine Indian

cuisine without this delicate vegetable, which is
mixed into various chut-
neys and used to thicken
soups or bind sauces.

In another phase of
okra's journey, the ancient
Egyptians learned about
it from Nubian Africans.
Not long after, the plant

Illustration 51. Okra pods

conquered Arabic gardens and kitchens, where it is called "*bamia*." Okra
is highly valued there because its seeds smell like musk, the erotic perfume from the sex glands of musk stags.[1] (Okra is a close relative of the
"abelmosk" [*habb-al-misk*], the "son of musk," as they share the genus
[*Abelmoschus*].) Musk is the favorite perfume of the Islamic countries: it
is the scent of seventh heaven. The Houris, the doe-eyed ladies of pleasure in paradise, supposedly wear scarves scented with musk fragrance.
Musk has long been mixed with the mortar used for building mosques;
even centuries later, the otherworldly scent within the walls still beguiles
those who pray there. Arabs and Turks mix crushed okra seeds into coffee
and cooling fruit drinks (*sorbet*); the seeds are sprinkled into clothes and
chewed to improve the breath.

From Africa, okra headed west as well as east. Arabian conquerors
brought musk to Spain and western Europe; by 1600 the vegetable was
introduced to Brazilian cooking. Black slaves brought with them on their
reluctant, harrowing journey to the New World—along with other cultural elements, such as mojo magic, certain dance and drum rhythms,
tales, certain speech rhythms and intonations, ecstatic religious cults, voo-
doo—specific ways of cooking and seasoning, as well as many aspects of
African healing, in addition to the seeds of their favorite plants,[2] including
what West Africans called "okra" and the Bantus called "*gombo bambia*"
or "*guimgumbó*." From this came the word "gumbo"; indeed, in former
times blacks were also called "gumbo" in the southern states, especially
those who escaped. Even today, both okra the plant and gumbo the okra

stew are soul food for American blacks. Fried chicken and catfish, collard greens, pork belly, testicles, tripe, and other innards (*chitterlings* or *chitlins*) were—and to a degree still are—all part of soul food, seasoned in a more or less west-African style. In Louisiana, the dried and powdered okra leaves used to thicken soups and stews are called "gumbo filé." African Americans in the southern states dried the leaves and the halved fruits for winter, and roasted the seeds to brew a sort of coffee.

African Americans also preserved their ancestors' practices using okra for healing. Poultices made of the leaves ease pain and soften tissue: the plant's mucous compounds serve as an emollient that, used topically, soothes infected tissue and softens scarred and hardened tissue. Ingested okra is both anti-inflammatory and anti-ulcerogenic, and aids treatment of digestive diseases and lung ailments. According to Indian as well as African lore, the hibiscus family makes genital organs more mucilaginous. Okra and other kinds of hibiscus are therefore used as a strengthening agent. It is said that *Hibiscus mochatus* will restore the manly strength of even an eighty-year-old man. Historian George Bancroft (1800–1891) reported that southern slave women observed an okra diet before having an abortion to make the uterus slithery and soft.

I got to know okra through a friend of mine, an old Texan who loved the plant and generously shared its seeds. But though he grew it with great success, not every gardener will fare as well with the plant; perhaps one needs a certain Southern magic to do so. As far as the African soul of the plant goes, a jazz musician friend from New Orleans—who conjured the coolest, most bizarre riffs on a clarinet I've ever heard—confided to me that his secret was eating several portions of okra every day. He felt the slimy vegetable brought him "into the groove," that it smoothed the sound he played and protected his lungs in smoky nightclubs. Just like his favorite dish, his music, jazz, also has African roots. "Jizz," or "jizzm" (possibly the word from which *jazz* is derived), is a vulgar expression for both semen, life-carrying slime, as well as for the smooth rhythmical movement of the act that makes life possible. Jazz is, then, sex as sound.

The association of okra to sexuality can also be found in India, where the god Ganesh is worshipped with hibiscus or okra blossoms. Ganesh, the elephant-headed god who loves to dance, dwells mainly in the root chakra (Muladhara); his trunk symbolizes the penis.

The sensual imagery associated with okra might not please everybody; it certainly would not have pleased my rather puritanical neighbors in the small Ohio town where I grew up. That should not, however, stop them from enjoying a meal of this delicious, nutritious vegetable.

Garden Tips

Cultivation and Soil: Okra can be easily cultivated in areas where vineyards thrive and tomatoes, cucumbers, and melons grow well. After two months the tender, unripe pods can be harvested for use as a vegetable; cut crosswise, the pods have a pentagonal shape. After another two months the plant will produce ripe seeds; a smart gardener will grow the seedlings in a green house or in a nursery in peat pots before planting them out into the garden. Okra needs a good spell of summer heat, rich, well-draining soil, and plenty of water. It is a rapid-growing, heavy feeder that should be planted in a fully sunny location that has been well composted and well manured.

Sow seeds lightly in rows or in hills after all danger of frost is past and when the soil is warm. Note that, as the seeds rot easily, a rainy period just after planting could cause the seeds to rot, in which case replanting may be necessary. Once the plants are a few inches tall, thin them to stand twelve to sixteen inches apart. (LB)

Recipes

Okra Stew with Garlic • 4 Servings

4 potatoes, peeled or unpeeled, cubed • 4 garlic cloves, peeled
• 4 tablespoons olive oil • 1 pinch of cinnamon • sea salt
• black pepper • 1 pound okra

In a medium pan, sauté the potatoes and garlic in 2 tablespoons of the olive oil for 20 minutes. Season with the cinnamon, salt, and pepper to taste. In a separate large skillet, sear the okra in the remaining 2 tablespoons of olive oil for 3 to 4 minutes or until tender. Add the potatoes and garlic to the skillet. Mix well and serve hot.

Okra with Coconut • 4 Servings

1¾ pounds (800 grams) okra, chopped • 3 ounces (85 grams) coconut flakes • 3 tablespoons ground coriander • 1 tablespoon turmeric powder • 1 pinch cayenne • 5 tablespoons butter • 2 teaspoons caraway seeds • 2 teaspoons black mustard seeds • salt • 1 teaspoon sugar • lemon juice • 6 ounces (175 milliliters) coconut milk

In a large bowl, mix the okra with the coconut flakes, coriander, turmeric, and red pepper and let rest for about 10 minutes. In a big frying pan, melt the butter and sauté the caraway seeds and mustard seeds until brown. Add the okra and coconut to the pan and sear for 5 minutes. Add the lemon juice and coconut milk and simmer for about 20 minutes or until okra is tender. Serve immediately.

TIP: Use a big frying pan for searing the okra; otherwise it will get too slimy and juicy.

Onion (*Allium cepa*)

Family: Amaryllidaceae: daffodil family; formerly Liliaceae: lily family

Other Names and Varieties: baby onion, gibbon, green onion, long onion, onion stick, precious onion, salad onion, scally onion, spring onion (in Britain), syboe, table onion, yard onion

Healing Properties: thins blood, lowers blood sugar levels, arouses desire (aphrodisiac), stimulates the heart (cardiotonic), strengthens the immune system (antimicrobial, antioxidant, antiviral), clears mucus (expectorant), promotes urination (diuretic)

Symbolic Meaning: sacred plant of Isis, goddess of the moon; menstruation, fertility; absorbs poison and disease; potent etheric life energy; poverty

Planetary Affiliation: moon, Mars

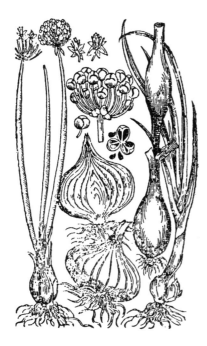

Illustration 52. Shallots and onions (Joachim Camerarius, Neuw Kreütterbuch, *1586)*

The onion is one of the world's earliest cultivated plants. In the Neolithic period it was grown in India, China and the eastern Mediterranean. The Greek historian Herodotus (484–425) noted how an inscription on the Cheops (Khufu) pyramid in Egypt indicates the quantity of onions, garlic, and radishes eaten by the slaves who built it. And the Bible tells us how the Hebrews longed for the onions of Egypt as they trekked through the desert; such is, incidentally, the origin of the German expression "longing to go back to Egyptian onions"— longing for the good old days.

Illustration 53. Ancient Egyptians watering and harvesting onions (depiction in chamber tomb no. 3 in Beni Hasan; copy of the original by Percy E. Newberry, 1893)

In classical Roman times cultivated people avoided those who reeked of onions, and "onion eater" was a derogatory term. Nonetheless, Varro, a Roman contemporary of Caesar, wrote, "Our grandfathers were very decent people even though their words smelled of garlic and onion."

The onion has historically remained one of the cheapest foods on the market; as such it has long been an ally to the poor, as both food and as an important healer—especially for those unable to afford a doctor's visit. Even today it is still a super star among the healing plants used in folk medicine. Poultices made with finely chopped, steamed onions are successfully used for many ills, including sinus infections, abscesses and boils, lung inflammations, middle-ear infections, and tonsillitis. Swiss pastor and herbal healer Johann Künzle (1857–1945) subscribed to traditional usage when he announced: "chopped, steamed onions pull sickness out so strongly that they become black and smelly; the onions soak up the poison of the disease."

Belief in the bulb's ability to soak up poison and negative "radiation" was shared from England to eastern Europe. The English would hang a bunch of onions in the kitchen to "soak up bad luck," and even wore an onion as an amulet or rubbed raw onion on the soles of the feet in order to draw sickness out of the body. In Bohemia and in the Erz Mountains, consecrated white onions were hung in the living room on Three Kings' Day "because they attract and neutralize fevers." Similarly, Dutch country folk would hang a linen satchel of chopped onions over a sick child's bed.

From such practices, it was but a small step for the onion to be used apotropaically—as means of warding off dark magic. Onion was believed to keep at bay not only sickness and plague but also wicked witches, bad spirits, and vampires. Italian lore claims that carrying an onion in the pocket protects from the evil eye. Serbs would tuck an onion into the bosom of a young bride to protect her from any bad wishes envious neighbors might harbor toward her. And such superstitions regarding onions spread well beyond Europe. In India in times of cattle plague farmers hang red-painted onions on a rope across the village entrance. In China it was common to wear an onion "necklace" during a cholera epidemic. In many places it was considered a good omen for a convalescent to dream of an onion, a signal guaranteeing returning health.

One can certainly rely on onions to help cure a cold. Anti-inflammatory, expectorant, and sedative onion syrup (onion juice reduced in honey or sugar) is popular in many places for bronchitis or a persistent cough. This recipe is known in India as well as in America, brought from Europe by the Pennsylvania Dutch. For a runny nose Swiss natural healer Alfred Vogel (1902–1996) recommends onion tea—sliced onions brewed with boiling water and steeped, to be sipped throughout the day. Inhaling the steam of cooking onions is beneficial for colds as well; for headaches and fever a steamed, chopped onion poultice can be wrapped around the soles of the feet.

Folk medicine similarly recommends holding a hot onion poultice for fifteen minutes on muscles cramped with lumbago. Rheumatic joints, sciatic pain syndrome, and neuropathic pain—even insect bites and warts—can all be treated with freshly chopped raw onion. In a similar treatment, raw, salted onion slices can be wrapped on corns overnight.

And what does modern analysis say to all of this? It attests that the sulfur compound allicin—that which causes tears to flow when onions are cut—has an antiviral, antimicrobial effect. In addition allicin strengthens the immune system by increasing the activity of killer cells. It hinders cholesterol oxidation in the blood, thus protecting against arteriosclerosis. Regular "onion eaters" have better blood values; this is because allicin slows platelet adhesion and accelerates the dissolving of blood clots. It also hinders nitrifying bacteria and therefore the development of carcinogenic nitrosamines in the intestines. But the benefit to blood doesn't end there; the phenolic acid and flavonoids in the onion also have a beneficial effect on the circulatory system, including lowering the blood sugar levels of diabetics. These research results confirm famous modern-day herbal healer Maurice Mességué, who advises that diabetes patients and heart patients include plenty of onions in their diet.

The onion, a triennial plant of the onion-garlic or allium genus, originates from the Asian steppes, an extreme climate to which it is completely adapted. In the moist springtime the small, marble-sized baby onions or "sets" begin to bud and start to soak up light and warmth into early summer. Later, when the weather becomes drier, the succulent, half-subterraneous bulbs—that is, the full-sized, mature onions—are formed. The following year these sprout and shoot into blossom and seed. In the meantime, in order to survive the dry, icy cold winter of the steppes, the bulbs store the watery life forces of the moon in their layered skins, enriching them with sulfuric glycosides. According to the alchemists of old, sulfur is a transporter of light and warmth. It is this combination of lunar water from the moon and fire energy from Mars that gives onions their extraordinary healing power.

Wild leeks and onions of various kinds are also to be found in the steppes of northern America, where Native Americans gathered them for both food and for healing. (Indeed, the name "Chicago" derives from a word of the Fox Indians that means "a place that stinks of wild onions.") Just like their Eurasian counterparts, Native Americans used onions for insect bites, infections, and inflammations; they drew poison and pus out of carbuncles and abscesses with onion poultices or reduced onion syrup (a method particular to the Iroquois). To help heal colds and sinus infections, Black Foot Indians put onions on red-hot rocks and breathed in the caustic steam. Nursing Native American women drank onion tea so as to transfer its healing qualities to their infants in their milk.[1]

Onions have a long history in the folk customs, symbolism, and healing practices in India, China, and the eastern Mediterranean. For example,

Illustration 54. Onion (drawing from Hortus Sanitatis, 1491)

the Chinese symbol for "intelligent" (*ts'ung*) is the same as for "onion." Chinese midwives traditionally touched the head of the newborn with an onion so it would grow to be intelligent.

The onion was also a sacred plant in ancient Egyptian five thousand years ago. Onion bulbs were offered to the gods and placed into the hands, on the eyes, or on the genitals of mummies. Sacred oaths were sworn on onions. The delicate, juicy plant was dedicated to the great goddess Isis, and it was forbidden for her priests to eat onions. Isis is the mistress of the periodicity of the moon and women's rhythms. Egyptians believed that the growth of the onion was connected to the moon's phases just as women's menstruation is. The Egyptian hieroglyph for the moon in its waning and waxing form is an onion. The moon gives the plants their life energy and rules over life's liquids. As the mistress of the moon, the goddess also rules over the waters, the cosmic milk of life. The onion absorbs this cosmic milk; when a person eats that onion, the glands are activated—including the reproductive glands. Thus, the onion also became a symbol of lust and procreation. The ancient Egyptian word for testicles—separate from the moon *hieroglyph* mentioned above—was the same as for onion. Indian Ayurveda also claims that onions nourish a man's seed (*shukra*), for which reason doctors prescribe it to increase the amount of semen. Indeed, Indian penitents and ascetics (*sannyasi*) who have sworn off worldly matters and procreation avoid eating onions and garlic under any circumstances.

Classical antiquity and early Christianity saw another aspect of the onion's various members of the lily family: they were seen as symbols of purity, innocence, and virginity. In Greece it was believed that lilies sprang out of the earth from milk that dripped from the breasts of cow-eyed

Hera, the queen of heaven. For Christians the lily became a symbol of Virgin Mary's immaculate conception: archangel Gabriel floated down from heaven with a white lily in his hand when he announced the conception to Mary. These beliefs are based on the perception that lily plants are not strongly bound to the earth; their roots are shallow, and the way the bulbs round out at the bottom resembles a drop of water. These bulbs symbolize the path taken by incarnating souls as they pass from high heaven, crossing over the gateway of the moon down to the material sphere of the earth. But also they symbolize the return from earth back to the eternal womb of being.

Kitchen onions and garlic don't just belong to the watery moon and the gentle white goddess; they also contain the pungency of Mars, the god responsible for fiery drive. For this reason the Greeks believed onions stimulate sex drive and general vivaciousness. With the Romans it was no different—as this Roman saying regarding male impotence declares: "If onions cannot help, nothing will!"

In their conquest of northern lands Roman legionaries brought cultivated onion varieties that they planted in their gardens. The Celts and Germanics were enthused about this new "leek," especially since bear's garlic, also called "ramsons" or "wild garlic," was already considered sacred by the northlanders, who regarded it as vitalizing, blood cleansing, and aphrodisiacal. This foreign "leek"—for which the barbarians used various names, such as *ynnlek, allouk, oellig, ublek* or *ullig*—found its way into each woman's house garden, where it remained. German botanist Hieronymus Bock (1498–1554), who had heard about the Egyptians' worship of the sacred onion, commented: "We Germans can also not do without such godly goods. . . . There are many who believe that if they eat some raw onion on an empty stomach the first thing in the morning they will be protected from bad, poisonous air for the entire day. . . . Many use it for lustful pleasure, and others use it medicinally." Furthermore, he noted that in Germany hardly anything was used more for baking pies than onions. To this day in southern German regions onion pie is a specialty. Every year on the fourth Monday in November Berne, Switzerland, holds an onion market (*Zibelemärit*) where one can enjoy onion pie and onion soup and where over one hundred thousand kilos of skillfully wrought colorful onions braids are sold.

Of course onion soup is also a famous French specialty, which, according to Maurice Mességué, is actually for "*longue nuits de folie* (long nights of [sexual] foolishness)."

For the peasant culture of Europe the onion played an important role as a healing plant, a plant for the time of Lent, and a comestible good. It is no wonder, then, that an intricate lore developed around cultivating onions. Seed onions were put into the soil in the sign of Capricorn so that they would become firm and hard—whereas in Aquarius they would rot and in Sagittarius they would shoot up without making a bulb. When planting them in the soil it was recommended to do so angrily, swearing, which would make the onions fiery. It was also thought that onions planted on Good Friday, the day the Lord was nailed to the cross, would be pungent, making "lots of tears flow" when eaten.

European peasants used onions as an oracle during the twelve days of Christmas. A teacher of mine, the old Swiss peasant philosopher Arthur Hermes (1890–1986), would peel twelve onionskins and name them after the months. Then he'd sprinkle some salt on them; the next morning he'd assess how much moisture had accumulated on them overnight. In this way he forecasted how much precipitation there would be in the following year's corresponding months. "The oracle is always right!" he claimed. This onion oracle is known all over Europe. Young women also used the onion as a marriage oracle. On Christmas Eve they would put one onion for each bachelor they knew in a corner of the warm living room. On Three King's Day (January 6) they would see if any had sprouted. If none had sprouted there would be no wedding in the coming year.

At the more esoteric level, opinions differ regarding onions. Like the Indian *sannyasins,* some people avoid eating onions so as to not enmesh the spirit in sensuality. Others, such as the Dutch alternative healer Mellie Uyldert (1908–2009), see in the onion the power of spiritual sublimation. She believed the plant absorbs etheric life force of the soil, which it stores it in its shallow-rooted bulb; then, in the second year, the energy shoots upward into flower, leaving the skins lifeless hulls. To her, this signifies that onions enrich our lower chakras with life energy—the energy needed to pull the soul upward into the spiritual realm. Onions, in other words, refine and spiritualize the subtle energies: "Onions help us sublimate, give us the strength to ascend from matter to spirit—for that reason it makes good sense to eat onions for each meal" (Uyldert 1984, 102).

Garden Tips

Cultivation:

Set Culture: Sets are little pickling onions used to produce scallions (when young) or cooking onions (when picked later in the season). They are of the Ebenezer type, which are either yellow or white onions. Look for plump, medium-sized sets that have not yet sent out shoots, as they will provide the best onions. Plant the sets carefully, root end down, covering them with a half inch of soil. Give them ample moisture and keep them free from weeds. In five weeks or so you can pull some as scallions, leaving the remainder to harvest at the end of the season.

Plant Culture: Plant onions are bought in bunches (usually 50 to 100 to a bunch). Red slicer onions of the Bermuda type are grown from plants, as are the large yellow and white sweet Spanish varieties. Like sets, they are planted early in the spring at their natural depth.

Seed Culture: Sow seeds thickly in rows in early spring and thin the young plants to stand two to three inches apart. They can be further thinned during the growing season and used as needed.

Of Special Note: Pinch off the flower buds as soon as they appear; this prevents the neck from becoming large and stunting the bulb. When the tops begin to wither and fall over, the onions are mature. Pull the onions a few days later, during a sunny period, leaving them on the ground for a day or two to cure naturally from the sun and wind. (LB)

Soil: Onions need deeply prepared, fertile, loose soil.

Recipes

Spring Onion Soup with Thyme Bread • 4 Servings

1 pound (455 grams) spring onions (green onions), chopped • 3 table-spoons olive oil, plus 2 tablespoons • 1 tablespoon honey • 1¼ cups (300 milliliters) white wine • 1 quart (945 milliliters) vegetable broth • ½ cup (115 milliliters) cream (18% fat) • 1 teaspoon horseradish • ground nutmeg • black pepper • 4 slices of bread • some fresh thyme leaves • 4 tablespoons Parmesan cheese, grated • 2 tablespoons olive oil

SOUP: Sauté the green onions in 3 tablespoons of the olive oil until brown. Stir in the honey, wine, and vegetable broth. Simmer for about 40 minutes. In a small bowl, mix the cream and horseradish. Transfer the soup to a serving bowl. Just before serving the soup, gently stir in the cream mixture.

THYME BREAD: Place the bread slices on a baking sheet. Arrange the thyme leaves on the bread. Sprinkle the Parmesan on the bread. Drizzle the remaining 2 tablespoons of olive oil on the bread. Broil the prepared bread in the oven until crisp, checking every few minutes, up to about 10 minutes. Serve with the soup.

Onion-Grape Soup with Roasted Feta Bread • 4 Servings

1 cup (225 grams) white or yellow onion, finely chopped • 3 tablespoons fresh thyme leaves • 2 tablespoons olive oil, plus 1 table-spoon • 1 tablespoon honey • ¾ cup (200 milliliters) white wine • 1 quart (945 milliliters) vegetable broth • ½ cup (115 grams) grapes, both red and white • 4 slices whole wheat bread • herbal salt • pepper • 3 ounces (85 grams) Feta cheese, sliced ½ inch thick

ONION-GRAPE SOUP: In a large pan, sauté the onions and thyme leaves in 2 tablespoons of the olive oil until browned. Add the honey. Add the wine. Let simmer for 5 minutes. Add the vegetable broth and simmer on low for 20 minutes. When ready to serve, transfer the soup to a serving bowl. Add the grapes just before serving.

FETA BREAD: Preheat the oven to 350 °F (175 °C). Place the bread slices on a baking tray. Season the bread with herbal salt and pepper. Drizzle the remaining 1 tablespoon of olive oil on the bread. Place the Feta cheese slices on the bread. Bake at 350 °F (175 °C) until brown. Serve with the soup.

Parsnip (*Pastinaca sativa*)

Family: Umbelliferae: umbellifer or carrot family

Other Names: chirivía, grand chervis, panais, parsnip herb, parsnip root, pastinacae herba, pastinacae radix, pastenade

Healing Properties: arouses desire (aphrodisiac), reduces fever, stimulates menstruation (emmenagogue), alleviates stone ailments, alleviates stomach ailments, promotes urination (diuretic)

Symbolic Meaning: gives life-energy; formerly eaten in Europe during the time of fasting; dedicated to the patron of swine, Antonius

Planetary Affiliation: Jupiter, Venus (Culpeper)

The parsnip is a biennial Umbelliferae with a fleshy, aromatic, white-yellow storage root. Though the seeds can be obtained in any organic seed store and the vegetable is well known in culinary circles, it is unfortunately no longer commonly known. It used to be very common in Europe. In fact, until the eighteenth century parsnips were even more popular than carrots. The vegetable is not as crisp and delicate as carrots but it has both more bulk—a ripe root can weigh up to one pound—and more nutritional value.

During the times of knights and minnesingers, the parsnip was a most popular vegetable. One particularly intriguing medieval recipe calls for sautéing and baking parsnips with almonds, chestnuts, raisins, nutmeg, and expensive spices. Their distinct flavor goes very well with roast venison, mutton, or beef. But parsnips were just as popular in the humble kitchens of the simple folk as they were in the cuisine of the aristocracy. Before potatoes replaced them, parsnips were an important filling and nourishing ingredient to stews and soups, as the root contains a lot of sugar, starch, and fatty oils. It was often used to strengthen the old, the weak, or the convalescent. Even into the nineteenth century milk with parsnips was given to help those with consumption—those experiencing the continual depletion, emaciation, loss of strength, and appetite of the then-fatal disease tuberculosis.

Illustration 55. Parsnip root and leaf

Parsnips that are sown in the spring can be harvested in late fall, but those who know the vegetable agree that the roots taste best after having been nipped by a frost. As such, they really should be left in the ground through the winter and then harvested in early spring. In the springtime they taste sweeter and are easier to digest because the stored starches slowly turn back into sugars. Parsnips were the ideal food during the forty days of Lent—the prescribed time for fasting, from Ash Wednesday until Holy Saturday (the Saturday after Good Friday). During Lent, occurring as it did during a dark time of year, food supplies became scarce. Parsnips were ideal because they are filling and contain a lot of vitamin C, which activates the glands and combats winter scurvy. In northwestern Europe during fasting time parsnips were eaten with pickled herring, boiled eggs, and mustard greens. The Irish brewed a tasty parsnip beer—some malt and yeast were added, but no hops. Later, the Irish also distilled parsnip alcohol and even made parsnip jam.

The flat, schizocarp parsnip seeds were widely used for seasoning. In eastern Europe, where indigenous plants still have a higher standing than in the affluent West, parsnip seeds (usually ground) are used as seasoning in soups, salads, sauerkraut, and pickles. Interestingly, though the root causes flatulence, the seeds are carminative, and thus reduce flatulence.

The young leaves and tips of the stalks are also good seasoning (in small doses) for soups and meals with lentils, peas, or carrots. It is reported that each spring, famous explorer Alexander von Humboldt (1769–1859) had his cook prepare the following soup in order to maintain good health: bear's garlic, daisy blossoms, yarrow sprigs, stinging nettle sprigs, plantain

leaves, chickweed, chervil, ground
ivy leaves, and parsnip greens were
sautéed in butter, onions, and flour,
then deglazed with broth.

The root vegetable not only
makes humans healthy and robust,
it is also good for animals. Parsnips were grown in fields to fat-
ten pigs and keep them healthy
over the winter. The holy hermit
St. Anthony, who is the patron
saint of pig herders, butchers, and
brush makers (they used to be
made mostly with pig bristles) is,
of course, also the patron of pig
fodder. Thus he is the guardian of
the parsnip root. Since St. Anthony
is also the protector against pests
and bubonic plague, the common
folk believed that eating parsnips
would help them avoid these ter-

*Illustration 56. Blossoming parsnip
(Joachim Camerarius,* Neuw Kreütterbuch, *1586)*

rible scourges, though no proof is known to support that claim. Parsnip
roots were also fed to cattle; milk and butter were richer if cows were
given parsnips to eat in the winter months along with hay and other
roughage. Such butter was claimed to taste as good as that of cows that
ate fresh grass.

All in all, the parsnip enjoyed a long period of popularity up until the
early nineteenth century, when potatoes began to dominate agriculture—
at which point parsnips faded into obscurity.

It still remains a mystery as to where and when parsnips were first
cultivated. Archaeologists have found its seeds at excavation sites of the
late Neolithic lake dwellers in the foothills of the Alps, but we cannot
know whether the plant was cultivated or gathered wild. In any case, the
wild plant is a native of Europe. Surely it was one of the plants that Old

Stone Age gatherers dug out with a dibble and carried to their camps in nets and baskets. The Celts, Germanics, and Slavs and also occasionally the Romans cultivated whole fields of this root crop. It is reported that Roman emperor Tiberius (42 BC–37 AD) liked the hearty flavor so much that he had the vegetable imported from the provinces along the Rhine. (You may recall that the emperor had greenhouses built for growing cucumbers.) Unfortunately, we know nothing more specific about parsnip: up until the seventeenth century, hardly any linguistic distinction was made between parsnips, carrots, parsley roots, skirret (*Siam sisarum*), or, indeed, any other edible roots. The name also gives us no clues; *parsnip* (from the Latin *pastinare* = to dig out; *pastinum* = digging fork) merely means "a dug-out root."

The seeds of this once very important vegetable came to the New World with the first settlers, specifically to Virginia (where the tribe of the Indian princess Pocahontas lived) and Massachusetts. The plant soon escaped garden confines and seeded itself out as a wild invasive species. Even today it is found growing wild throughout North America, especially along waysides and in fallow fields. The Native Americans took to the new vegetable, cultivating it in their gardens. Parsnips soon became part of the winter supplies of the Iroquois—along with corn, pumpkins, beans, and nuts; when these stockpiles were destroyed in 1779 by General Sullivan on a punitive expedition against the insubordinate natives, the resulting famine forced the Iroquois to surrender.

As Rudolf Steiner (1861–1925) formulates it, parsnips, like other umbellifers, have a strong "etheric body." The biennial absorbs so much etheric life energy in the first year that its root becomes massive and juicy. Simultaneously it opens itself so much to cosmic light energy that it becomes filled to the very tip of its root with aromatic essential oils. These astral forces let the plant "explode into space" in the second year, so that it blossoms and produces seed. Another way of putting it would be to say that parsnips show a very dynamic yin-yang polarity, which accounts for their healing nature.

In its wild form in particular, the parsnip has been known for ages as a healing plant. Its concentrated, life-giving energy is what makes it an ideal food for those suffering from consumption. Dioscorides (~40–90 AD), the ancient master of phytotherapy, prescribed it as a means "to make the female womb able to conceive"; also, "it creates a desire for coitus." Leonhart Fuchs (1501–1566) wrote: "Drinking the cooked-out root provokes desire in married couples" (*Neuw Kreuterbuch,* 1543). Folk sayings echoed the view: "Leaves and seeds cooked in wine and drunken mornings and evenings, helps infertile women be able to conceive." The German name "buck's herb" was given to the parsnip not only for its aphrodisiacal nature but also for its strong odor. Its essential oil, which contains caproic acid esters, makes it smell somewhat like a billy goat.

According to Rudolf Steiner, cosmic astrality manifests itself in plants in their aromatic oil. This astral energy has the ability to set life energy into motion. When we take the parsnip, especially its seeds, into our bodily microcosm, it also sets our fluids into motion—stimulating the digestive, sexual, and excretive glands. Thus, traditional folk medicine recommends a tea made of the seeds or dried leaves as a diuretic and to stimulate the gall bladder. Such an infusion is good for dropsy, kidney and bladder stones, a weak stomach, and fever, as well as for functional weaknesses of the sexual organs (erectile dysfunction and ejaculation difficulties). Dioscorides prescribed parsnips to help the flow of menstrual troubles. Leonhart Fuchs also wrote: "if the root is inserted into the vagina, it will drive a dead foetus out."

In England, more so than elsewhere, parsnips remained a treasured vegetable for a long time. Nicholas Culpeper (1616–1654) described the medicinal effect as "opening," diuretic, carminative, cleansing, and good for the bite of wild animals (probably as a cataplasm). Because of its effect on the urinary-genital system, he placed the plant under the rule of Venus. The big yellowish, nourishing, sweet root shows that Jupiter is involved as well. The root also contains inulin and some fats.

John Wesley (1703–1791), founder of the Pietistic Methodist movement in England, didn't just care about the souls of the poor, the exploited workers of the early Industrial Revolution; he also cared about their health. As they could obviously not afford doctors and medication, and were generally undernourished, the revivalist preacher wrote a booklet for them: *Primitive Physic: An Easy and Natural Way of Curing Most Diseases.* In it he listed simple naturopathic treatments and local domestic plants that were both free and easily found. For example, he suggested applying to cancerous abscesses a poultice made of mashed parsnip leaves and stalks; for asthma and tuberculosis he recommended eating parsnips. The booklet became very popular among the settlers in America, where there were few doctors; thus parsnips became an integral part of American folk medicine as well. Ironically, had the settlers asked the Native Americans, they'd have learned the healing properties of the plant were already well utilized.

Garden Tips

Cultivation: The seed is slow to germinate and will be helped by being soaked overnight in cool water. Sow thickly in rows as soon as the ground can be worked in spring. Apply a light layer of mulch in order to conserve moisture in the soil, for the seeds must remain damp in order to germinate at all. Thin the seedlings to two to three inches apart and then increase the thickness of the mulch to keep weeds at bay. Parsnips are a long-season crop. Begin to harvest after the first hard frost and continue for as long as possible. The flavor of this root vegetable is greatly improved by a couple of hard freezes, which turns its starches into sugars; in fact, you can leave parsnips in the ground until just before the ground freezes too hard to to be dug. As with carrots, scatter a few radish seeds in the row to act as a marker. You can harvest the radishes just as the parsnips are making good progress. (LB)

Soil: Like all deeply growing root crops, parsnips prefer deeply prepared, loose, sandy loam. Heavy clays will inhibit root growth. As a slow grower, it does not require highly fertile soil, but a good application of aged manure, made before planting time, will aid its progress.

Recipes

Parsnips with Basil Vinegar and Basil Sauce • 4 Servings

½ cup (115 milliliters) vegetable broth • ¼ cup (60 grams)
fresh sweet basil leaves • 1 pounds (500 grams) unpeeled parsnips, cubed
• 1 cup (225 grams) peeled or unpeeled potatoes, cubed • 1 tablespoon
basil vinegar • 2 tablespoons olive oil • ½ cup (115 milliliters)
cream (18% fat) • sea salt • pepper

In a large pan, bring the vegetable broth to a boil. Add the basil, parsnips, and potatoes and cook about 15 minutes. When the parsnips and potatoes are tender but still firm, lift them out of the broth into a serving dish and keep warm. In a small bowl, mix the vinegar, olive oil, and cream. Add this to the vegetable broth. Season with salt and pepper to taste. Simmer the broth mixture uncovered for about 30 minutes or as long as it take to reduce by about half. Transfer the mixture to a serving dish and serve as a sauce with the vegetables.

Parsnips with Mustard • 2 Servings

2 parsnips • 1 egg • 2 tablespoons flour • 1 tablespoon mustard
• 2 tablespoons parsley, finely chopped • ground coriander • herbal salt
• white pepper • ¾ cup (175 grams) bread crumbs • 3 tablespoons butter

In a medium pot, boil the parsnips in slightly salted water until tender but still firm, about 10 minutes. Let cool. Cut the parsnips into wheels, about ¼ inch thick. In a medium bowl, mix the egg, flour, and mustard until smooth. Add the parsley, coriander, herbal salt, and pepper to taste. Add the parsnip wheels to the bowl and marinate for 1 hour at room temperature. Put the bread crumbs in a bowl. Dredge the parsnip wheels on both sides in the breadcrumbs. In a large skillet, fry the parsnips in the butter until golden brown.

Pea (*Pisum sativum*)

Family: Fabaceae, Leguminosae, or Papilionaceae: bean, legume, or pea family

Other Names and Varieties: English pea, garden pea, Mange tout, snow pea, sweet pea

Healing Properties: helps prevent appendicitis, lowers cholesterol, can prevent conception, strengthens the immune system (ideal for cancer diet)

Symbolic Meaning: dwarf food, fertility, food of the dead,

Planetary Affiliation: Venus

The pea deva, the spiritual entity that shows itself in the form of a pea plant, is a pronounced friend of humanity. Pea seeds, along with vetch, wild pistachios, almonds, and various wild grains, numbered among the foods gathered by Mesolithic foragers in the Near East and west Asia. When the first tribes became sedentary some ten thousand years ago, this bean family member crept into the very first emmer and barley fields as a weed; soon it became a field crop on its own, turning into a valuable source of protein for humans and animals. The pea plant migrated up the Danube Valley into northern Europe with the swidden farmers and was cultivated at the time of the Linear Pottery Culture, the culture of the earliest central European agriculturalists. Because the pea, like all legumes, binds nitrogen with the help of rhizobia, it greatly enhanced soil fertility. Thanks to this plant these matrilineal cultivators were able to remain longer in one place before soil exhaustion led to decreasing harvests, forcing them to slash and burn a new section of primeval forest. The peas were eaten cooked into a thick soup (peas porridge), which, alongside grain porridge, was a mainstay for these tribes.

Today's tender sweet peas (sugar peas) were yet unknown—not to mention snow peas. It was not until the seventeenth century that Dutch gardeners began to cultivate and market sugar peas, which are eaten unripe. Fresh sugar peas, which were incredibly expensive, were a new sumptuous delicacy, the absolute fashion among the wealthy. The queen of the French

Illustration 57. Garden pea

"Sun King," Louis XIV, is recorded to have complained, "The young princes want to eat nothing but peas!" These popular tender peas were also introduced to North America, and Thomas Jefferson had them grown on his estate.

Over time a lot of lore, superstitions, and rituals accumulate around such an important and old cultural plant. Ultimately, as small as it is, the pea came to play a more central role in European folklore and fairy tales than did any other vegetable. More than a few fairy tale heroes won both a princess and a castle with its help. As peas porridge is said to be a favorite dish of the wee folk, dwarves, and good house spirits, in order to please them a small bowl of it was traditionally placed in a dark corner of the house on Christmas Eve.

According to the German fairy tale "The Fairies of Cologne," the wee folk used to come secretly in the night to relieve those sleeping of much of their unpleasant work. They helped with carpentry, sewed, baked bread, washed clothes, cleaned, and swept. They would probably still do this to this day had it not been for a curious tailor's wife who thought she'd have no peace until she'd find out what they looked like. Toward midnight the nosy woman tossed a bucket of peas on the steps and lit a lantern; lo and behold, there she caught sight of the wee folk stumbling and tripping over the peas in their hasty flight. After that incident the helpful dwarfs left the city of Cologne forever, leaving the people to do their work themselves. The story is meant as a warning for all those who pry into nature's secrets out of mere curiosity; or, as e. e. cummings put it, the tale speaks to the "naughty thumb of science" prodding sweet nature. Just like the fairies of Cologne, the ethereal beings that work wonders in nature shy away from rude curiosity and cold intellect.

In the original Brothers Grimm fairy tale "Cinderella," doves take the place of helpful fairies. So that Cinderella would miss the ball given by the prince, her stepmother commanded she do an impossible task: sort out the good peas from the spoiled ones; but with the help of the doves, she is able to finish in time

Illustration 58. Curiosity drives off the fairies of Cologne (nineteenth-century sketch)

and attend the ball, where of course she wins the prince. And then, let's not forget, there is the story of the princess and the pea.

Folk tales also tell of nasty dwarves who plunder pea fields at night, breaking open the pods and trampling the bushes. In order to stop this naughty behavior, it is advised to go into the field before midnight and beat the ground around the pea beds with switches and whips. In doing this there's a chance one may knock off one of the dwarves' invisibility-rendering magic hats; this accomplished, there's a good chance to grab one of the tiny plunderers and force him to exchange the hat for a gift, such as a divining rod for finding hidden treasures. On the other hand, it might be wiser to let the dwarves continue enjoying the peas in exchange for a rich harvest that they *won't* trample.

Land cultivators the world over have historically acknowledged the importance of ritually feeding the dead, and this custom is even today especially strong in China, Africa, and Latin America. Understandably, they give these departed ancestors foods they had especially enjoyed during their lifetimes; in return, the living hoped their fields would be blessed with good harvests, their animals with good health, and, of course, their descendants with good fortune. In early Egypt (twelfth dynasty, 1900 BC), among the foods offered to the dead was the unpretentious pea. Gypsies—who originated from the northwestern regions of the Indian subcontinent—offered peas for the departed; Europeans offered peas and peas porridge. Indeed, despite scientific enlightenment, despite the Church's warning against this sinful *superstitio,* this excessive religious observance, the practice continues in the European countryside to this day. Some prevailing beliefs: those who eat or cook peas (even only the husks) during the Holy Week will soon have a corpse in the house—perhaps their own; whoever sits on a pillow made of pea straw on New Year's Eve will soon die; anyone who eats peas during the twelve days of Christmas will get boils on the arse or will become hard of hearing—or their chickens will stop laying eggs. Or, there's always the possibility, as is said in Germany, that grim old Bertha—a reminiscence of the archaic European goddess of death and rebirth—will cut open the offender's stomach and stuff it with pea straw.

What is the deeper meaning of these winter solstice taboos of foodstuffs? During this sacred time peas are food for the dead and taboo for the living. It was general knowledge that the ancestral spirits visit during the twelve days of Christmas. Since they entered the house through the chimney, the hearth must be very clean, with a bowl of peas, hemp seeds, or millet porridge placed near it in offering. In Bohemia until only recently it was a custom to pour a portion of peas porridge at all four corners of the living room, making the sign of a cross with each pouring; though it was said to be "for the mice," it was mostly likely originally meant for the ancestral spirits.

Nearly all cultures know the custom of the funeral feast: the final farewell meal in which the departed loved one participates "in spirit" before beginning the long journey into the hereafter. In Mecklenburg, Germany, peas porridge is part of the traditional funeral feast. In Freiburg,

Germany, it was the custom to serve peas porridge to the beloved departed at midnight during the wake.

The traditional cultures, such as that of peasant Europe, did not experience time as linearly as we do, but as a cycle, as a revolving wheel. In the yearly cycle, midsummer and midwinter stand opposite to each other. Peas are considered off-limits during the winter solstice festival, they are heartily enjoyed in the summer. While eating peas at Christmas may be punished with blemishes of the skin, their consumption during midsummer is recommended for healing such ailments. Indeed, in Swabia, Germany, peas cooked in the St. John's midsummer fire are believed to have particular healing power.

Most traditional peoples believe that ancestors send fertility from the other realm. So for the cultures that make offerings of the pea, it's not surprising that the small vegetable is associated with fertility magic in both house and barn. In the twelve days of Christmas, the farmer's wife mixed peas into chicken fodder so the hens would produce plentiful eggs and the rooster would maintain virility and continue to crow vigorously. Baltic peasants would add peas to the pig food on New Year's Day for similar reasons. Another custom was to walk around one's orchard and knock on the tree trunks with a sack full of peas; the idea was that there should be as many fruits on the trees at harvest time as there were peas in the sack.

It is only logical that what works in the barn and orchard must also work for people. In many places peas played a major role in wedding festivals and festivities surrounding birth. Peas and cereal grains were thrown over the bride, or peas were put in her shoes. In some places peas are thrown against the windowpanes during bachelor parties or eve-of-wedding fests. And while modern people may shake their heads about such "silly" superstitions, who of us truly knows the extent to which the power of visualization can subtly influence ethereal realms? If nothing else, faith in such rituals frames the actions we take in our daily lives in the process of working toward our highest goals—the perseverance of which can make all the difference.

We've discussed how agricultural peoples of yore imagined the life force evident in both plant growth and the animal drive as that of a natural deity or *daemon*. This entity, whose brimming strength makes it hard to tame, was honored and celebrated in so-called "mystery dramas" at sacred points in the yearly cycle. In the European countryside this force of nature was personified as a "grain bear," "corn mother," "harvest queen," "field wolf," or "stag"—or as a "pea bear." In the winter nights, especially during the Christmas period or during Lent, this daemon was represented by a young man dressed in pea straw. Like a dancing bear, the young man would be led by a "bear trainer" on a chain through the village. The young man acted wildly, grumbling and growling at the young women he tried to snatch—to their delight. In Thuringia during Lent a hairy "bear" ambled through the villages begging for alms. In the Rhineland on Ash Wednesday the pea bear rampaged through the streets; to increase fertility, the women tried to pluck some of the pea straw from his coat to put under theirs hens' nests, or under their own beds. In some locales, the pea straw worn by the young man was later burned in the traditional public spring bonfire—part of the effigy of "old man winter" or the "old winter witch" that was set aflame. Folklorists recognize remnants of archaic sacrificial rites in these practices. As the Oxford scholar Robert Graves (1895–1985) claimed, in the late Neolithic era potent male animals or even young men were sacrificed to the earth goddess.

From the beginning of its influence the Church tried to ban such old beliefs and customs. For example, at the Synod of Liftinae in Belgium in the year 743 AD, the "*Indiculus Superstitionum et Paganiarum* (Small Index of Superstitions and Paganism)" listed prohibited pagan customs such as the "bawdy festivals in February." Nonetheless, many of the rituals managed to live on unabated even into our modern times.

In the autumn, while the cutters harvest the fields, the vegetation daemon flees into the last sheaf of grain. This sheaf is then decorated and carried triumphantly on the harvest wagon through the village. In some places the one who bound this last sheaf is wrapped in pea straw and decorated with horns; in him, the "pea bear" momentarily takes on visible form.

For the pre-Christian Germanic peoples the pea bear was seen as an incarnation of strong, hairy, thunder god Thor (Anglo Saxon *Thunar*,

Old High German *Donar*), whose nickname was "Osborn" (Scandinavian *Asbjørn*), which means "divine bear." When Thor, the favorite god of the country folk, throws his lightning hammer across the sky in a thunderstorm, the fields turn green. In northern Europe, a Thor's hammer was placed into the lap of the bride at the wedding to ensure she will be as fertile as the fields. Until recently in eastern Germany the "pea bear" accompanied the bridal procession, certainly a remnant of archaic fertility magic. In many areas it was customary to eat a porridge of peas with bacon on Thor's day—Thursday. Even today in Swabia, Germany, peas porridge is eaten on Thursdays during the advent time, the four weeks leading up to Christmas, so as to ensure money won't run out in the coming year. (The divine bear, as a harvest god, is thought of as rich.) In Swabian custom, during the last three Thursdays of advent one must throw dry peas against the windowpanes. Local priests claim that such is a sign of the "coming appearance of the savior," but it is more probable that the peas are considered the roaming spirits that bring fertility. The patter reminds of the hail that often announces Thor's presence.

The pea, thus, was not only popular as an important cultivated plant; it was essentially believed to be divine. For medieval Christians each pea has the signature of the sacramental chalice engraved in it—it is the navel of the seed. Of course, the pea had to have its own patron saint: St. Notburga of Tyrol (Austria). Patches of wild peas still grow in the area where she once lived— because, it is said, she often fed the poor with peas porridge.

> Peas porridge hot, peas porridge cold,
> Peas porridge in the pot, nine days old.
> —Traditional English nursery rhyme, ~1760

The Pea As a Healing Plant

It would seem that such a revered plant would also play an important role in healing lore, but that is not the case. Nursing mothers traditionally applied peas porridge to treat their nipples when they were sore from nursing—but this was probably nothing more "sympathetic medicine," as peas resemble taut nipples. Similar "sympathetic magic" was practiced when the birth pains began. Peas were put over the fire; when they began to cook—according to the belief—the birth would take place. Peas were also said to cure warts. The unsightly verruga was rubbed with a pea, after which it was put in a satchel and thrown out; whoever later picks up the bag by chance will get the wart. (This cure is considered even more effective using a pea stolen from a neighbor's field.)

It was not until the twentieth century that the pea revealed its hidden medicinal properties. Peas are good for diabetics; they can lower harmful LDS cholesterol and, to a small degree, blood sugar levels. They are also helpful in cancer and AIDS diets because they contain protease inhibitors, which trap oxygen radicals and reduce inflammation. As a result of British research in 1986, it was discovered by chance that pea dishes help prevent appendicitis.

Dr. S. N. Sanyal, a biophysicist from the University of Calcutta, "discovered" that the pea, long considered a symbol of fertility, is actually rich with contraceptive substances. It contains m-Xylohydroquinone, which dampens fertility by intervening in the production of progesterone and estrogen. Dr. Sanyal showed that female fertility was reduced by up to 60 percent; for males the sperm count was substantially lessened. But such was, indeed, merely scientific verification of what Asian medicine had already long known; Indian women have traditionally cooked a soup out of pea pods in order to delay conception. Interestingly, in Tibet, where peas are a major source of nourishment, the population remained stable over hundreds of years. (Carper 1988, 180) Note, however, that this is not to say that pea extract can effectively replace the near-perfect efficacy of the birth control pill.

Why does the pea produce sexual hormones, as do other pulses? Ecologists presume that via these hormones such plants practice birth control on their natural predators. How so? At times when the climate is too cold or too dry for optimal growth, the plants produce these hormones in abundance so as to reduce the chance of being consumed out of existence. But during optimal conditions, when they themselves are abundant, they produce such small amounts of these fertility-reducing hormones that they have little or no influence on their predators.

It seems that the deva of this particular philanthropic legume still communicates actively with the more sensitive among us. It was through the pea that Augustinian monk Gregor Mendel (1822–1884) discovered the laws of genetic inheritance. For years in his cloister garden in Brno, Moravia, he tirelessly crossed smooth yellow peas with wrinkled green ones, recording the results. Though few showed interested in the monk's obscure hobby at the time, his pea cultivation research has become the cornerstone of contemporary genetics studies.

The famous Findhorn Garden in northern Scotland owes its status to the pea deva. Dorothy Maclean, a "highly sensitive person," got her first message from plant devas through the pea plant. That it was this ancient cultigen that "talked" to her is no coincidence: she had always, since childhood, cherished the plant, loving how it grows, how it flowers and smells. This empathy, rather than the scientific experimental method, brought her into contact with what she called the "soul of the pea kingdom." The message she received: if humans open their hearts to plants, then miracles such as seen in Findhorn can happen.

Garden Tips

Cultivation: Few garden crops are as highly prized as peas, which can be planted in spring as soon as the soil can be cultivated. A few light frosts will not hurt them. The seeds can be treated with a bacterial inoculant so that they produce more nitrogen. Because the pea is a trailing plant, it appreciates a trellis to climb on. As soon as the plants are big enough to climb they should be mulched to keep the roots cool. Sugar peas should be harvested when the pods are full but not yet hard. Snow peas (edible pod peas) should be picked just as the peas inside begin to form in the pod. (LB)

Soil: In order to grow well peas like loose, sandy soil that is well composted and well fertilized with *natural* fertilizers.

Recipes

Cold Pea Soup with Mint • 4 Servings

1 pound (455 grams) unpeeled early potatoes, cubed
• 1 quart (945 milliliters) vegetable broth • 1 pound (455 grams)
fresh peas • black pepper • herbal salt • 1 pinch vanilla powder
• dab of honey • ½ cup (115 milliliters) cream (18% fat)
• fresh mint leaves (as garnish)

Simmer the potatoes in the vegetable broth for about 20 minutes or until tender. Add the peas and simmer for about 10 minutes. Let the soup steep for about 15 minutes. Blend with an immersion blender until smooth. Transfer to a covered container and chill in the refrigerator for about one hour or until cold. When cold, transfer the soup to a serving dish. Season with the vanilla, honey, salt, and pepper to taste. Mix in the cream. Garnish with mint leaves.

TIP: This soup pairs nicely with croutons freshly roasted in olive oil.

Pea Salad with Garlic Croutons • 4 Servings

1 pound (455 grams) fresh peas (without pods) • ½ pound (225 grams)
tomatoes • 2 onions, finely chopped • 1 bunch parsley • bit of lovage
• bit of honey • 1 tablespoon balsamic vinegar • 3 tablespoons
hazelnut oil • sea salt • pepper • 2 slices bread, cubed
• 4 to 8 garlic cloves, chopped • 2 tablespoons olive oil

In a medium-large serving bowl mix the peas, tomatoes, and onions. In a separate small bowl, mix the parsley and lovage with the vinegar. Add honey to taste. Pour this mixture over the vegetables until they are evenly covered. Season with sea salt and pepper to taste; let rest for 10 minutes.

Fry the bread cubes and the garlic in the olive oil at a low temperature until golden brown. Let cool for a few minutes before sprinkling them over the salad.

Potato (*Solanum tuberosum*)

Family: Solanaceae: nightshade family

Other Names: Murphy (Irish potato), spud, tater, tuber

Healing Properties: builds up base levels (ideal for the stomach), reduces acidity; taken externally: as a poultice eases joint inflammation, rheumatism, and swollen lymph nodes

taken internally: the juice eases heartburn and stomach ulcers,

Symbolic Meaning: stupidity, egoism, lack of inspiration, materialism

Planetary Affiliation: moon

After rice, the potato is the second-most-cultivated nutritional plant worldwide—darling of the agricultural industry and private vegetable gardens alike. Potatoes will grow for anyone, even those who do not otherwise have a green thumb. Some children enjoy harvesting them almost as much as searching for Easter eggs. And when it comes to the potato patch, even the most hard-boiled rationalist will at some point dabble in magical thinking: perhaps planting the spuds right after the full moon, or consulting the Farmer's Almanac for which day the moon will be in an earth sign (Taurus, Virgo, Sagittarius). In Switzerland and other alpine countries, many gardeners note whether the moon is ascending or descending, that is, whether it's on its way to the highest zodiac sign (Gemini) or heading back down to the lowest sign (Sagittarius). Why? When Luna comes down from the higher zodiacal signs to the lower ones, it is believed she brings life energy down into earth, which is, of course, ideal for the tuber. Then there are other guidelines for when to plant, these concerning the "sidereal moon," that is, the quality of the sign in which the moon finds itself at the time. For example, old garden rules claim a moon in Virgo is unfavorable because then the shrub will blossom continually, later producing measly, thin tubers; or, if planted when the moon is in Sagittarius, the potatoes will be small and hard; in Aquarius and Pisces they will be watery; in Cancer they will be wormy and scabby. Other signs are favorable, though: if one plants when the moon is in Gemini and Libra, the harvest will be double; when in Leo and Taurus, the potatoes will be big. Furthermore,

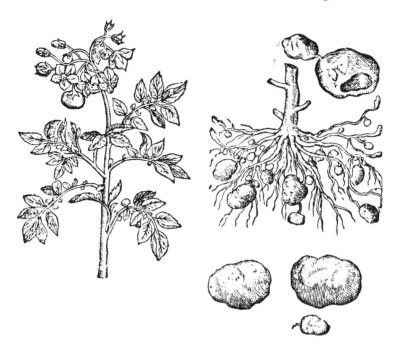

Illustration 59. One of the earliest drawings of the potato (Carolus Clusius, Rariorum Plantarum Historia, 1601)

gardeners consider how close the moon is to the earth: when it is closest (perigee) vs. when it is farthest (apogee). It's considered best to put the spuds in their beds at the time of moon's perigee. And then there is also the "synodic moon" to be considered: when it waxes and wanes. As you can see, potato planting can be a complicated business. But there is also an old saying claiming "the dumbest farmer has the biggest potatoes." There is some truth to this, for such a farmer relies on his gut instinct and intuition, which is often more reliable than abstract intellectual rules when it comes to working with living organisms.

Nowadays, one can hardly imagine life without the nourishing, starchy tuber. From scalloped potatoes to potato salads, from chips to French fries, there are more potato dishes in the Americas than can be mentioned in one breath. Most regions have their own kinds of potatoes and their own favorite dishes; in Europe, these are as varied as are the different

Illustration 60. Potato-shaped vessel of the Peruvian Chimú culture

dialects. From dumplings in Saxony, *lefsa* (soft flatbread) in Norway, and *rösti* (like hash browns) in Switzerland, potatoes are used in both salty and sweet dishes. A simple potato soup was known to be the favorite food of German emperor Wilhelm II (1859–1940).

Fries and chips, which are as much a part of international modern life as are hamburgers and cola, have had interesting beginnings. When French fries (*pomme frites*) were first made in France in the eighteenth century, they were considered for a long time to be a refined dish fit only for aristocracy. (Thomas Jefferson brought the recipe back from France and served thick-cut fries at Monticello.) More than a century later, this treat led to the accidental invention of the potato chip. A guest in a fancy resort in Saratoga Springs, New York, had ordered the French potato delicacy; being fastidious, he sent the fries back to the back to the kitchen, claiming they were too thick. The hotel's cook, a mixed-race African American/Native American named George Crum (1822– 1914), made a new batch with thinner strips, but the guest was still not satisfied. Finally Crum decided to fry them so thin they couldn't be "skewered with a fork." Rather than being upset, the guest was delighted. Soon these "Saratoga Chips" became the specialty of the house (Panati 1998, 388).

But, despite their long-beloved status, potato dishes were not always so popular. In Europe, when the Spanish first brought the tubers from South America toward the end of the sixteenth century, this nightshade plant was viewed quite skeptically because it was common knowledge that nightshades, such as belladonna or angel's trumpet, can be very poisonous. At this stage the plant was assumed to have aphrodisiacal and possibly healing properties. Ultimately, it was mainly curious pharmacists or pastors interested in botany who first planted this "apple of the earth" (French *pommes de terre*) or "American truffle" (the German word for potato, "*kartoffel*," comes from the Italian *tartufolo* = truffle). Indeed, the first potato planted in Germany was in an apothecary garden in Breslau in 1587. But the European royalty was also interested in the exotic plant, and passed it on from court to court, letting their cooks experiment in their kitchens. Of course, one must be careful when experimenting. Sir Walter Raleigh (~1554–1618), who received the plant from an aristocrat, got solanum poisoning from eating the berries instead of the tubers. Queen Elizabeth I (1533–1603) didn't fare any better when she had potato leaves prepared and served as a sort of spinach; she had received the plant as a gift from the New World from Sir Francis Drake (~1540– 1596), pirate in the service of her Majesty.

Except for the tubers, the nightshade plant is indeed poisonous. Though the potato does not contain tropane alkaloids (atropine or sco-polamine) found in belladonna or henbane, the green portions of the plant do contain solanine, which is nearly as poisonous as strychnine. Even small amounts cause stomach pain, cramps, and diarrhea. The sola-nine in the potato plant functions to both disrupt the skin-shedding metamorphosis of hungry insects and protect its tubers from rot.

Not surprisingly, at first country folk didn't want anything to do with this exotic tuber. Because of the "signature" of the tubers, the peasants feared eating them might give them leprosy, tumors, or scrofula (lymph-adenitis). In some regions the plant was even officially forbidden, as in Besancon in 1630, where the city council declared: "The potato contains poisons that can cause leprosy." Puritans and the Russian Orthodox did not eat them because they were not mentioned in the Bible; being there-fore not the "Word of God," they must be of the devil. Even today anthro-posophists are careful with potatoes, recommending sick people avoid this bloated, proliferous tuber, claiming it dampens the spirit and encourages uninspired materialistic thought.

Only hardship and famine taught people to value the potato. This first occurred in the seventeenth century in British-controlled Ireland. The periodic uprisings by rebellious Irish were suppressed by the British tactic of burning or trampling the fields, an approach that, though effective in destroying grain fields, left potatoes unharmed; potatoes thus helped stave off famine. Then, during colonization the English overlords confiscated the best soils to grow grain and raise beef cattle, which were intended for export. Before long practically all that was left for the Irish to eat were potatoes and skimmed milk.

In Germany, Scandinavia, and Poland it was abject poverty that led to the widespread eating of potatoes. The first potato fields in central Europe were planted in 1680 in impoverished Vogtland, where it was proverbially said:

> *Potatoes for breakfast,*
> *at midday in the soup,*
> *for supper in their skins,*
> *potatoes 'til I drop!*

The rulers of the Age of Enlightenment during the eighteenth century soon recognized the potential of the potato. The economist Adam Smith (1723–1790), the prophet of modern capitalism, recommended mass cultivation of potatoes as a cheap source of food for the working classes. He believed the tubers, which have more nutritional value and produce more bulk per acre than do wheat and other cereal grains, would be more economical.[1] More peasants could be relieved of tilling the soil—so he calculated—and put to work in the mills and factories.

In France, pharmacist Antoine-Augustin Parmentier (1737–1813) pointed out to His Majesty Louis XVI that *pommes de terre* would be good food for the masses; unfortunately, the people weren't willing to oblige. During the famines of 1780s the clever, upper-class tactician ordered potatoes to be planted in parks and empty lots in and around Paris, the fields patrolled by day by armed guards. In the evening, however, the guards left their posts. Thinking they were outfoxing the pharmacist, during the night the rabble plundered the fields stealing potatoes—just as they were intended to do. Soon Parisians took a fancy to these exotic "earth apples." The rulers in Prussia and in Russia were less subtle: they simply ordered by decree that all subjects plant potatoes—while simultaneously highly taxing flour. As a result, the consumption of cereals between 1690 and 1790 was halved. In turn, the people came to appreciate potatoes, but not just as food—since it's also enjoyed distilled as high-proof potato spirits, potato whiskey, or schnapps.

Illustration 61. Antoine-August Parmentier made potatoes popular in France in 1780 (Brendan Lehane, The Power of Plants, *1977)*

Prehistoric hunters and gatherers in Monte Verde, Chile, foraged for wild potatoes as long as 10,000 years ago. Later, on the foggy, moist slopes of the Andes where it is too cold for corn, the ancestors of the Incas cultivated potatoes—*papas*—by creating level terraces that they irrigated. In time they developed some three thousand varieties: white, yellow, red, purple, and brown; big and small, sweet and bitter. (The bitter ones were used only as fodder for lamas and alpacas.) The Incas felt that the potato connected them to the great Earth Mother and to their ancestors. The tuber was also connected to the jaguar spirit, which at times had to be appeased with bloody rituals. They also prayed to Axomama, the potato mother or goddess. In a ritual similar to how European peasants paid tribute to the last sheaf of grain they cut, the Indios honored Axomama in a "ceremony to renew the potato." First they spread out the harvested potatoes on the ground to let them freeze for three nights; then, after stomping them with their feet until all of the water squeezed out, they dried them in the sun. To this day these freeze-dried potatoes—*chuños*—are the main staple of the Quechua and Aymara people.

Illustration 62. Incas harvesting potatoes (Spanish drawing, sixteenth century)

The potato deva, a truly mighty being, has changed the destiny of humanity. The Spanish fed their Indian slaves working in the silver mines of Potosí with *chuños* stolen from the Incas' larders. With the immense wealth obtained from this mined silver, the Spanish lords financed both their world power ambitions and the Counter-Reformation. But, despite such ill-begotten treasure, the geopolitical center of power migrated—thanks to the potato—from southern to northern Europe. The potato preferred the cool and moist Atlantic climate to that of the hot and dry Mediterranean. Plus, due to its high vitamin C content, the potato became an ideal winter food, putting an end to pernicious scurvy. Soon, potatoes could feed entire armies of soldiers and, a little later, factory workers; potato alcohol also helped the populace to bear the brutality of early industrialization. In this way the productive tuber greatly facilitated the Industrial Revolution in northern Europe.

Potatoes supposedly arrived in the North American colonies in 1621 when the governor of Bermuda, Nathaniel Butler, sent two large cedar chests containing "Spanish tubers" and other vegetables to Governor Francis Wyatt of Virginia at Jamestown. Nearly two hundred years later, Thomas Jefferson, always interested in horticultural novelties, grew them on his estate. But during their early American history potatoes were grown only sporadically in vegetable gardens; they didn't become a major staple until the influx of the Irish and central and eastern Europeans in the middle of the nineteenth century.

The potato literally revolutionized nutrition in Europe: after its ascendancy, oatmeal, millet, and root vegetables like parsnips, skirret, and rampion vanished from dining tables. The potato tuber, which was thereafter eaten at nearly every mealtime and is easily digested, contains lots of vitamins, proteins, and amino acids (lysine, leucine, valine, etc.), as well as starch and even trace elements (aluminum, nickel, zinc, and iodine, among others). The introduction of the potato enabled Europeans to live longer, healthier lives and reproduce more.

Unfortunately, overreliance on one crop is a dangerous gamble, as was keenly felt in 1845, the fateful year the potato blight (*Phytophthora infestans*) suddenly appeared in Ireland, rotting and blackening the harvested potatoes. The fungus was especially devastating because all the potatoes were basically a single variety; as they had an extremely narrow genetic basis, they could offer little resistance to the invasive fungus. By the time this blight had lasted three consecutive years, the Irish population had been reduced by half: one-fourth of the Irish starved to death, and one-fourth—some two million people—emigrated, mainly to North America. The beleaguered newcomers, however, were not particularly welcome, being as they were both Catholic and inclined toward alcohol, neither of which suited the Puritan ethos. In addition, the narrow nourishment of potatoes and skimmed milk over several generations had left the Irish rather small in stature. All in all, the resident Caucasian Americans were afraid the Irish "dwarves" would genetically ruin their race. Of course, thanks to the better nutrition to be found in the States the children of the Irish immigrants soon grew as big and strong as their compatriots.

The potato blight raged in other parts of Europe as well, inciting many millions of poor peasants, especially from Scandinavia, the Netherlands, and the German-speaking countries, to make the hard decision to emigrate to the New World. As a result, most of today's Caucasian Americans are the descendants of potato blight refugees.

Potatoes As Healers

It's to be expected that healers in Europe appropriated for their own purposes the tuber that had conquered the dining table. At first, seventeenth-century doctors, who didn't yet distinguish between pota-toes and sweet potatoes,[2] believed that the longish tuber could improve a man's potency. Indeed, for Shakespeare potato fingers were a symbol of lust:

> *How the devil Luxury, with his fat rump and*
> *potato-finger, tickles these together! Fry, lechery, fry!*
> —*Troilus and Cressida*, Act 5, Scene 2

Henry Hudson (~1565–1611), British commentator on Shakespeare's works, wrote: "It is said that potato fingers have lust and prurience because it is believed that the potato strengthens the body and creates lust." This misconception, however, didn't last long.

In traditional folk medicine it is believed that to carry a potato around in one's pocket helps against rheumatism. Poultices of mashed potatoes or fresh potato juice are used for gout, rheumatism, and lumbago. Raw, grated potatoes mixed with oil are used for burns, sunburn, and cracked skin. Hot potato poultices are used for infections, bronchitis, swelling, including of the lymph gland, lumbago, and other pain. Raw juice is drunk for stomach ulcers.

Potatoes are said to make people plump and sluggish—the infamous "couch potato." In truth, potatoes on their own are ideal for keeping a slim figure; it is only the oils used in preparing them that makes them fat-tening. In increasing quantities of high-pH bases in the digestive system, potatoes help to prevent stomach acidity, constipation, and liver damage. New research suggests they may be anticarcinogenic because they contain protease-inhibiting agents that neutralize viruses and carcinogens as well as Chlorogenic acid, which guards against cell deterioration. In addition they have an antioxidant effect.

But even today there are still critics of the humble potato. Anthro-posophists assert: "Creative thinking has diminished in Europe since the time that eating potatoes became popular." They claim that potatoes make people dumb and egocentric, and that they are partially responsible for the present spiritual state of modern humanity. "The potato," said Rudolf

Steiner (1861–1925), "is digested in the head." One of Steiner's followers proclaims that potato consumption does not support inner awareness, that in the long term it can even harm the midbrain and the development and functioning of the brainstem" (Walter 1971, 102). Rudolf Hauschka, another anthroposophist, fears that even the children of excessive-potato-eating parents will have a hard time mastering their cerebral functions. Impressive tuber indeed!

Garden Tips

Cultivation and Soil: Though potatoes are basically undemanding, it is best they always have a fresh, new place in the garden each year. They should never be planted in the same bed in the following year, or following tomatoes, either; since both are nightshades, they can share diseases. The day before planting, cut the seed potatoes so that there is at least one eye to each cutting with plenty of flesh around the eye; let them dry overnight. Till the soil well the next day, making rows about two feet apart. Well-aged compost can be incorporated at this time. Hoe very shallow trenches and lay the potatoes in, eyes up. (LB)

Recipes

Olive-Potato Ravioli with Browned Butter • 2 Servings

Dough: 1 cup (225 grams) whole wheat flour • 2 eggs, plus 2 egg yolks, whisked • 3 tablespoons olive oil • 2 tablespoons vegetable broth • Filling: 4 ounces onions, finely chopped • some fresh thyme leaves • 2 tablespoons olive oil • 2 ounces black, pitted olives, chopped • 1 cup (225 grams) mashed potatoes • herbal salt • pepper • ground nutmeg • 1 egg yolk, whisked with ½ teaspoon water • 2 ounces butter

Dough: Knead the ingredients into a dough. Transfer to a covered container and refrigerate for 4 hours.

Filling: Sauté the onions and thyme in the olive oil until browned. Add the olives and mashed potatoes. Season with salt, pepper, and nutmeg to taste. Set aside.

Raviolis: Preheat the oven to 350 °F (175 °C). Roll out the chilled dough into a 3-inch log. Slice into rounds about ½ inch thick. Prepare a baking sheet with grease or with parchment paper. Taking 1 dough slice at a time, dab about 2 teaspoons of the filling in the middle of the dough slice. Brush the rim with egg yolk whisked with a few drops of water. Fold the dough in half to create half-moons; pinch the edges together to seal. Place the ravioli on the baking sheet and brush with egg yolk. Repeat with the remaining dough. Bake the ravioli at 350 °F (175 °C) for 10 minutes, or until golden brown. Transfer the baked ravioli to a serving dish.

Browned butter: In a small pan, gently heat the butter until slightly browned, about 5 minutes; be sure not to burn it. When ready to serve, drizzle the butter over the ravioli.

Halved Baked Potatoes • 4 Servings
4 unpeeled potatoes, cut in half lengthwise
• 2 tablespoons olive oil • salt

Preheat the oven to 350 °F (175 °C). Prepare a baking sheet with parchment paper. Rub each potato half with olive oil. Sprinkle cut sides with salt. Place each half, sliced side down, on the baking sheet. Bake at 350 °F (175 °C) for 20–30 minutes or until a fork goes through easily.

Pumpkin and Squash (*Cucurbita pepo, C. maxima, C. moschata*)

Family: Cucurbitaceae: gourd family

Other Names: gourd, Jack-o'-lantern, pepo, vine

Healing Properties:

Flesh: eases kidney ailments, obesity, and stomach ailments

Seeds: eases prostate hyperplasia and urinary infections, expels worms

Symbolic Meaning: world egg (Native Americans, Africans), primeval union of yin-yang, luck-bringer, long life (China), shortness and elusiveness of life (Christian); honoring the dead; end of summer; Halloween and St. Martin's Day

Planetary Affiliation: moon and Jupiter

On December 3, 1492, on the island of Cuba, Christopher Columbus became the first European to lay his eyes on a pumpkin field. He knew at once that the opulent pumpkin plant, with its big, rough leaves and tendrils, yellow-gold blossoms, and rotund orange fruits is an "Indian" variety of the *Cucurbita,* or *Curbita,* the melons (*Cucumis*) and gourds (*Lagenaria*) of the Old World.

In northern Europe, aside from cucumbers and poisonous bryony, the latter of which was used in occult rituals, not much attention was paid to this plant family—perhaps because these plants need a lot of warmth and are very sensitive to frost. Watermelons had been known in Mediterranean countries since ancient times, and were served—like ice cream today—as common refreshments. And gourds, with their hard, dry shells, were used by the Romans to make containers, drinking vessels, and rattles. But otherwise the *cucurbitas* were considered to be commonplace. This American pumpkin, however, was of a completely different caliber.

For North and South American natives the pumpkin was a nutritional mainstay, and one of the oldest plants cultivated. Like corn and beans, it was regarded as an incarnated goddess descended from the heavens. Pumpkin seeds found in caves in Oaxaca, Mexico, and other places are dated to be some 10,000 years old. These were wild plants, though—the flesh scant and bitter. They were gathered for their seeds, which contained valuable protein and oils. Over the course of several thousand years, Native American gardeners bred and cultivated hundreds of squash varieties of different sizes, shapes, and colors—acorn squash, banana squash, chayote, crookneck, flying saucer (also called "scallop squash" and "pattypan squash"), golden nugget (also called "Oriental pumpkin"), zucchini, and many, many others—all of which have delicate, easily digestible flesh.

Illustration 63. "Santa Maria," flagship of Christopher Columbus, the first European to see a pumpkin

In the Americas of today gardeners still produce a striking variety of this plant family, all referred to as squash. Because the white settlers had no word for this unusual vegetable, they took over the Narragansett Algonquian word "*askutasquash*" ("green thing eaten raw"), which they simplified to *squash*. (In Britain, where the term "squash" refers to either a pressed citrus fruit juice or a game similar to tennis, the vegetable is called "vegetable marrow.") Americans distinguish between winter and summer squash, the former kinds (*C. maxima, C. moschata*) have a round stem and are eaten when fully ripe; the latter (*C. pepo*) have a square stem and are usually eaten before they are ripe. Most of the various members of this plant family need a very long period of sun to ripen; therefore in northern climates only a few kinds thrive. Among these various summer squash, the extremely productive zucchini ("*courgette*" in France and Britain) is an all-time favorite in personal vegetable gardens. Blossoming continually, each plant repeatedly produces long, green, cucumber-like fruits—so many that a single family cannot consume

Illustration 64. Extraterrestrial "pumpkin head"

them all. One solution to this "problem" is to fry some of the blossoms in batter—a first class delicacy!—before they get a chance to ripen.

The giant pumpkin (*C. maxima*) is probably the largest vegetable of the entire plant kingdom. In the year 1900 at the Paris World's Fair (*Expostition Universelle*) a 400-pound pumpkin with a diameter of three feet broke the established record; in 2014 a Swiss accountant grew a pumpkin weighing more than a ton (2,323 pounds). With possible genetic manipulation, the future might bring us even bigger pumpkin monsters.

As it was for the Native Americans, the pumpkin also has cult status in modern America: as both Halloween jack-o'-lanterns and pumpkin pie at Thanksgiving, the harvest time festival. This celebration and feast serves to remind us of the Pilgrim Fathers who were saved from starvation by the local Amerindian tribe, the Wampanoag, in the winter of 1620. Sadly, we tend to forget that the Wampanoag were shortly afterward expelled and nearly extinguished by these very settlers.

By the end of the sixteenth century pumpkins were also grown in the gardens and fields of the Old World. Nonetheless, it took Europeans a long time to warm up to eating them as a vegetable. Even today in France pumpkin is mainly used as cattle fodder. The huge berry—botanically speaking it's a berry!—instead inspired fantasy visions, both then and now. Charles Perrault (1628– 1703) incorporated it into his version of "Cinderella" by having the fairy godmother turn a pumpkin into Cinderella's carriage. And "galactic boat people," extraterrestrials that have supposedly crashed in the Mojave Desert, are generally called "pumpkin heads" (which is, of course, also a term for a nitwit).

Records suggest a variant of Halloween has been celebrated since the Megalithic age, the era when Stonehenge was built. Then it was an end-of-the-year-festival, when winter was about to set in and the spirits of the dead temporarily left the "other world" to roam about begging for food. The Celts called these holy days "Samhain," and celebrated them at full moon in November; in later eras they were known as "All Hallows' Eve." In order to receive blessings and protection from the departed, and to avoid being spooked or haunted, people would set out food offerings and lights on their doorsteps. The lights consisted of lanterns made by hollowing out big turnip roots, carving faces into them, and placing candles inside. The lit-up

Illustration 65. Before pumpkins came to Europe, lanterns were carved out of turnips for "All Hallow's Eve (Halloween)

turnip roots represented the full moon, as it was thought the sprits of the dead traveled on moonbeams. (Since Classical antiquity, European Christians believed the souls of the dead ascended first to the lunar sphere, the first rung on the "ladder of heaven.") When the descendants of these people came to America, they replaced the turnip with a pumpkin, and the festival became more secular and commercial, in time morphing into the trick-or-treat holiday we know today.

Anthropologists consider the important Mexican holiday *Día de Muertos* (The Day of the Dead) to have originated some three thousand years ago. To this day candied pumpkin meat is offered to the departed as food on this holiday, now celebrated on November 1. This is yet another example of how, as a lunar plant, the pumpkin has long had a strong association with the dead. For another, in Slovakia it was the custom to boil garlic and squash stems in water with which to wash down the chairs and table where a dead person had been lying in state; the room was then sprinkled with this water. These precautions, it was believed, ensured the ghost would not come back to haunt the room.

As pumpkin and various other squash vegetables came to be known throughout the Old World, each region developed its own relationship to the quaint plants. For the Chinese, the pumpkin became a symbol for the primeval oneness of yin-yang; for the Africans it is the world egg, with the seeds of all beings within it. Because of the pumpkin's plentiful seeds, to the Turks it symbolizes the female ovary, protecting from the "evil eye." In Cairo pumpkins are hung to protect from the evil eye.

In rural South Africa pumpkin also became part of the folklore and healing lore. The Zulus and other Southern African peoples cook the yellow blossoms into a kind of relish that is eaten with corn mush, and roasted seeds are a popular snack. The herbal healers of the Zulus, the *inyanga*, cook pumpkin leaves and put them on the chest as hot compresses for pneumonia. They also recommend a tea made of the roots for rheumatic pains and ground seeds to get rid of tape worms.

Illustration 66. Woman and child carrying a pumpkin on their heads (illustration by K. Paessler, Gärtner Pötschkes Großes Gartenbuch. 1945)

The Spanish, who strictly discern between categories of "hot" and "cold" in their traditional healing, prepare the seeds (*semena frigida majora*) as a remedy for cooling intense, lustful passion and for lessening "hot" seminal fluid. In 1643, Nicholas Culpeper confirmed the "cooling" nature of the plant by placing it under the rule of the moon.

In southern and western France pumpkins are cultivated only as animal fodder; the French cannot imagine finding them tasty. Eastern Europeans, however, befriended pumpkins readily, approaching the plant in a typical Slavic way, pickling its flesh as they pickle its cousin, the cucumber. Hot pumpkin soup and even pumpkin porridge are also popular in these regions. The American favorite, pumpkin pie, on the other hand is considered an exotic dish.

The country folk in Europe also transferred onto the pumpkin the notions of sympathetic magic applied to other big vegetables. Pumpkin seeds, they believe, should be sown on Whitsuntide (Pentecost) Sunday when the church bells ring—so "they will grow to be as big as church bells." (You may recall a similar belief having to do with cabbage.) For the same reason the seeds should be carried in a big bucket or basket. In Breslau, a woman with big buttocks would sit on the seeds so the pumpkins would grow as big as her bottom; for the same reason one should also tell a big lie while sowing the seed in the ground. In Lausanne, Switzerland, peasants brought the seeds to church to be blessed on Annunciation Day (March 25), the day when the archangel Gabriel announced to the Virgin Mary, she was with child; in the same way that Mary's belly would grow big and round, so should grow the pumpkins. Other days serve as well: in some regions sowing on May 25, the day of St. Urban, "brings a big turban," whereas the Polish plant on the day of St. Stanislaus (May 8).

If one sows before sunrise on April 30, St. Walpurgis Day—a festival diametrically opposed to the fall festival of Samhain (Halloween)—the seeds will thrive as fast as witches fly. (We earlier noted the same belief associated with cucumbers.) In Brittany pumpkin seeds are sown on Good Friday so they will "resurrect" in big style.

The Healing Power of Pumpkins

Native Americans well knew the healing benefits of pumpkins. The Mayans used the juice in salves to treat burns. For round worms and tapeworms, the Aztecs made a medicine out of pumpkin seeds, onions, and wormseed (*Chenopodium ambrosioides*); for bladder and kidney diseases they made a medicine out of the pulp. The Catawba chewed the seeds to cure kidney problems; the Cherokee and Menominee used them as a diuretic and to cleanse the urine for bedwetting, dropsy, burning sensations while urinating, and cramps in the urinary organs.

Folk medicine concerning the pumpkin is quite similar in Europe, where it was traditionally believed the plant derived some of its healing properties from the abundant life energy it radiates. As a bland food, pumpkin flesh is recommended for stomach troubles and kidney/bladder ailments. Fresh pumpkin pulp is applied to furuncles, abscesses, varicose veins, and cankerous sores. Pumpkin seed oil is used to heal cracked skin and wounds, especially burns.

By at least the nineteenth century Europeans discovered something the Aztecs had known centuries earlier: pumpkin seeds get rid of worms. Eating just about ten ounces paralyzes the worms; after thirty minutes they can be excreted with the help of a half tablespoon of castor oil. (The famous Bavarian herbalist and healer Sebastian Kneipp [1821–1897] recommended wormwood tea [*Artemisia absinthium*] be mixed with the ground seeds.) Modern medical research has shown that the seeds help with benign swollen prostate gland; they contain delta-7 sterols, which resemble the male sex hormone, and dihydrotestosterone—as well as vitamin E and selenium, which have both anti-inflammatory and antioxidant effects. And cancer researchers in South Africa are currently studying pumpkin seeds for their peponin, which is thought to block the production of HIV-1 enzymes.

As we see, given its many health benefits—and no known side effects—there are plenty of reasons to include tasty pumpkins in one's diet.

Garden Tips

Cultivation: Before sowing, soak the seeds in milk until they are swollen. After there is no more danger of frost, plant the seeds into raised mounds. You can spur growth by adding liquid compost in the middle of the growing period. Pumpkins thrive very well—and will not get aphids—if grown with nasturtiums and angel's trumpet. (LB)

Soil: The pumpkin is a frost-sensitive heavy feeder; it grows best in sandy loam that has been well supplied with rotted manure. A midseason application of compost tea will spur growth. Any kind of quash plants also thrive well when planted into an old compost pile.

Recipes

Pumpkin Salad with Blueberry Sauce • 2 Servings

3 tablespoons mayonnaise • 1 tablespoon olive oil • 1 teaspoon honey • 4 tablespoons fresh blueberries • 1 tablespoon apple vinegar • a bit of freshly ground ginger • herbal salt • white pepper • 1 cup (225 grams) pumpkin, grated • 4 to 6 leaves of endive lettuce

In a medium bowl, mix the mayonnaise, olive oil, honey, vinegar, and blueberries. Season with ginger, herbal salt, and pepper to taste. Add pumpkin, stirring until it's fully covered in the sauce. Set the endive leaves on a serving dish. Spoon the pumpkin mix onto each leaf and serve.

Pumpkin with Yellow Boletus • 4 Servings

½ cup (115 grams) onions, finely chopped • 1 cup (225 grams) fresh yellow boletus, chopped • 2 bay leaves • 4 sage leaves • 2 tablespoons olive oil or lemon olive oil • 1 cup (225 milliliters) white wine • 1 cup (225 milliliters) vegetable broth • 1 cup (225 milliliters) cream (18% fat) • ½ cup hominy • herbal salt • 2 pounds (905 grams) pumpkin, cubed

In a large pot, sauté the onions and boletus with the bay leaves and sage leaves in the olive oil for about 5 minutes until nicely aromatic. Add the white wine and mix well. Add the vegetable broth and cream and bring to a boil. Add the hominy to slightly bind the mix. Add herbal salt to taste. Simmer, uncovered, for about 20 minutes. Stir in the pumpkin. Simmer, covered, for about 5 minutes.

TIP: Fine butter noodles go well with this soup.

Radish (*Raphanus sativus*)

Family: Cruciferae or Brassicaceae: mustard family

Other Names or Varieties: black Spanish round, crimson giant, daikon, perfecto

Healing Properties: inhibits fungi and bacteria; activates gallbladder and liver; helps prevent gallstones, kidney stones, and bladder stones; improves intestinal flora; prevents scurvy (antiscorbutic); promotes urination (diuretic)

Juice: clears mucus (expectorant)

Symbolic Meaning: quarrel and strife, hardy vitality, affluence (Japan), spring and the perpetual renewal of life (Near East), an attribute of the wind and weather gods, St. Peter and Donar

Planetary Affiliation: Mars

Even though the radish is said to have originated in Northern China and has been cultivated there for thousands of years, most Europeans also consider it a native plant (Schwanitz 1966, 127).[1] Black, white, purple, and red radishes rank among the favorite crops in Europe and the U.S. Radish roots were part of the daily food supply of the slaves who built the Egyptian pyramids, and the ancient Greeks used various radishes medicinally. Roman admiral Pliny the Elder (23–79 AD) who wrote a thirty-seven-volume treatise on natural history (*Historia naturalis*) after his retirement from the military, reported that the Egyptians were mainly interested in the oil from the seeds. He also noted that radishes thrive in cold climates so well that in "Germania" a single one grew to the size of a newborn baby.

"*Radih*" (from the Latin *radix* = root) is the Old High German word for radish. In Bavaria they still call radishes "*radi,*" which they eat with their "soul food," Bavarian veal sausage with sweet mustard, and their locally brewed beer. (Only the Japanese and Chinese eat more radishes than these southern Germans do.) In earlier times, "liquid bread" (beer) eaten with grated, salted radishes kept the country population healthy over the long winter months, as radishes contain enough vitamin C to protect against

Illustration 67. Radish (Joachim Camerarius, Neuw Kreütterbuch, *1586)*

scurvy. In addition the root has vitamins A, B1, and B2, phosphor, and a lot of potassium. The glucosinolates in radishes also have an antibacterial and antifungal effect, which helps prevent colds. And those not minding their P's and Q's (pints and quarts) in the tavern could protect their livers by eating plenty of fresh grated radishes, which trigger hepatic metabolism and increase gall secretion. Bavarians prefer the quite strong black radish, usually grated and generously salted; sometimes it's doused with fresh cream and eaten with buttered bread.

The radish is—like most cruciferae, such as cabbage and horseradish—packed with vitality. Thanks to its sulfuric oils it can take cold outside temperatures, and it keeps well throughout winter in a cool, moist cellar or in a sandbank. The Bavarians say the radish compares to a strapping example of the male species: it is a kind of vegetable Arnold Schwarzenegger. Popular belief in Southern Germany and France claims men who eat a lot of radish will have a stronger erection due to the gases that accumulate in the lower body regions. Otto Brunfels (1488–1534), botanist and official city physician of Basel, Switzerland, noted, "Radish is also said to encourage unchastity." The radish—as doctors of earlier centuries knew—has the signature of the masculine planet Mars. This is made obvious by its pungency and red color and by its effect on the Mars organ, the gall bladder. This gland, which produces bitter bile, was also seen in earlier times as the organ in which anger had its seat. (What in English is referred to as "breathing fire and brimstone" is called in German "spitting gall and poison.")

Because Mars rules over the radish, it follows
that it was a symbol for quarrel and strife in the
Middle Ages. It was believed that especially quar-
relsome spirits—such as the legendary and unruly
mountain spirit Rübezahl (in Polish, *Liczyrzepa;* in
Czech, *Krakonoš*) at home in the mountain range
between Bohemia and Silesia—were especially
enthusiastic about this fiery tasting root vegetable. In the old "language of flowers," with which
court damsels and knights communicated without
having to speak, wearing radish leaves or flowers
meant: "Through you I have had to suffer a lot
of pain and sadness." Wherever the radish plant
appears in old paintings it has a similar meaning.
For example, in Albrecht Dürer's 1496 painting *The
Prodigal Son,* a young man kneeling in a pigsty has
turned his back on a radish, meaning he is regretful
and wishes to leave any disputes behind him.

So that the radish did not cause too much
strife, precautions were taken to consecrate it.
Radish consecration was traditionally done on the
day of the festival of the Chair of St. Peter (February 22). This apostle was known for his choleric
nature, which was brought to peace only through
the gentle hand of the Lord himself. The European

*Illustration 68. Rad-
ish (Otto Brunfels,
Herbarum Vivae
Eicones, 1532)*

belief that St. Peter is responsible for the weather leads one to assume
that the radish was under the protection of the thunder god Thor in
pre-Christian times. Thor was also known to be very potent, earthy, and
occasionally extremely hot tempered—he cast thunderbolts and lighting
by throwing his mighty hammer.

The Healing Power of Radishes

The statement that radish "sweetens the blood" has some truth in it, as
it affects the acid-base balance of life's precious fluid. A stressful lifestyle

Illustration 69. Radish in blossom

together with a diet that contains too much sugar can lead to an increase in the carbon dioxide level in the blood, making it slightly acidic; this in turn can lead to burgeoning health issues. The black radish in particular helps to raise the pH level of the blood to its normal balance of 7.4.

This pungent taproot has been prominent in traditional folk medicine since early times. The juice is rubbed into the scalp to vitalize the hair and make it grow. Radish seeds are cooked into a brew to counteract mushroom poisoning. Peasant dairy farmers use the crushed leaves to heal cows' udders. Radish slices are placed on corns to soften them. An effective syrup to treat a chronic cough or bronchitis was made from radishes: a hollowed-out radish was filled with honey or sugar water and let stand for about ten hours, after which the syrup was taken a spoonful at a time. Radish juice rubbed on the skin helped restore a rosy glow to a pasty, sallow complexion. (In India there is also a cure made of ground radish seeds to help against leukoderma.) All of the stone ailments (calculosis)—gall, kidney, and bladder stones—were treated with radish juice. In particular, English herbal doctor Nicholas Culpeper (1616–1654) prescribed the juice mixed with wine for gallstones.

The radish is also cherished in India, where it is called "*muli*" (root); the word is also found in the *Mula*dhara chakra, the "root" chakra. Indian hepatitis patients are given radishes, especially radish juice. As in traditional European healing lore, the juice is mixed with honey and salt for coughing and lung ailments. Ayurveda prescribes radish juice for urinary retention and painful urinating; for lithiasis (stones and gravel) one cup of radish juice daily is prescribed for two weeks.

Modern phytotherapy confirms most of the traditional uses of radish for healing. It is good for keeping a base milieu in the intestines and improves intestinal flora. The nineteenth-century Bavarian herbalist Sebastian Kneipp recommended eating it without salt. Its high potassium content makes radish into a diuretic, a desiccating agent for those with gout and rheumatism. It's also good for a cold because it dissolves mucus and has an anti-inflammatory effect on the mucus membranes in the nose, sinuses, and throat. And as a tonic for the liver and gall bladder it is hard to surpass.

Radish Customs and Use Around the World

In earlier times—and to a degree today—gardeners carefully observed sowing times. It was believed that radishes sown on certain days—St. Kilian's Day (July 8), St. John's Eve (June 23–24), and Corpus Christi (celebrated 60 days after Easter Sunday)—would thrive especially well. If sown when the moon is in Aquarius or Pisces they would be juicy; in Sagittarius they would shoot into flower; in Cancer or Capricorn they would grow lots of small roots; and in Aries they would taste especially strong. The Pennsylvania Dutch chant while sowing: "As long as my arm, as thick as my leg!" If the radishes developed long "tails" it was thought a strong winter was about to come.

Radishes are cultivated all over the world. European settlers brought the radish to North America, where it was quickly picked up by the Native Americans. Since that time gardeners distinguish between the hardy, fall kinds that keep well and the summer kinds, which are consumed immediately. In Europe there are some twenty different kinds of both radish types. Small, red radishes are a relatively new cultivation that originated in Italian Renaissance gardens before spreading throughout eighteenth-century Europe. These small red radishes are actually not even roots—they are thickened root crowns (hypocotyl); the actual root is the small thread or tail below the crown.

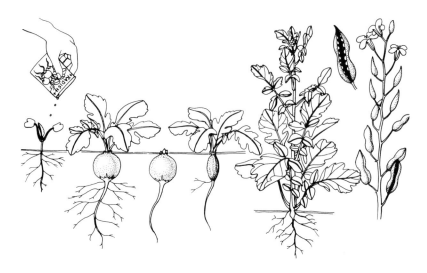

Illustration 70. Radishes in their biennial growth period (illustration by Molly Conner-Ogorzaly, from B. B. Simpson and M. Conner-Ogorzaly, Economic Botany, *1986, 217)*

Eastern Asia knows an abundance of radish varieties. In China and Japan the roots are eaten both raw and cooked, the leaves cooked as a vegetable. Varieties with seeds especially rich in oil (oilseed radishes) are used to make nutritional and lamp oil. Original China drawing ink is made from the soot of the flame of radish oil. Then there are edible radish seed pods, which are eaten in salads or as a vegetable. When my red radishes go to seed, I add the delicious pods to mixed vegetables in the wok.

The biggest radish is the mild Japanese daikon, which is cooked as a vegetable, used as animal fodder, and pickled like we pickle sauerkraut. And as they can grow up to three feet long and weigh up to fifty pounds, it is no wonder they are a symbol of wealth in Japan.

Garden Tips

Cultivation: Radish seeds sprout quickly. Like alfalfa, cress, or mung beans, they are also good for sprouting in winter in dishes as a source for vitamins. For spring cultivation the seeds can be sown right in with carrots, as they are good row markers and are harvested long before the carrots need the space. Fall radishes are sown about sixty days before the first frost, so they will mature during cooler weather. Watering during any late summer heat spells will help cut their bite. Note that they will shoot to seed once it becomes too hot for them to thrive. (LB)

Soil: As taproots, radishes prefer loose, sandy loam that is free of obstructions. And just as for carrots and parsnips, the soil should be well-composted—just not to the depths needed for the longer taproots.

Recipe

Radish-Grape Salad with Pumpkin Seeds • 2 Servings

Salad: 2 black radishes (or a bundle of red ones) • ½ cup (115 grams) red grapes • 1 ounce (40 grams) pumpkin seeds • Sauce: 1 tablespoon red wine vinegar • 3 tablespoons olive oil • some fresh lovage • 1 ounce (40 grams) raw pumpkin seeds, chopped • honey • sea salt • white pepper

Grate or slice the radishes in thin slices. Put in a serving bowl. Cut the grapes in half and add to the bowl. In a separate small bowl mix the vinegar, olive oil, and lovage. Season with honey, salt, and pepper to taste. Pour over the radishes and grapes, tossing until evenly covered. Sprinkle with the pumpkin seeds and serve.

Red Beet and Swiss Chard (*Beta vulgaris*)

Family: Amaranthaceae: amaranth family; formerly Chenopodiaceae: goosefoot family

Other Names: beetroot, beta, chard, borscht, mangelwuzel, mangold

Healing Properties: regulates acidity, builds blood, activates liver metabolism, inhibits tumors

Symbolic Meaning: keeps us "grounded"; spirit of rationality

Planetary Affiliation: Mars, Saturn (Culpeper); sugar beet: Jupiter

> The beet is the most intense of vegetables. The radish, admittedly, is more feverish, but the fire of the radish is a cold fire, the fire of discontent not of passion. Tomatoes are lusty enough, yet there runs through tomatoes an undercurrent of frivolity. Beets are deadly serious. Slavic peoples get their physical characteristics from potatoes, their smoldering inquietude from radishes, their seriousness from beets.

With these lines the red beet, otherwise denounced as a boring vegetable, stepped on to the stage of world literature from the first page of Tom Robbin's 1984 novel *Jitterbug Perfume*. And though an old Ukrainian proverb warns that "a story that begins with a red beet ends with the devil," Robbins was willing to take that risk.

Unlike all other vegetables, the red beet exits our body with the same color it had when it entered. Borscht, the favorite soup of the eastern Slavic peoples, is red due to red beets, which are a significant part of eastern European folk culture. (Though this root vegetable is not quite as well known in western Europe, health enthusiasts do know about vitamin-and-mineral-rich red beet juice and tasty beet salad made with cooked red beets and onions.)

Many years ago, an elderly woman told me that red beet "builds up blood." At the time I could barely hide my skeptical smile; just because the red beet turns the stool red does not mean it's good for the blood. To me, such was as much an old superstition and outdated "signature teaching"

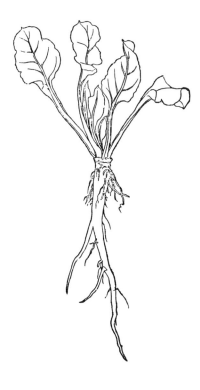

Illustration 71. Swiss chard (Otto Brunfels, Herbarum Vivae Eicones, *1532)*

as Enlightenment scientists considered of similar claims made by ancient Greeks and Romans, including Dioscorides, Galen, or Pliny the Elder. But, despite criticism, traditional folk belief held on to this claim—which was based on experience handed down from generation to generation.

It turns out that recent clinical research supports the traditional folk belief. Red beet juice is given for leukemia, anemia, and malaria as it is thought it helps regenerate and increase red blood corpuscles. The juice also traps radicals and contributes to lowering elevated blood fat levels, the latter of which has a positive effect on the health of the heart and circulatory system. The traditional folk medicine belief that expectant mothers should eat plenty of red beets is another example: it so happens that the juicy globes contain exceptional amounts of folic acid, a vitamin substance that helps the embryonic vertebrae develop properly so that there is no risk of spina bifida.

Swiss herbal healer Alfred Vogel (1902–1996), popularly known as "the little doctor," considered red beet juice supportive in case of viral flu, Hodgkin's disease, blood pressure ailments, irritated appendices, and—because of its iodine content—goiter. It activates gall bladder and liver metabolism. Research done by Dr. Alexander Ferenczi in 1961 made headlines when he claimed to have discovered anti-tumor properties in betaine, which is responsible for the color of red beets. In his study, patients who'd drunk one liter of fresh beet juice daily for three months showed a stronger blood count than did the control group. It should be noted that, though such was a medical study, establishment medicine strongly doubts this positive effect. But naturopaths point out that not all red beet juice is alike; only beets that are grown organically (without artificial nitrate fertilizer) and get full sunlight can produce juice that has therapeutic value. But whether the juice actually helps heal X-ray and other radioactive damage—as medical doctor S. Schmidt from Germany claims—is another question.

Chinese traditional healing lore uses the red beet globe to strengthen the heart, regulate conditions of agitation, rev up

Illustration 72. Red beet in full blossom (Leonhart Fuchs, De Historia Stirpium Commentarii Insignes, *1543)*

a sluggish liver, ease the hormonal concerns of menopause, and improve the blood. Ayurvedic medicine also praises the beetroot as a blood builder since it supports a healthy base-acidic balance, which helps to prevent the body tissue from becoming overly acidic. As in the European tradition, Ayurveda also uses the juice for liver disease, constipation, and intestinal ailments. For bad skin, pimples, pustules, or even scabs on the scalp, Indian medicine prescribes the following: the water in which red beets have been cooked is mixed with vinegar in a 3:1 juice:vinegar ratio to be used externally or massaged into the scalp. It is interesting to note that in 1649 Nicholas Culpeper noted a similar recipe—a decoction of red beet water with vinegar—for cankerous abscesses, boils, tumors, blisters, frostbite, scabies, dandruff, and even hair loss. Culpeper, who was

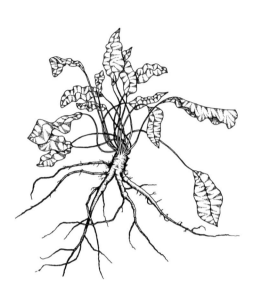

Illustration 73. Wild chard: precursor of the red beet, sugar beet, Swiss chard, and Good King Henry

also an astrologist, puts the plant under the rule of Saturn because of its "mineral nature." Others stress the influence of Mars because of its blood building properties and its color.

Like spinach, orache, and Good King Henry (which we discuss among other forgotten, rare, and less-known vegetables), the red beet is a Chenopodium or goosefoot plant. Chenopodiums thrive best on salty, alkaline, strongly mineralized soils of the salt steppes, along seashores, as well as on rubble and garbage dumps near human settlements. The original wild plant (*Beta vulgaris* var. *maritime*) still grows as a tough-leafed beach plant on the coast of the Mediterranean, the Caspian Sea, the Dead Sea, and the North Sea. Prehistorians assume that foragers as far back as the Stone Age gathered the plant for soups. Surely they cooked it with meat and other ingredients as by itself it has a rather caustic, unpleasant, bitter taste—due to its saponins and oxalic acid, substances that make the teeth feel "dull."

The oldest archeological findings of this plant are from a New Stone Age settlement (4000 BC) in Holland. Ethnobotanists assume, however, that it was first cultivated intentionally in the Mediterranean area, specifically in Sicily. From the wild form, primitive farmers selected and cultivated two kinds: a beetroot (usually red, but sometimes yellow) and a leaf vegetable—the precursor of Swiss chard. We also know that "*silqua*," as the bulb was called in the antique Near East, was cultivated in the gardens of the Babylonians and Phoenicians in the second century

BC, and that red and white beets were sold in Athenian markets in the fourth century BC.

Since seed bundles of red beets or Swiss chard were found in Roman military camps and civilian settlements in the Rhine-Main river areas, it's clear the Romans brought the cultivated "*beta*" (from this Latin term comes our word "beet") to their cold, foggy provinces in northern Europe. But, apparently, the Germanics and Celts were not particularly interested in the new vegetable, content as they were with their turnip (*Brassica rapa* subspecies *rapa*) or the yellow turnip or rutabaga (*B. napus*). And though Charlemagne (742–814) ordered the cultivation of the *beta* throughout his Western European land holdings, and monks cultivated it in cloister gardens, for hundreds of years red beets scarcely had a place at the northern table.

Not until the sixteenth and seventeenth century is the vegetable—the red root globe as well as the leaf chard—mentioned again. At that time Europeans were turning away from the otherworldly mysticism of the High Middle Ages and beginning to focus more attention on the material world and its laws. Interest in alchemy gave way to interest in the "hard science" of chemistry; the belief that good or bad health was the result of witch's spells or demonic influence gave way to belief in logical reasoning and mechanical natural laws—as presented by enlightened medical doctors. Similar to the potato, which came somewhat later to northern Europeans, the *beta* played a significant role in the nutritional paradigm change that took place at that time. (From there European settlers brought the beet to America and though it is not clear when the plant arrived, it was well known there by the eighteenth century.)

To better understand how the beet fit into the nutritional paradigm it behooves us to take a closer look at one of the basic ideas of alchemy. The alchemists, the forerunners of our empirical scientists, distinguished three states of matter, three formative, active building principles in nature: *sal* (salt), *mercurius* (mercury), and *sulfur*. They described *sal* as absorptive, receptive, concentrating, consolidating, and hardening. The power of "salt" is focused in the human anatomy in the head, with its hard skull and its ability to concentrate thought and gather impressions from the senses.

With plants the *sal*-force is the strongest in the root, the densest part of its anatomy, which takes up water and minerals from the surrounding soil.

The second state of matter, *sulfur,* is the diametric opposite of *sal.* As a principle "sulfur" is a centrifugal force, bringing about dissipation, dissolution, and evaporation. In the human being this pole is found in the lower body: in the reproductive and digestive organs and in the function of excretion. In plants the sulfur processes take place in the blossom, where the plant dissipates itself in scent, nectar, and abundant seed production—thus communicating with its environment.

The principle of *mercurius* is characterized by rhythm and fluctuation between the two outer poles. In human anatomy this is expressed in the inhale/exhale working of the lungs as well as in the heartbeat, with its rhythm of systole and diastole animation. In plants the mercurial principle is located in the region between the root and the flower, namely in the stalk and leaf regions where rhythmic growth takes place and gases—oxygen and carbon dioxide—are exchanged between the plant organism and the atmosphere.

If we apply this threefold system to the red beet, we recognize that the *sal* pole is predominant in the plant. The root bulb greedily absorbs and concentrates various minerals—calcium, phosphorus, potassium, magnesium, iron, copper, sulfur, iodine, boron, lithium, strontium, chlorine, and also traces of rare minerals such as rubidium and cesium. Like other members of the goosefoot family, this plant is immune to salt. It even takes to a bit of cooking salt sprinkled in the rows before sowing! By contrast, the sulfur pole of the red beet is very weakly developed, almost atrophied. Its tiny, unspectacular blossoms, without color and without scent, are barely noticeable. It is as if the colors normally found in the flowering pole have slid down two stories, right down into the soil. The sweetness, the nectar, which is usually concentrated in the blossom, is also drawn down by *sal* power into the root. Indeed, the bulb has so much sugar that in ancient Greece beet juice was boiled down to syrup and used as a healing elixir instead of honey. Crystallized beet sugar, to which we are increasingly addicted to in this materialistic age, is also the result of a *sal* process.

It is interesting to note that, as Western Civilization became more head-oriented and materialistic, *beta vulgaris* became a more interesting plant for the Europeans. During the time of the Enlightenment in the eighteenth century—when rational thinking became dominant over gut intuition, and when the traditional medieval European three-field system was replaced by modern agricultural methods—this plant started to play a new and important role. At this time a new kind of beet was developed that was lighter in color and had more bulk, known as the fodder beet, mangelwurzel, or field beet. Fields that had previously been fallowed for one year were now planted on a large scale with these

Illustration 74. Salt, mercury, and sulfur in the archetypal plant (illustration by Lambert Spix, from Wolf D. Storl, Der Kosmos im Garten, *2001)*

field beets. They were stored over the winter in big insulated heaps or shredded in silos similar to sauerkraut and served as fodder to the cows, swine, and other animals—thus the name "fodder beet." This beet made it possible to bring more animals through the winter; as a result the meat supply for the population, especially for the well-to-do citizens, noticeably improved.

Beta vulgaris contributed another achievement to the way of life at that time. The chemist Andreas Sigismund Marggraf (1709–1782) demonstrated that this new beet contained considerable amounts of sucrose that was identical to precious cane sugar. Toward the end of the

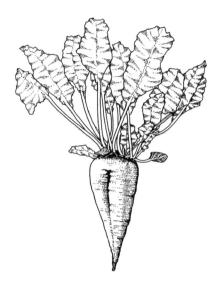

Illustration 75. Sugar beet

eighteenth century, pharmacist Franz Karl Achard (1753–1821) cultivated what became known as "the white beet of Silesia": a bulb with a sugar content of 8.8 percent (today it contains around 20 percent). At that time, with Napoleon having conquered most of mainland Europe and a British navy embargo on all the ports, the continent was cut off from sugar imports from the Caribbean. But, thanks to the sugar beet, a mighty new industry grew in the shadow of the embargo. Granulated sugar, hitherto a scarce commodity available only to rich aristocrats or for medical use in apothecaries, suddenly became a cheap mass product—with wide-ranging results. The working masses thereafter could afford to generously spread their bread with energy-rich sugar beet molasses at breakfast and sweeten their substitute chicory coffee. Candy stores, alcohol stores, and soft drink companies flourished, as did dentists. To wit: Europeans became severely addicted to sugar. (Few people realize that sugar is an addicting drug!)

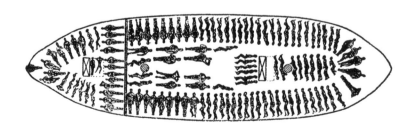

Illustration 76. Cultivation of sugar beets ended slavery in Central America; shown here, the loading plan of a slave ship

But the thus-lessened health of the sweetened Europeans had a significant benefit for humanity: the slavery-based sugar plantations in the Caribbean soon became unprofitable, ultimately leading to slavery being prohibited and abolished. In benefitting human beings who had been considered nothing more than working machines, the beet could be thought of as a plant deva, one that helped to establish human rights and "democratize" human culture.

Garden Tips

Cultivation: There are few plants that are easier to grow than red beets and Swiss chard. Sow the seeds directly in the bed as soon as the earth is ready in the spring; later, thin the plants to about eight inches apart. Swiss chard can be picked as soon as the leaves are nearly of a desirable size, as they will continue to grow after being cut. The fresh greens from thinning out red beets are delicious when prepared like spinach. (LB)

Soil: Both red beets and Swiss chard grow well in any good garden soil as long as they have a sunny, open spot. Note that the vigorous roots can grow as far down as six feet, breaking up the subsoil and improving drainage wherever they roam.

Recipe

Red Beet Salad with Olive Sauce • 2 Servings

10 ounces (285 grams) raw red beets, cut into fine strips • 2 green onions
• 1 cup alfalfa sprouts • 3 ounces (100 grams) dried, pitted black olives
• 2 ounces (80 grams) hazelnuts, ground • 4 tablespoons cold vegetable
broth • 2 tablespoons olive oil • 2 tablespoons wheat germ oil • herbal
salt • black pepper • ½ cup lovage, finely chopped (for garnish)

Mix the olives, hazelnuts, broth, olive oil, and wheat germ oil in a blender on high until smooth. Season with salt and pepper to taste.

In a serving bowl, mix the onion and alfalfa sprouts. Arrange the beet strips on the spouts. Pour the olive sauce over the beets and sprouts. Garnish with the lovage and serve.

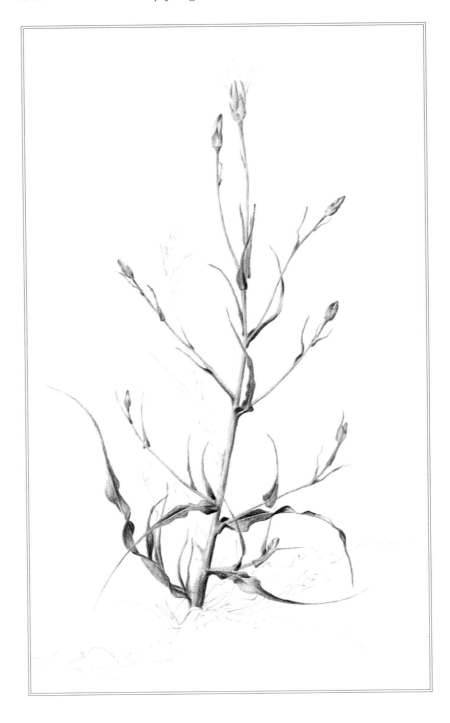

Salsify (*Scorzonera hispanica*)

Family: Asteraceae or Compositaceae: composite, daisy, or sunflower family

Other Names: black oyster plant, goat's beard, serpent root, Spanish salsify, viper's herb, viper's grass

Healing Properties: reduces cough, strengthens immune system, softens tissues, promotes urination (diuretic); ideal for diabetes diet

Symbolic Meaning: sun plant, enemy of snakes, Lemurian plant

Planetary Affiliation: Saturn, moon, and the sun with the influence of Jupiter

Relatively few people know of the root vegetable salsify. If we are familiar with it at all, it's been in the form of small, bite-sized white root morsels. Once tasted, they surprise us with a fine, mild, almost sweet flavor similar to asparagus. It is even called "winter asparagus" in some places in Europe. Freshly dug from the garden bed, however, one sees that the cylindrical roots are at least a foot long and have a coal black, coarse rind similar to that of comfrey, which protects them from frost and drought and makes them absolutely winter hardy. When the fresh roots are peeled, they are white and milky, and break easily.

Permanent agriculture enthusiasts like salsify for how well it fits into the idea of an "eatable," self-regenerating eco-system. This vegetable needs very little care; in favorable conditions it will even sow itself, becoming a permanent part of the garden. That said, the root will nonetheless not develop as well without a gardener's care. For example, after harvesting, if the top part of the root is replanted many small edible roots will grow out of it. The buds can be sautéed and added to a vegetable dish or a salad (Heil 2001, 123). Incidentally, if the seeds do not sprout, they are too old—after just one year they don't sprout well.

Salsify must be sown early enough in the spring in order to have fully developed roots by harvest time; if they are sown too late the roots will be spindly in the fall. They can be left in the garden all winter, covered with a protective layer of mulch and harvested as needed—as long as there

Illustration 77. Salsify

are no root voles or other such varmints in the garden, as salsify is one of their favorite roots. The vegetable has many vitamins (including vitamin E), fructose (inulin), and manna sugar.

Though one of salsify's many names is "black oyster plant," note that it is different from the oyster plant (*Tragopogon porrifolius*). Indeed, the popularity of salsify was such that it eventually pushed *Tragopogon porrifolius* from both vegetable gardens and dinner tables. (We cover the oyster plant in the Forgotten, Rare, and Less-Known Vegetables section to come.)

Salsify is a relatively new vegetable, as it's been around only since the middle of the seventeenth century, first cultivated in Italy and then in France. Before that it was gathered in its wild form, its tasty young leaves added to soups; it's thought that the wild plant crossed over the Alps with the Romans. As a wild plant salsify prefers a Mediterranean-like climate in plant communities with grasses and bushes. It's certainly to be found near vineyards and in meadows in northern Europe. European settlers brought it to North America, where it now is often considered an invasive weed, one that grows wherever suits its needs. (I have seen it growing wild in Wyoming, for instance.)

In southern Italian and Spanish folk medicine, the root has long been eaten as a treatment for heart ailments, arteriosclerosis and dizziness. As it (like comfrey) contains wound-healing allantoin, it was also used externally to treat snakebites and other poisons as well as pox and other skin problems. The genus name *"scorzonera,"* which derives from the Italian sc*orzonera*, refers to *scorzone*, a kind of "black, poisonous viper." Pietro Andrea Mattioli (1501–1577), an Italian herbal doctor in the service of

Emperor Maximilian II, wrote: "This herb has recently become known and appreciated in Hispania, having helped many people who had been bitten by snakes. After this was successful, it was discovered that it also helped for other kinds of poisoning and also even pestilence." This explains some of the other names of the wild plant: *natter weed, viper root, natter milk,* and *viper's grass.* The pale purple or yellow blossoming cruciferae has even been praised as "snake's death." Mattioli continued: "Many write that the juice of this plant is so powerful that when the snake, as they call it, *scorzo,* is even touched by it, it goes rigid. And if the juice is dripped into the snake's mouth, it will die soon afterward."

The root also found its place in rural veterinary medicine. For example, if the hind legs of a pig go lame, then one should "place a piece of the black root in a crack in the wall and say the following, 'Dragon, dragon, dragon, out of the stall!'" A vegetable in such a service most certainly deserves the name "power root"!

Its traditional use as a healing plant for snake bites, poisoning, and pestilence was no longer relevant when gardeners first began to cultivate the plant as a vegetable, a debut—ultimately as much cultural as culinary—that coincided with the Enlightenment. Salsify is first mentioned as a vegetable in Switzerland in 1690, when a certain Mr. Zwinger soberly commented, ". . . with butter, salt, and seasoning eaten in the fall and winter months it is pleasant and healthy fare—it is good for the bodily needs and is enlivening." Indeed, since King Louis the XIV, the "Sun King" of France, often suffered from indigestion, he had large amounts of *scorsonère* cultivated in his garden in Versailles, convinced as he was that it was an excellent remedy for debauched stomachs that had just enjoyed lavish meals. (It so happens that the root contains mucilage, which soothes the stomach.) It is mainly because this mightiest of sovereigns showed interest in this hardly known vegetable that it was soon *en vogue* all over Europe.

Equally in vogue at this time was coffee. We mentioned earlier that expensive coffee was often stretched with the addition of roasted chicory roots; roasted salsify roots served just as well. Also fashionable at this time were silk stockings and gowns; when it was discovered that silkworms greedily devour salsify leaves, the plant came into use as silkworm

Illustration 78. Salsify, a delicate winter vegetable

fodder. Salsify was also a favorite vegetable in Victorian England; unfortunately, since the servants were expected to peel the sticky black roots until they were perfectly clean, most of the vitamins and minerals were lost in the process. (Modern nutritionists recommend cooking the roots in the skins and peeling them, or not, once they're cooked—the skin then comes off easily.) And Russians, who learned about salsify in the nineteenth century, were so enthused that gardeners there developed "Russian giant salsify"—the kind cultivated everywhere today.

Like chicory, lettuce, dandelion, field sow thistle and goat's beard, salsify belongs to the subfamily of composites, *Lactuceae* or *Cichorioideae,* that contain "milk" or latex. They usually blossom yellow (though sometimes blue) and have ray florets (what we see as individual petals surrounding the central "disc" of a daisy-like flower). The Tau-Saghyz (*Scorzonera tau-saghyz*) is a kind of salsify from the steppes of Kazakhstan that has a fair amount of milk; as such, it was cultivated in the former Soviet Union as a substitute for rubber latex.

The Cichorioideae plant group is very much ruled by the rhythm of the sun. Their blossoms open at sunrise and close at sunset, and their faces follow the sun's path across the sky. Many members of this subfamily were once referred to as "brides of the sun" or as "lazy girls" (since they go to sleep right at sunset). Given both the plants' tendency to flower yellow and the positive effect they have as a liver tonic, herbal astrologers like Nicholas Culpeper (1616–1654) recognized in them the signature of the sun and/or Jupiter. In mythology, sun gods and thunderbolt-carrying storm gods like Jupiter are known to be the enemies of poisonous snakes, worms, and dragons—as such, it's no surprise the reputation of salsify is seen as related. The milky juice, or latex, of the plants demonstrates that they also carry the signature of the moon. Saturn can be seen in both the root's black skin and its ability to withstand drought and cold. On the basis of its Saturnic signature, doctors of yore tried it as a remedy for bubonic plague ("Black Death") and for melancholy resulting from too much "black bile."

Occultists of all colors and persuasions apply special meaning to the milky juice of these composites. The Dutch wise woman and herbalist Mellie Uyldert claimed the bitter milky substance contains the power of materialization, incarnation, and solidification. This juice, she believed, is a remnant of the cosmic amniotic fluid in which the embryo of the earth once floated; it is a remnant of the Lemurian-era milky atmosphere in which primeval plant and animal organisms lived and from which they nourished themselves; it is a kind of "mother's milk" that enables spiritual beings to incarnate into earthly matter. Theosophists and occultists like Mellie Uyldert believe that when the moon split off from the earth the earth began to dry out, the atmosphere became thinner, and the creation became more solidified. Only some of the plants, such as milky composites, the spurge family, and the poppy family kept some of this primeval milk in their bodies. This milk still has some of the healing power of the old Lemurian atmosphere, which is calming, purifying, and purging.

It's anybody's guess whether this occultist/theosophic story about the sunken continent of Lemuria is only a subconscious, "clairvoyantly perceived" memory of our own embryonic status or a tale of actual cosmic occurrences. But, regardless, even in our own times salsify purportedly does have healing properties. It strengthens the immune system. Thanks to its inulin[1] and mannitol (manna sugar) content, it's ideal for diabetics. A decoction (without salt) of the root suppresses coughs and is a diuretic—good for gout patients. Applied topically, the decoction has a softening and healing effect on scalp eczema, acne, and other skin blemishes. According to Konrad Kölbl, a modern master of healing lore, salsify furthers brain functions and strengthens the entire bodily organism. It does this thanks to its high calcium content, which is important for bone metabolism. Koelble claims it is especially beneficial in a radioactively contaminated environment, as the calcium helps hinder radioactive isotopes from accumulating in the bones. What appears to be just another unorthodox claim has been scientifically validated: calcium in the diet does indeed help reduce the uptake of ionized radiation.

Garden Tips

Cultivation: Sow seed in the open garden in the early spring. Mulch the rows after the plants have established themselves in order to keep the soil moist and cool and to discourage weeds. The roots can be dug for use once they reach an ideal size. Note that, like with many root crops, a light autumn frost will improve their flavor. They can be stored in moist sand in the cellar. (LB)

Soil: Salsify likes well-drained and loose soil such as a sandy loam. Since the roots grow six to eight inches long, the soil should be prepared to at least that depth.

Recipe

Salsify with Chervil Lemon Sauce • 4 Servings

1 pound (~400 grams) salsify • 2 tablespoons lemon juice
• 2 tablespoons butter • 1 pound (~400 grams) potatoes, peeled or unpeeled, cubed • ½ cup (115 milliliters) vegetable broth
• ½ cup (115 milliliters) cream (18% fat) • ground nutmeg
• sea salt • black pepper • fresh chervil, finely chopped

Prepare a large bowl of water; add a splash of milk. Thoroughly scrub the salsify but do not peel. Cut into ½-inch-thick slices and immediately place in the bowl of water. (Alternatively, sprinkle with lemon juice; the goal is for them to stay white inside.) In a large pot melt the butter over medium heat. Add the salsify and potatoes and mix thoroughly. Cover and cook over medium low heat for about 10 minutes. Add the vegetable broth and cream. Simmer until salsify and potatoes are tender. Season with salt, pepper, and nutmeg to taste. Transfer to a serving bowl. Just before serving, stir in the chervil.

Spinach (*Spinacia oleracea*)

Family: Amaranthaceae: amaranth family; formerly Chenopodiaceae: goosefoot family

Other Names and Varieties: Amsterdam, Bloomsdale, summer supreme, winter queen

Healing Properties: base rich, nutritional vegetable activates digestion; cooked juice for coughing, asthma

Symbolic Meaning: green life force; promoted as superfood: Popeye and agribusiness

Planetary Affiliation: Venus

Spinach and other related goosefoot plants originated in the sparse steppes of central Asia. In Turkestan, Afghanistan, and eastern Persia (Iran), the hot and dry summers evaporate the moisture, leaving the soil glistening with salt and alkaline. But the alkaline soil was not a problem for these plants, since the protoplasm of the Chenopodium family is fairly resistant to the influence of salts and alkalines. This is a characteristic that predestined the plant for modern mass cultivation on irrigated fields, which tend to become salty. These plants can also easily take the mineral salts of artificial fertilizers.

The primeval precursor of today's garden spinach greened in the moist, cool spring and quickly grew to lush tufts; the long-day plant blossomed in the bright summer days and made seeds; after dying off in the fall, only a fruit capsule remained. To protect itself from being devoured by hungry animals, the fruit pod had spikes, but these were lost later in the process of cultivation.

It is probable that prehistoric nomads in the central Asian steppes gathered wild spinach leaves in the spring, adding them, along with various other greens, to meat broth. We know that ancient Persians cultivated "*aspinakh*" as a garden vegetable. It was later made known to Allah's sons when they invaded the Persian realm in the seventh century BC; they modified the Persian name to *isfinaj*. The juicy green leaves—which were as green as the victorious flag of the Prophet—fascinated the Arabs. As they cherish good food, they appreciated how this new leafy green pairs so well with the many delectable dishes of their cuisine; but the plant appealed to their poetic vein as well. Was the plant not similar to Islamic warriors in many ways—the bristly external seedpods protecting a soft and delicate interior? Ibn-Al Awwam, an Andalusian scholar, declared spinach to be "the crown prince

Illustration 79. Arabic merchants spread the cultivation of spinach

amongst vegetables." In no time Arabic doctors also discovered the healing properties of the plant. Spinach—so it is written in tenth-century medical writings—is good for the liver when suffering from jaundice and activates bowel movement, and the cooked juice helps for coughing and chest ailments.

Just as the Romans once brought along vineyards wherever they set foot, the Islamic conquerors brought the cultivation of spinach from India to Spain. In the dialect of the Spanish Moors it was called "*ispinag,*" which sounded to the Spanish like "*espinada,*" which means thorny; out of this developed the Medieval Latin word "*spinachia*"; this is how we eventually got our word "spinach."

In the sixteenth century spinach appeared in European gardens and began slowly but surely replacing the leafy greens that had been cultivated until then. Indeed, most of the leafy greens used before spinach have been forgotten. These plants included garden sorrel (*Rumex acetosa*), garden orache (*Atriplex hortensis*), purple amaranth (*Amaranthus lividus, A. blitum*), garden patience (*Rumex patientia*), and Good King Henry (*Chenopodium bonus-henricus*). Here and there spinach, this "barbarian" potherb, numbered among the "nine greens" or "seven greens" gathered

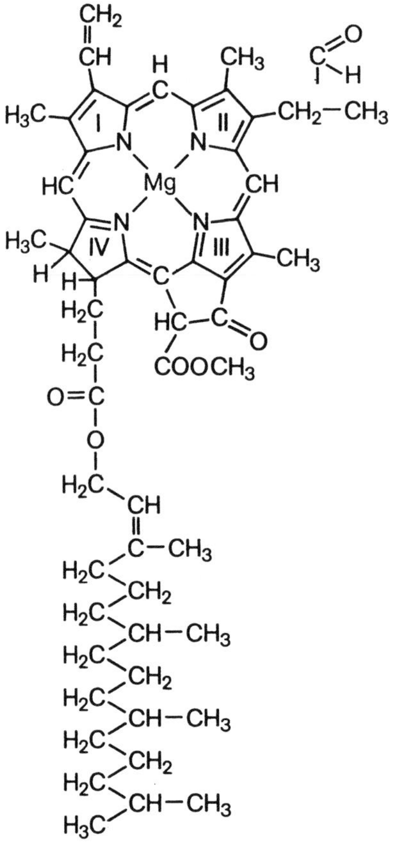

Illustration 80. Molecular structure formula of chlorophyll

in the spring and added to soups or baked into breads. This spring tradition served as a "blood cleansing" after the long winter, ensuring good health throughout the rest of the year. After the Christianization of Europe these greens were traditionally eaten on Maundy (Holy) Thursday (the Thursday preceding Easter); on this sacred day in Bohemia spinach donuts were eaten.

Folklore has very little to say about spinach—no myths, no fairy tales, and no traditional uses tell us anything about the deva of this plant. We do know that, like other leafy vegetables, spinach was sown on days when the moon finds itself in a water sign—Pisces, Scorpio or Cancer—so it would have many lush leaves. Fire signs were strictly avoided, as it was believed the plant would only shoot and produce a lot of seeds.

It was not until the first half of the twentieth century that spinach became popular, developing an almost cult status. This happened for several reasons. First, in 1913 chemist Richard Willstätter (1872– 1942) discovered the basic chemical structure of green leaves: chlorophyll.

He was able to show that the molecular structure of chlorophyll is identical to that of blood; the only difference is that in the middle of the molecular ring chlorophyll has a magnesium atom, whereas the hemoglobin of blood has an iron atom. But this wasn't just a scientific breakthrough—the news also made waves among food gurus and health nuts. Green leaves and red blood! The green leaves capture the enlivening strength of the sun's rays and mediate it to the blood, cleansing and regenerating it.

The tabloid press of the times celebrated chlorophyll as "the color of life." The green plant pigment now appeared to be a powerful substance; indeed, it was believed the very source of health had been found. Of course, it wasn't long before the green substance was commercialized, particularly in the United States. The 1920s saw all kinds of green soaps, toothpastes, deodorants, and mouthwashes. Even pills and other medications were dyed green with chlorophyll—physicians counted on the resulting placebo effect speeding recovery time. Green vegetables, especially those with a high iron content, were suddenly "in," and standing tall among them stood mighty spinach.

There was another reason for the sudden popularity of the leaf vegetable. In the first decades of the twentieth century, the U.S. government invested hundreds of millions of dollars in irrigation projects with the aim to turn the desert in the southwestern states and California into an agricultural paradise. In the process the newly established agribusiness, which was gradually eliminating small family farms, began flexing its muscles. Deserts morphed into endless irrigated fields that mass-produced strawberries, peas, tomatoes, lettuce, and spinach for the North American food market. The result? In just one example, in 2011 70 percent of the lettuce consumed in the entire U.S. was grown in Salinas Valley, California—the "salad bowl of the world"—where with massive chemical and technical input agricultural "technicians" bring in five harvests per year. Practically overnight an entire packing and transporting industry arose, which offered work for cheap seasonal laborers brought in from Mexico. Now, for this investment to be worthwhile, obviously demand for these products had to be stimulated—as directed by major promotional campaigns advertising a new way of life. Hollywood stars disclosed their secrets for longevity and good looks: drinking orange and tomato juice and eating corn flakes and oodles of spinach, whose iron and chlorophyll keeps them fit and healthy.

Illustration 81. Blossoming spinach plant (Leonhart Fuchs, De Historia Stirpium Commentarii Insignes, *1543)*

Around this time came advancements in the technology of conserving food in tin cans. In order to bring canned spinach to the consumers, scientists from government institutions were commissioned to make the new food product palatable. Their assignment was to rationally and objectively research the nutritional aspects of spinach. Unfortunately, many were in pay of the agribusiness lobby, and so not surprisingly positive results poured in from all directions. The *Biochemical Journal* (volume 10, 1926) reported that laboratory rats fed with spinach grew faster than those not fed with it. They reportedly grew even faster than a control group fed with cod liver oil (the health tonic of the day regularly given to children). The bottom line: if children eat a lot of spinach they will grow up to be big and strong.

One other conclusion came from the studies: spinach leaves have an antirachitic effect, especially when they've been radiated with a mercury vapor–quartz iodine lamp. (At the time many children suffered from rickets, which caused bowlegs and skeletal damage; this resulted from Louis Pasteur's research making it fashionable to cook milk before drinking it, a practice that destroys the milk's vitamin D, which is needed for strong bones.) The bottom line: if children eat a lot of spinach they won't get rickets. In 1927 *American Medicine* reported that scientific evidence showed that this "king amongst vegetables" helps prevent anemia, heart arrhythmia, kidney ailments, dyspepsia, hemorrhoids, and all kinds of states of nonmotivation and debility. At the same time extensive analytic research was conducted on the vegetable's ingredients and substances: saponins (which are beneficial for digestion), glucoside, flavonoid, amino acids, and of course chlorophyll; plus minerals such as calcium, phosphorus, potassium, magnesium, sodium, and iron—lots of iron. Interestingly, however, it turns out that it's a myth that spinach has a lot of iron! Even more interestingly, the assertion that spinach contains plentiful iron resulted from a typo. In one of the first analyses, the percent period was placed one digit too far to the right, noting the iron content as ten times what it really is. Also of note: no great pains were taken to publicly correct the mistake.

As a result of the perpetuation of this error, doctors, especially children's doctors and gynecologists, advised their patients to eat a lot of spinach for its high iron content. Too often such doctors felt compelled to diagnose "iron-deficiency anemia." Just as there are fashionable sicknesses, there are also fashionable diagnoses. In ancient times it was "bad fluids" (according to the humoral teachings); in the nineteenth century it was psoriasis, sycosis, and syphilis; in the first half of the twentieth century it was gastritis, colitis, arthritis, focal infections, and anemia. The symptoms of anemia are paleness, cold hands and feet, loss of appetite, dizziness, headache, weight loss, and a general loss of physical and mental robustness. That the social conditions of the times—poverty, unhealthy living and working conditions—could be responsible for the anemia seems to have not occurred to anyone; instead, the sole cause was attributed to iron deficiency. Women and children were especially at risk. Women lose a lot of blood during menstruation, and pregnancy and nursing both leach their energy. Small children grow quickly, consuming a lot of iron, as do youths, especially if they have fallen victim to the habit of masturbation (according to the medical theory of the time). As such, it was concluded that children and women, especially pregnant and nursing women, should eat as much spinach as possible.

Unfortunately, the children did not comply when the—oh, so healthy!—slimy, green glob was dished onto their plates. Given the difficulty of the sell, educational measures needed to be taken—and this is where Popeye came into the picture. Popeye is a tough little guy and no one shoves him around. As children could identify with him, they were ready fodder for the jingle everyone in my generation could sing:

> *I'm Popeye the sailor man,*
> *I'm strong to the finish*
> *cause I eat my spinach,*
> *I'm Popeye the sailor man.*

Whether any tots became convinced that miracle spinach turned the sailor man into a superman is debatable. In any case, some friends of mine who were children at that time told me it did not fool them—that the canned stuff tasted awful no matter how highly Popeye praised it.

Today, the spinach hype has been brought down to earth. Eaten occasionally—fresh, not canned—spinach is indeed a nutritious vegetable. But as daily fare for weak constitutions and convalescents, as fortification for small children and pregnant or nursing women, it is not at all a good idea—and for people with kidney problems least of all. (Recall that in 1927 *American Medicine* recommended spinach for kidney ailments.) Modern-day gardener John Seymour correctly pointed out that if Popeye had eaten just one-fourth of the spinach he ate on television he would have surely have died of oxalic acid poisoning. Like other Chenopodium family members (Swiss chard, orache, Good King Henry) or related knotweed family plants (rhubarb, sour dock), spinach contains considerable amounts of oxalic acid (126 mg per 100 g). Oxalic acid binds with calcium and magnesium found in the body,

Illustration 82. Popeye the Sailor Man tanking up on spinach, which gives him superhuman strength

leading to decalcification of the bones and teeth. It also binds to the calcium in mother's milk. In the process are built up calcium oxalates, tiny sharp crystals that damage and congest the kidneys and also lead to urinary stones. In fact, two-thirds of all urolithic calculi are oxalic stones. How smart of all the children who refused to ingest the canned green slime!

Even separate from the oxalic acid concerns, the iron content of spinach happens to be relatively low (5 mg per 100 g)—*and* it's usually in a compound state and thus not accessible to the organism. And so, those told to ingest more iron should instead eat, for example, stinging nettle, which happens to contain no oxalic acid. But in the meantime, research has shown a light on the popular iron-deficiency anemia diagnosis. We know now that the body sequesters iron; this means the iron level in the blood drops when the body is suffering an infectious disease or when a woman menstruates or is about to give birth. Since most pathogenic bacteria need iron to grow and reproduce, they "starve" when the body withholds its iron levels; as such, this is a perfect example of the innate "wisdom of nature." In cases of pregnancy or infection, a diagnosis of iron-deficiency anemia is definitively false, and the resulting prescription of iron pills and ferruginous preparations are counter-productive.

Another problem with commercially grown spinach is that it absorbs and accumulates many nitrates, plus heavy metals like cadmium. Excessive use of nitrogen fertilization to make the leaves lush and green contributes its share of unsavory ingredients as well. Although nitrates are not very dangerous, they do hinder the building of vitamin A in the body and can cause problems with the thyroid gland in children. However, it can become problematic when nitrogen-fixing bacteria change nitr*ates* into nitr*ites*. For this reason one should never warm up cooked spinach or keep spinach in opened cans for any length of time. High amounts of nitrites can cause blue baby syndrome in infants, a disease that disrupts oxygen transport into the blood.

So where does all this back and forth information leave us? Despite these reservations, spinach remains a tasty vegetable that's rich in vitamins, minerals, and bases—especially young tender leaves. Spinach has iodine, which is good for the thyroid, plenty of vitamin C, and large amount of vitamin A, which helps with chapped skin, dry conjunctiva, and night blindness. (A mere 100 grams of fresh spinach provides an adult's recommended daily intake of vitamin A.) Spinach also contains large amounts of beta-carotene, a precursor of vitamin A and an antioxidant, which according to recent research helps prevent cancer. In 1969, Japanese experiments with guinea pigs showed that spinach is able to lower blood cholesterol levels. Spinach also counteracts hyperacidity and activates pancreas, intestinal lining, and gall secretion. Cooked spinach juice helps against a dry cough. And as for its oxalic acid content: quickly blanching the leaves loses a lot of the acid.

In any case, one should eat only organic spinach that has been fertilized naturally with compost. It is also best to pick the leaves on sunny afternoons, when the nitrate content in the leaves is lower.

Garden Tips

Cultivation: Sow seed in the open ground as soon as the soil can be worked. Thin plants and then begin to pick for table use by cutting every other plant, giving a chance for the others to spread out. Mulch is especially important for keeping the soil cool and the weeds down. (LB)

Soil: The idea is to give spinach plenty of water and nitrogen, grow it quickly, and harvest before hot weather comes along. Spinach cannot tolerate an acidic soil, and so enough limestone should be incorporated to raise the pH to a neutral condition. Nitrogen is especially important for fast and tender growth.

Recipe

Spinach Strudel with Juniper Sauce • 4 Servings

Strudel: 21 ounces (600 grams) fresh spinach • 2 tablespoons butter
• 1 ounce (50 grams) cranberries • 1 teaspoon honey • 1 tsp. vanilla
marrow or extract • herbal salt • pepper • 10 ounces (285 grams) pastry
dough • egg yolk, whisked • **Sauce:** ½ cup (115 grams) onions, chopped
• ½ cup (115 grams) red beets, cubed • 4 small pine twigs or
20 juniper berries • 2 tablespoons honey • 1 tablespoon vinegar

• 3 ounces (80 grams) gorgonzola • 2 cups (½ liter) red wine
• 2 cups (½ liter) vegetable broth • 1 shot glass gin
• 1 to 2 tablespoons lentil flour for binding • herbal salt • pepper

Sauce: Put the onions, beets, pine twigs, honey, vinegar, gorgonzola, red wine, vegetable broth, and gin in a large pot and simmer on low heat for about 1 hour. Pour the sauce through a sieve into another container; discard the pine twigs in the sieve. Return the sauce to the pot and thicken with lentil flour. Bring to a boil once more. Season with salt and pepper to taste.

Filling: In a small pan on medium heat, briefly sauté the spinach in butter. Let cool. Add honey and cranberries and mix together. Season with salt, pepper, and vanilla to taste.

Strudel: Preheat the oven to 350 °F (175 °C). Grease a baking sheet. Roll out the pastry dough to ¼ inch thick. Spread the spinach mixture evenly over the dough, leaving a half-inch margin around the edge. Roll into a strudel shape and place on the baking sheet. Brush with the egg yolk (whisked with a few drops of water for more sheen) and bake for about 45 minutes at 350° F (175°C) or until golden brown. Transfer the strudel to a serving dish.

Tomato (*Solanum lycopersicum, Lycopersicum esculentum*)

Family: Solanaceae: nightshade family

Other Names and Varieties: apple of paradise, gold apple, love apple; beef tomato, cherry tomato, pear tomato, yellow tomato

Healing Properties:

Taken externally: fresh juice helps disinfect wounds

Taken internally: increases pancreas secretion; regulates bowel movement; inhibits tumors (anticarcinogenic); ideal in diets for gout, kidney and heart ailments, rheumatism

Symbolic Meaning: temptation, Eve's apple, love madness, egoism, sex and fertility

Planetary Affiliation: Mars, Venus

Next to potatoes, tomatoes are definitely the favorite of cultivated garden fare. The tasty, beautifully colorful, juicy vegetable—though technically a fruit—has won the hearts and tables of people all over the world. But that was not always the case. When in the early sixteenth century the Spanish discoverers first saw tomatoes in Central America, they were more than skeptical about eating them, having immediately recognized the tomato as a nightshade plant. During this era of witch persecutions and the Inquisition in Europe, nightshade plants—such as henbane, belladonna, mandrake, and angel's trumpet—weren't just known to be extremely poisonous: they were also considered evil, belonging to the devil. For the Spanish conquerors, nightshades were associated with witches and their wicked brews and salves that led to licentiousness, whoring, and other damnable activity.

There was also another practice that did not exactly speak for the innocent plant. Spanish chroniclers reported in disgust that the Aztecs sacrificed their war captives, cutting out their still-beating hearts in offering to the sun god. The remaining meat of at least some of the victims was later prepared in a stew seasoned with tomatoes and chili peppers and

Illustration 83. Tomato blossoms (illustration by Molly Conner-Ogorzaly, from B. B. Simpson and M. Conner-Ogorzaly, Economic Botany, *1986)*

served to noblemen. (While scholars do not agree on the extent to which cannibalism was practiced by the Aztec nation, they do agree that it took place on occasion, especially for ritual purposes.) According to the conquerors, it would be hard to find anything more devilish on God's earth. (It did not occur to them that they themselves came from a culture that cruelly tortured other—mainly completely innocent—human beings in God's name, and where pyres burning "witches" were constantly aflame.)

Of course, the Aztecs also used tomatoes as medicine; unfortunately, most of their recipes for healing are hard to follow. For instance, to treat "facial star disease" a mask was made of lizard manure, soot, and tomato juice. The drink for convalescing and general strengthening—fresh-pressed tomato juice, ground pumpkin seeds, yellow paprika, and cooked agave juice—certainly sounds much more pleasant. For asthma and other lung ailments they put cooked tomatoes, made as hot as possible, on the chest, rubbing them in with copal resin as soon as they were cool enough.

For the Mayans, tomatoes were daily fare. They believed that tomato juice increases red blood (in which life force resides) in humans, and thus strengthens the body. They also treated skin infections and hemorrhoids with fresh tomato juice (Rätsch 1996, 272).

Tomato comes from the Aztec word "*tomatl,*" which means something along the lines of "a firmly swollen thing." European botanists came up with other names for the suspicious fruit. First was *lycopersicum,* "wolf's peach." The "peach" of this name they got from a not very detailed description of an old Egyptian poisonous plant—presumably mandrake—that also has golden yellow berries and that the renowned Roman doctor Galen had mentioned in his writings. The "wolf" derived from the fact that heathen Europeans called all plants that are poisonous, caustic, or even "malicious" "wolf plants." The distinguished German physician and member of the Royal Society, Dr. Michael B. Valentini (1657–1721), wrote: the tomato "is called 'wolf's peach' because, though it is pleasing to the eyes, if people eat it, it can kill them, just as wolves can." The fruit was also called "apple of insanity" (*mala insana*) and "golden apple of a stinking smell."

Illustration 84. The Spanish associated barbarous human sacrifice with tomatoes

Other botanists of the sixteenth century thought of friendlier names for the new plant, such as "love apple" (*poma amoris*) or "paradise apple." But even in these names convey a basic mistrust, a fear of eroticism and sensuality. The fruit, juicy and red like voluptuous lips, and full of slimy seeds, reminded scholars of fatal female temptation. In Germany, a hot chick is still called a "hot tomato"—who might though turn out to be a "sour" or "fickle tomato"—and a temperamental woman is called a "tomato with pepper" (Bornemann 1991).

When tomatoes first became known the scholars of the time puzzled as to whether it could be the forbidden fruit that once grew on the Tree of Forbidden Knowledge in the Garden of Eden. Their suspicion derived from the report of Christopher Columbus of his third voyage, which had taken him to the mouth of the Orinoco River on the coast of South

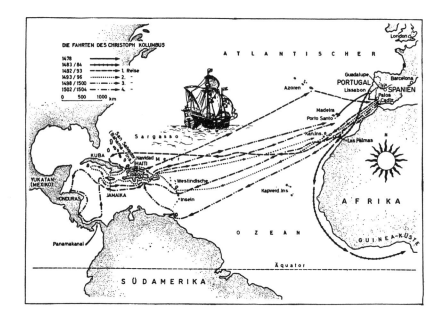

Illustration 85. The Voyages of Christopher Columbus

America. Columbus wrote that the region was beautiful beyond measure, the vegetation was lush, the animals were peaceful, and the natives were handsome and pictures of perfect health. In all seriousness, he believed he had landed on the border of Paradise, the Garden of Eden described in sacred texts. Could it be that the many wild tomatoes that grew there were descendants of the forbidden fruit? The name "paradise apple" noted earlier became relatively widespread. For example, such was the name used in the countries belonging to the Habsburg Empire—Bohemia, Silesia, Yugoslavia, and Tyrol; in Scandinavia they are still known as "paradise apples": *paradisaeble, paradisaepple*. And today in Vienna only strangers buy "tomatoes" on the famous Naschmarkt; the Viennese buy *Paradeiser*. In the Odenwald, near the Rhine, locals still call the fruit "Adam's apple" in memory of the first victim of female seduction.

Even though people were suspicious of this exotic "love apple" or "gold apple," it did find a place in European gardens—as a decorative plant. As an expression of his otherwise inexpressible hopes and wishes, many a suitor pooh-poohed the usual gift of flowers, giving the lady he hoped to win a basket of ripe, lush red tomatoes instead. For a long time tomato juice was considered to be a secret love potion, one that in the eyes of the Puritans "leads to licentiousness"—as wrote modern-day ethnobotanist Christian Rätsch, an expert on aphrodisiacs.

Gradually, however, the tomato's medicinal properties were discovered. According to its signature, the red fruit was believed to heal wounds. The fresh juice was trickled into wounds in order to prevent the buildup of pus and the development of erysipelas. Those who were versed in medical lore experimented with tinctures made of fresh stems. They got the idea from the similar fruits of the bittersweet nightshade, which was used for pustules and skin diseases of a scrofulous nature, such as occurred from syphilis and the misuse of mercury salves. According to the way of thinking of the times, it was only logical that this "love apple" could alleviate the symptoms of venereal disease, the disease with which the goddess of sensual love, Venus, had smitten humanity. After all, it was Columbus's sailors who first contracted the dreadful sexually transmitted disease, bringing it back with them from the New World. The medical doctrine of the time stated that the place where a sickness originated was also where the cure could be found.

But it would take until the sixteenth century before Europeans ever considered eating tomatoes. The Italians were the first to dare to eat the dreaded fruit. Perhaps it was a rejected lover who wanted to take his own life with the *poma amoris,* the apple of love; perhaps it fell onto his toasted bread, or into his pasta of olive oil, garlic, and parsley. In any case, botanist Joachim Camerarius the Younger (1534–1598) wrote: "In Italy many have the habit of eating these fruits cooked with salt, vinegar, and oil, but it is a very unhealthful food." In time, Italy became the second home for tomatoes, which plunged into intimate wedlock with pasta. By the eighteenth century, entire fields of tomatoes were under cultivation in northern Italy. Farmers from the region of Parma were the first to conserve them by cooking the juice or drying the fruits in the sun.

It took the northern and western Europeans and North Americans very long to overcome the taboo of eating tomatoes. Though herbalist William

Illustration 86. For a long time it was believed that the tomato was the "apple of paradise" that had caused humanity to plunge to its perdition (Baum der Erkenntnis, 1531)

Salmon (1644–1713) reported seeing tomatoes growing in the early American colonies—in what is now South Carolina, in 1710—it was presumably only as an ornamental plant. An American colonel named Robert Gibbon Johnson was declared crazy in 1820 when he announced that on September 26 he would publically eat a whole basket of tomatoes while sitting on his open porch. On the appointed day more than two thousand curious onlookers appeared to witness the spectacle; to the astonishment of all—excepting himself, we presume—he survived.

In as late as 1866 in Northern Germany the "love apple" was still considered an ornamental plant, whereas in Southern Germany it was cultivated and eaten as a side dish or as an ingredient in soups. But still scientists and physicians has their doubts: they claimed that, as an acid-producing vegetable, the tomato acidifies the blood and body tissue and makes it susceptible to rheumatism, gout, and arthritis—and, worse, it supports cancer. (Today we know that exactly the opposite is the case.)

It was not until after 1920 that the tomato became really popular. Agribusiness cultivated huge fields of standardized hybrid tomatoes[1] in the new arable areas in the desert of Southern California. As a result the U.S. market was flooded with tomato juice, tomato paste, canned tomatoes, tomato soup, and ketchup.[2] For Hollywood stars, tomato juice became as much a part of the daily ritual as orange juice and spinach; and during Prohibition a popular cocktail, the "Bloody Mary," nicely disguised the vodka lurking within. Today the average American eats some fifty pounds (twenty-five kilos) of tomatoes a year.

Not long after, doctors found their way to attesting considerable health advantages to the newly fashionable and profitable vegetable. They [correctly] reported that tomatoes are good for dyspepsia, liver troubles, gout, rheumatism, and heart and kidney ailments. Fresh tomatoes increase pancreas secretion and stimulate bowl movement. In addition they are full of high-quality vitamins, including vitamin C, carotene (a pre-stage of vitamin A), thiamine, and vitamin E, the "fertility vitamin." Folk healers also befriended the vegetable. Modern-day herbal healer Maurice Mességué recommends it for acidosis (stomach acidity, such as in heartburn), constipation, for thinning the blood, and for gout-related ailments. He also recommends hanging the stems and leaves in closets to keep out moths and insects.

Anthroposophists, however, still have doubts about the tomato. They note that this nightshade plant just does not have the proper "power to grow upright," that the tomato is "weighed down with matter." The anthroposophically oriented botanist Alfred Usteri (1869–1948) was suspicious of what he called "a rapacious plant that thrives on its own composted waste and debris." He claims the tomato reflects the materialism that took root in the beginning of the fifteenth century and that is the mirror image of the human egoism that led to racism, nationalism, and consumerism. The tomato, thus, can cause diseases in the human being, which represent the physical expression of these mental configurations. In other anthroposophical writings there are also warnings about the "surplus expansive force" in the tomato, and about the "misguided formative forces that can help promote cancer, rheumatism, and gout" (Pelikan 1975, 186).

It is interesting to note that recent research indicates exactly the opposite: the tomato is anticarcinogenic. In fact, there are statistically fewer cases of cancer in areas where a lot of tomatoes are eaten. One study has shown that—thanks to the high concentration of the carotene lycopene— it is especially beneficial for lung cancer. The fruit's lycopene content makes it one of the top-rated antioxidant foods as well.

And what about the crazy imaginations that deemed the tomato a witch's plant that can cause insanity and hallucinations? Those myths have long since been cleared up as well. The glycoalkaloid solanine found in tomato leaves and stems is indeed poisonous; it can cause dizziness, nausea, gall and kidney irritation, cardiac flutter, profuse sweating, cramps, and unconsciousness—but it is absolutely not a psychedelic. Or maybe it is, just on another level? Or maybe it has a tendency in that direction? I would like to share an unusual, enlightening experience the tomato once gave me. I had been busy all day in a large biodynamic garden near Geneva, Switzerland, tying tomato plants to posts and pinching off side shoots. The aromatic evaporation of the plants in the closed-off plastic tunnel was almost overwhelming. As is usual when doing that kind of work, I let my thoughts wander. I was thinking about Buckminster Fuller's 1967 hypothesis of our "spaceship Earth" and about the fragile, thin film of chlorophyll upon which all life on earth depends. In my mind's eye I saw the unnecessary destruction of the forests and the spreading of the deserts. The thought that "we are living on a dying planet" overwhelmed and saddened me. But suddenly I felt "beamed" into another dimension. An angel or god—it must have been the tomato deva—said to me: "You are wrong. The green cloak of the earth is only an external expression of the fullness of life that flows through the entire universe. Life and consciousness belong to the essence of being, not just matter and energy, and they cannot be irrevocably destroyed. Do not worry, just do your work and do not be afraid!" That message came from such depth that it has become a lifeline for me. To this day I am thankful to the tomato for giving me this insight. I know that it is not an "uncanny spirit" that lives in the plant, but a strong and friendly one.

Garden Tips

Cultivation: Tomato seeds should be started indoors about eight weeks before the last frost. Tomatoes should be planted in an open place, for they need full sun and good air circulation for maximum growth and production. The soil can be well composted in advance of planting; an extra handful of well-aged compost may be thrown in the planting hole before you transplant. You should plan to stake your tomatoes. Drive in a stake at planting time and tie the young plant to the stake (tightly around the stake and loosely around the tomato stem.) After that allow just two main shoots to grow, pinching off any side shoots, until the plants have reached about two feet in height. After that you can allow side shoots to develop. Keep the shoots tied to the stake as they grow. (LB)

Soil: Tomatoes grow best in a sandy loam that offers good drainage and aeration. Never plant tomatoes where puddles form, for this indicates poor drainage and a great possibility of bacterial wilt, stunting, and fruit rot. Good air circulation is equally important, since this will help prevent blights and fungal diseases.

Recipes

Tomato Salad with Plums and Plum Vinegar Dressing
• 2 to 4 Servings

Salad: 4 ripe tomatoes, cut into ¼ inch slices, 4 firm, tart plums, cut into slices • sea salt • pepper • 3 ounces (80 grams) alpine cheese, coarsely grated • Dressing: 2 tablespoons plum vinegar • 5 tablespoons olive oil • 3 ounces (80 grams) onions, finely chopped • some chives, finely chopped

Layer the tomatoes and plums in a serving bowl. Season with salt and pepper to taste. Sprinkle the cheese over top. In a small bowl, mix the vinegar, olive oil, onions, and chives. Drizzle over the salad.

Tomato-Potato Soup with Marjoram and Nuts
• 4 Servings

1½ pounds (680 grams) potatoes , peeled or unpeeled, cubed • ¾ pound (~350 grams) onions, chopped • 2 tablespoons olive oil • 4 tomatoes, cubed • 1 quart (945 milliliters) vegetable broth • ground nutmeg • sea salt • pepper • fresh marjoram • 4 garlic cloves, chopped • 2 ounces (50 grams) raw pumpkin seeds • 3 ounces (80 grams) cottage cheese

In a large pot, sauté the potatoes and onions in the olive oil, covered, for about 8 minutes, stirring regularly. Stir in the tomatoes and cook for another 2 minutes. Pour in the vegetable broth. Bring to a boil and boil for 1 minute. Move the pot off the burner and season with ground nutmeg, honey, salt, and pepper. In a small serving bowl, mix the marjoram, garlic, pumpkin seeds, and cottage cheese; season with salt to taste. Serve with the soup.

Forgotten, Rare, and Less-Known Vegetables

"Business as usual." This adage is as true in the garden as it is in the kitchen. As creatures of habit, most gardeners doggedly sow and plant the same vegetables they've always sown. This despite the fact that the number of less-known vegetables ideal for the garden is so plentiful it could fill a book of its own. Here follow just a scattering of the forgotten vegetables I've grown at one time or another. They are all compatible with a typical northern climate, such as is found in northern Europe and most of North America.

Burdock or Gobo (*Arctium lappa* var. *edule*)

Family: Compositae: composite, daisy, or sunflower family

Other Names: bardane, smaller burdock, clotbur, cockle-button, cuckoo-button, hardock

Healing Properties: cleanses blood, lowers cholesterol, inhibits fungi and bacteria, supports liver and gall bladder, promotes urination (diuretic)

Tea from roots: promotes hair growth

Symbolic Meaning: bear plant, dedicated to Germanic Donar, or Thor, the "divine bear"; wards off lightening; fickle love (language of flowers)

Planetary Affiliation: Venus, Jupiter

Many have encountered wild burdock, whether they realize it or not. Though a native of the Old World, wild burdock has become a widespread invasive weed in the northern areas of North America. It is a "bear" among plants. (There's more on that to come.) It has leaves like elephant ears, a mighty taproot, and a flower head with many barbs. Many a girl has made acquaintance with hazelnut-sized burdock fruits when naughty boys tossed them into their hair and these capsules have been the undoing of many a long-haired dog and cat. But how many know that this plant with the nasty burrs is both healing and delicious? In eastern Asia—China, Java, and especially Japan—a cultivated form of the plant is highly valued for its roots and young spring shoots. The *gobo* or *takinogawa* is a favorite vegetable of the Japanese, so much so that it's cultivated on large, industrial plantations in order to keep up with the demand. The root—which, grown in loose, well-fertilized soil, can reach the size of a baseball bat—has a strong, nutty taste. In the "land of the rising sun," as the Japanese fondly call their country, the vegetable is added to soups, deep-fried as tempura, or mixed with sea weed, carrots, and other vegetables and sautéed in sesame oil, then seasoned with ginger and soy sauce. *Gobo* goes very well with rice and fish dishes. The young shoots taste similar to cardoon (an edible thistle plant); as they are rather bitter, they call for the right kind of sauce to make them tasty. In

Illustration 87. Burdock root

Russia a "Taiga stew" is made of two parts finely chopped burdock and one part sour dock. The Russians even use burdock leaves in soups and purées, but as they are very bitter they're difficult for Western taste to get used to (Koschtschejew 1990, 206).

Burdock root is very nutritious. It contains biotin, protein, vitamins C, B1, B6, B12 and E, and many minerals, including potash, sulfur, silica, and manganese. Like many composites, the carbohydrates in the plant are mainly made of inulin, which makes the root ideal for a sugar diabetes diet.

Burdock sprouts and grows quickly. And while the plant needs a lot of room and soil that is not compacted, its plants are very pest-resistant. As heavy feeders they appreciate plenty of compost as fertilizer. The roots of the biennial plant are harvested in the fall of the first year or in the spring of the second year; they are best three or four months after sowing, as then they are especially tender. In the second year they shoot to flower and seed, and the roots become too woody to eat. Harvesting these roots is the biggest challenge for the gardener. They can grow up to three feet long and break easily—to harvest them one must dig a deep trench next to the row and then carefully take the root out. This works best after it has rained and the soil is moist and loose. In Japan the roots are grown in wooden boxes; for the harvest one simply needs to lower the sides of the box. The roots can be stored very well in a sand heap. (Note: the black rind should be peeled off before cooking.)

Germanics and Celts of olden times regarded wild burdock as a plant belonging to the bear. Bear plants are especially big (hogweed, for example), mighty in healing (such as clubmoss, bear's garlic, or bearberry), or very hairy (such as the roots of meu [*Meum athamanticum*] or licorice root [*Ligusticum*] or bear's medicine). The Germanics dedicated the plant to their favorite god, Thor, the god of thunder and lightning; just like the burdock, Thor is a healer: big and strong and hirsute. Understandably, it was believed that the plant could help hair grow. In Europe one can still buy burdock root

Illustration 88. Thor, "the godly bear," for whom burdock is a sacred plant

oil that (used externally) is not only good for hair but also for rheumatism and joint and skin ailments.[1] The famous herbalist Maria Treben (1907–1991) described how, having lost a lot of hair as a young girl, she was advised by an elderly woman to boil burdock roots and wash her hair with the water. She wrote that after several washings her hair grew back so thick she could hardly brush it (Treben 2009, 130).

As the burdock was associated with the thunder god, Thor, it was called "*Toennersbladen*" (thunder leaf) in Northern Germany, where it was hung from roof gables to protect houses from lightning. Since Thor was known to slay all kinds of "worms" and "snakes" that cause disease, many rituals were practiced asking for his help. When requesting aid against maggots plaguing animals, for example, a supplicant would approach a burdock plant clutching a rock in one hand. Without speaking, the petitioner would think the following: *Burdock, I am strangling you. Burdock, I won't let go of you until the maggots have let go of the animal.*

As a majestic bear plant, the burdock truly has the signature of regal Jupiter, but Nicholas Culpeper (1616–1654) and other astrological doctors put it medically under the rule of Venus. The juice of the leaves was used as a diuretic, and a tea made of the seeds was given for urinary stones. In addition a tea of the roots and leaves was made for venereal diseases—syphilis raged in Culpeper's time—and for cleansing the blood. Today phytotherapists would agree: the whole plant activates gall bladder secretion and is both diuretic and sudorific, similar to—or even better than—sarsaparilla imported from South America. By cleansing the kidneys and skin, tea of burdock taken over a stretch of time helps cure gout as well as syphilitic and scrofula conditions. In addition the plant supports liver and gall bladder functions—in this case through Jupiter's influence. Thanks to its polyacetylene content, the plant also has bacteriostatic and fungicidal properties; as such the tea can be used externally for acne and boils and internally for flushing out toxic substances and uric acid, as well as for curing bladder infections and spleen, kidney, and liver ailments. Similarly, lupus can be treated internally with burdock tea and externally with burdock salve. The powdered root helps treat chemical poisoning. Skin tumors used to be treated with crushed leaves. Modern research has shown that all of the plant parts are effective in helping combat cancer (Mabey 1993, 41).

Just as in ancient times in the Old World, for the Native Americans, the bear was believed to be the "medicine man amongst the animals." A Dakota medicine man is quoted as saying: "The bear is quick-tempered and is fierce in many ways, but he is our herbal teacher. Whoever dreams of a bear will become a healer." As far as its healing properties go, burdock absolutely deserves its botanical name, "*Arctium lappa*" (Greek *arktos* = bear; Celtic *lapp* = paw). Since native peoples also believed that such a powerful plant was capable of driving off the devil, for protection burrs were sometimes braided into a cow's tail or put in one's own hair.

In France burdock is called "*bouton de soldat*" because soldiers used to replace lost buttons with burrs—a practice that became the model for the hook and loop fastener commonly known as Velcro. And in the language of flowers, burdock stands for "inconsistent love"—because it will cling to anyone.

Recipes

Burdock-Tomato Salad with Almond Dressing and Burdock-Snake Bread • 4 Servings

Salad: 1 cup (225 grams) burdock roots, stems, and leaves, cut into bite-sized pieces • 3 large tomatoes, sliced ¼ inch thick • Dressing: 1 tablespoon almond paste • 3 ounces (50 milliliters) vegetable broth • 1 tablespoon red wine or balsamic vinegar • 1 tablespoon wheat germ oil • 2 tablespoons sunflower oil • 1 tablespoon freshly ground black pepper • fresh herbs, finely chopped • Snake bread: 4 burdock roots, chopped • sumac or paprika powder • 2 pounds (905 grams) bread dough

SALAD: Put the burdock roots, stems, and leaves in a serving bowl and garnish with the tomatoes. Dressing: In a separate small bowl, mix the almond paste, vegetable broth, vinegar, wheat germ oil, sunflower oil, pepper, and herbs. Drizzle the dressing over the burdock and tomatoes.

SNAKE BREAD: On a floured, flat surface, mix the burdock roots and paprika into the dough and knead well. Option 1: Roll the dough into long "sausages" about 1 inch in diameter. Wrap each sausage around a fresh willow stick to roast over a fire, constantly turning until roasted golden brown. Option 2: Preheat the oven to 350 °F (175 °C). Shape the dough into buns about 3 inches in diameter. Bake in the oven at 350 °F (175 °C) for about 35 minutes. Serve with the salad.

Burdock Flower Buds with Herbal Sauce and Whole Grain Rice • 4 Servings

¾ cup burdock flower buds • ¼ cup fresh herbs such as parsley, thyme, or marjoram, finely chopped • ¼ cup olive oil • ⅓ cup white wine • ⅓ cup cream (18% fat) • herbal salt • black pepper

In a medium pan briefly sauté the burdock buds with the fresh herbs in olive oil, covered. Add the white wine and cream and simmer, covered, for about 10 minutes. Season with salt and pepper to taste.

Daylily (*Hemerocallis fulva*)

Family: Xanthorrhoeaceae: grass lily family; subfamily: Asphodeloideae

Other Names: ditch lily or fulvous daylily, outhouse lily, railroad daylily, roadside daylily, tawny daylily, tiger daylily, tiger lily, washhouse lily

Healing Properties: reduces inflammation, relaxes muscles, cleanses system, promotes urination (diuretic)

Symbolic Meaning: St. Josef, tenderness, purity; insouciance, nonchalance (Chinese)

Planetary Affiliation: moon, Jupiter

The daylily, with its funnel-shaped blossom, which can range in color from yellow/ocher to salmon, is a common garden flower that is easy to cultivate; once planted, the May-to-July bloomer is a reliable perennial. In the traditional folklore of Europe it was called "Saint-Joseph's-lily" (*giglio di San Giuseppe*) whereas the white lily belonged to his wife, the pure Virgin Mary. Though the plant blossoms profusely, each individual flower blossoms for only one day, from sunrise to sunset. Because of this Swedish botanist Carl Linnaeus (1707–1778) gave the plant the name "*Hemerocallis*" (from the Greek *hemera* = day, *kallos* = beautiful). The daylily reproduces not via seeds but via rhizomes—which makes it even more surprising that it grows wild in so many places. The plant's reproduction is ensured via the distribution of its root parts by rodents, voles, hamsters, and humans.

The daylily—which is in fact not even a lily but a member of the asphodel family—originated in eastern Asia. The plant was unknown in Europe before the Renaissance; this new kind of "lily" was first mentioned in the sixteenth century by French and Belgian botanists such as Rembert Dodoens, Carolus Clusius, and Matthias de l'Obel. An American botanist commented in 1812 that these flowers grew wild around Philadelphia. Nowadays daylilies can be found all over the midwestern states on roadsides and riverbanks and in wet meadows. Enthusiastic admirers have cultivated over thirty thousand different registered varieties.

In China, Japan, and Korea the daylily has been cultivated for thousands of years as a vegetable. The plants are mainly found growing in clusters on dykes between rice paddies. The young shoots are harvested in the spring and prepared like asparagus; they can also be added raw to salads. The buds are also very popular braised in a wok, deep-fried in batter, or added to soups. The blossoms (from the Chinese *jin zhen cai*), which are somewhat slimy and have a sweetish tangy taste, are good for garnishing a soup or as a decorative touch to a salad. In East Asia the dried blossoms—called "golden needles"—are used as seasoning. One may very well enjoy golden needle seasoning in a Chinese restaurant without knowing it. The short, fleshy storage root is also edible but it is fairly difficult to harvest and clean. The roots taste best in the spring when they are fresh and tender. They can be added to soups or boiled in salt water as a vegetable. They taste like a mixture between corn and oyster plant. The daylily is also nourishing: the roots contain protein and some oil; the blossoms contain beta-carotene and vitamin C.

Japanese aboriginals, the Ainu, who are known for their bear cult and full, bushy hair, gather the wild plant in great quantities. They dry the blossoms or pickle them in salt brine. The Chinese name for the daylily is "*xuan-cao*"—*xuan* means "forget worries"; *cao* means "herb." Thus, it is considered a plant via which one can forget one's worries. Eating a lot of the shoots is said to have an almost psychedelic effect—or in any case to be very relaxing. The effect must be very mild, though, as none of my drug-wise, old hippy friends knew about it, and as Christian Rätsch didn't mention it in his *Encyclopedia of Psychoactive Plants*.

As the plant is described as "sweet" and "cool," masters of herbal lore such as Nicholas Culpeper, had he known about it, could have confidently attributed the plant as under the influence of the moon and Jupiter.

In the ancient Chinese herbal book *Shennong Bencaojing* (third century BC), the daylily is mentioned as a healing plant. In Chinese folk medicine—which has more uses for the plant than official academic medicine does—it is known as a healing agent for jaundice and as a diuretic. The root is used for venereal and urinary diseases. It is added to pig meat dishes to strengthen those who have "feverish states of exhaustion"; for intestinal bleeding it is cooked in wine and drunk. Cooked mashed roots are applied hot as a poultice for inflamed breasts (mastitis). The blossoms are considered to be cleansing, calming, and relaxing; dried blossoms are used for hematuria. Tea made of the dried plant is considered relaxing, detoxifying, and pain relieving.

As eastern Asian folk medicine is not easy to follow, I have not included any specific recipes for the daylily. But there is no reason to not have this beautiful plant in one's garden and to try it out as a vegetable: with one significant caveat. It is very important to be certain you have the right plant (*Hemerocallis fulva*); there are many similar-looking plants that are rather poisonous, such as various lilies, irises, or daffodils. Do grow them, but grow them well informed!

Recipe

Daylilies with Onion Pie • 4 Servings

1½ cups (340 grams) shortcrust pastry dough • 1½ cups (340 grams) onions, chopped • 5 ounces (140 grams) daylily blossoms • 1 tablespoon olive oil • 7 ounces cream (200 milliliters) (18% fat) • 7 ounces (200 milliliters) cottage cheese • 2 tablespoons lentil flour • 2 eggs • 2 pinches ground nutmeg • herbal salt

Preheat the oven to 300 °F (150 °C). Grease a pie pan. Roll out the dough to about ¼ inch thick and fit into the pie pan. In a medium sauté pan, sauté the onions and daylily blossoms in the olive oil for about 10 minutes or until the onions are glassy. Take off heat and let cool. Spread the onions and blossoms evenly in the pie pan. In a medium bowl mix the cream, cottage cheese, and eggs until smooth. Season with nutmeg and herbal salt to taste. Pour this mixture over the pie. Bake at 300 °F (150 °C) for 35 to 40 minutes. Serve warm.

TIP: This dish pairs nicely with a green salad.

Good King Henry (*Chenopodium bonus-henricus* or *Blitum bonus-henricus*)

Family: Chenopodiaceae: goosefoot family

Other Names: all good, everlasting, fat hen, Mercury, poor man's asparagus, wild spinach

Healing Properties:

Taken externally: poultice eases rheumatic pains, scabies, and skin rashes

Taken internally: prevents scurvy (antiscorbutic)

Symbolic Meaning: plant of kobolds and alpine spirits, related to milk magic for summer pastures

Planetary Affiliation: Mercury

Like spinach, Good King Henry is a member of the Chenopodium family. It has three-pointed, deeply green leaves that resemble goose feet in shape and look like they have been slightly powdered. The tiny, colorless, plain blossoms cluster neatly in formation on a "truss" arising from one stalk.

Good King Henry was once one of the favorite leaf greens in Europe— that is, before the upstart spinach arrived and took its place. The tender green leaves are among the first to come in the spring. They can be prepared as one would spinach, and taste especially good with eggs. The tender shoots—that were once bleached by putting a bucket over the plant—were considered a delicacy. When they were about as thick as a pencil they were harvested, peeled, and cooked like asparagus. This dish is still eaten in parts of England and Scotland—known as Lincolnshire asparagus, it is eaten with mayonnaise, lemon butter, or herb butter.

In England and other northern European countries Good King Henry was considered a quite healthful food. Nicholas Culpeper (1616–1654), who preferred Good King Henry to spinach because it is firmer and— according to him—tastier, put the plant under the rule of Mercury. That is significant since Mercury is the healer among the gods. In English folklore the plant itself is even often referred to as "Mercury." An old proverb reveals the high regard for the plant: "Be thou sick or whole, put Mercury in your cole [vegetables]." Culpeper prescribed Good King Henry internally for driving winter scurvy out of the limbs and externally as a poultice for skin wounds, gout, and rheumatic pain. British shepherds gave the roots to their sheep to treat "coughing." Farming women gave the leaves to the hens so they would grow fat and healthy; indeed, "fat hen" is another English name of the plant. Leather tanners used the seeds to make Shagreen leather (Grieve 1982, 365). The British cherished Good King Henry so much that they took the seeds to their colonies in North America, where it promptly thrived as a wild invasive plant species.

But Good King Henry was also very much honored in other places,[1] and its various names all capture basically the same message—"all good": in German, *allgut;* in French, *toute bonne;* Dutch, *algoede;* Spanish: *toda buena;* Italian, *tutta buona;* and in Medieval Latin, *tota bona.*

It is said that St. Henry was the first to make a healing poultice out of Good King Henry and some other healing plants used for leprosy, but we do not know which St. Henry this was, as there were quite a few of them. The plant was known and used long before Europe was Christianized; the name of the patron saint was simply added to legitimize the continued use of the plant.

The German name for "Henry"—either "Heinrich" ("king of the hedge," from the Old Germanic *haganrich;* [*hag* = "hedge," *rig* = "king"]), "Heinz," or "Hinzl"—is, as Jacob Grimm noted, an old name for a kobold, an imp with flat feet like a goose. Just as we learned about the "The Fairies of Cologne" in the chapter on peas, such kobolds—or sprites, or pixies— were believed to attach themselves to homesteads or village settlements, helping people with their work, feeding and watering the animals in the barns, sweeping, chopping wood, and generally ensuring everything was running smoothly. They would also play practical jokes on any servants who were lazy. For their work, the kobolds enjoyed receiving a small bowl of milk with a small piece of bread once a week and on holidays as a gesture of thanks. They did not, however, like to be seen—except once in a while by children and fools, as they have pure souls. A tale from the Swabian Alps tells how an impudent fellow—surely an early overly curious scientist—once strewed flour or ashes on the floor to get prints of their goosefeet. Since they always try to hide their feet, this angered the kobolds, who disappeared forever. But the plant—in German called "*schmozenheiner*" (dirty Henry)—has ashy goose-feet-shaped leaves to this day. (Marzell 1943, 938).[2]

Other goblin-friendly herbs have been given the name "Heinrich" in German. These are often called "dog" plants in English, such as dog's mercury (*Mercurialis perennis*)—*böser Heinrich* (bad Henry) in Ger-

Illustration 89. Good King Henry (Heinrich Marzell, Wörterbuch der deutschen Pflanzennamen. 1943)

man—a purge plant that causes severe diarrhea and vomiting. Purple loosestrife and blueweed are both referred to as "*stolzer Heinrich*" (proud Henry) in German; various kinds of docks are *roter Heinrich* (red Henry), and knotweed is *eisern Heinrich* (iron Henry).

Good King Henry likes to grow around garbage dumps, alongside rural roads, and near house and barn walls. Since it flourishes under the direct sun and in soil saturated with cow dung and urine, it grows exceptionally well near the Alpine huts housing the workers who tend cattle pastured over the summer. Naturally, it is also part of the wild food cooked by herders and dairy folk (who stay up in the high Alps with the cattle over the entire summer season); stinging nettle, sour dock, and Good King Henry—often called "shepherd's spinach" in German—all grow around these huts and are, next to cheese and milk, part of the herder's cuisine. In many places milk magic is practiced with Good King

Henry. In the Ore Mountains and in Swabia, the root is used to neutralize wicked curses made on the milk. The shepherd speaks the following:

> *Good King Henry, you serve me well.*
> *My poor cow is not feeling well.*
> *Go up and down the village lane*
> *and bring back her health again.*

If the milk wasn't as pure as it should be, the milk vessels would be rinsed with a decoction made with Good King Henry.

Good King Henry was always in high demand as a healing plant. The alpine shepherds used it for open wounds, swellings, and tumors; they wrapped and fastened the leaves over the affected area. In older times it was used for leprosy, consumption, and pleurisy. It was made into healing salves under the name "smear dock." In Switzerland it was known as "home plant"—growing as it did near the house and barn; its healing strength was thought to ward off the demons that harm the cows and their udders (Hoefler 1990, 25). In Valais, Switzerland, anyone stung by stinging nettle would rub the afflicted area with Good King Henry, saying:

> *In Nomeni Patri*
> *Rub nettle and nettle petal*
> *With Good King Henry*
> *And don't let the nettle settle*

Good King Henry has some interesting near relatives that are also almost completely forgotten garden vegetables: including lamb's quarters (or pigweed), an excellent wild vegetable; cultivated garden orache (*Atriplex hortensis*); and Strawberry Blite. Jesuit's tea (*Chenopodium ambrosioides*), a highly aromatic and effective vermifuge, is a relative, too—as is quinoa (*Chenopodium quinoa*), the delicious seed grain from Peru, and the mystic tumbleweed that rolls across the plains in the West.

Good King Henry well deserves to be introduced to your garden. It likes well-fertilized, moist soil and a sunny place. In my experience—and not surprising given its habits—it grows well next to house walls, where it comes back year after year, making very little work for the gardener. Who knows, maybe a friendly kobold will move in right along with the plant.

Recipes

Good King Henry Vinegar • 2 Quarts

7 ounces (200 grams) fresh Good King Henry leaves • 1 dash vanilla powder • 2 quarts (2 liters) fruit vinegar • 4 tablespoons honey

Put the Good King Henry leaves in a large (more than 2 quarts) jar. Add the vanilla powder and vinegar. Lightly screw on the lid and let stand for three weeks at 70 °F (24 °C).

Stir the honey into the vinegar. Through a fine cloth, pour the vinegar mixture into sterilized jars and seal.

Pane Nero • 4 Servings

1 pound (455 grams) flour • 1 to 2 ounces (40 grams) yeast • 1 cup water (235 milliliters) • 1 pinch herbal salt • 1 tablespoon black mustard or finely ground pure wood ash • ½ cup (115 grams) Good King Henry leaves • olive oil (for brushing)

In a large bowl mix the flour, water, yeast, salt, and mustard or ash. On a flat, floured surface, work into a dough. Cover and let rise at room temperature for 2 hours. Mix the Good King Henry leaves into the dough. Cover and let rise for 1 hour.

Preheat the oven to 350 °F (175 °C). Grease a baking sheet. Shape the dough into a loaf and place on the baking sheet. Brush with the olive oil. Bake at 350 °F (175 °C) for 50 minutes or until golden brown.

Green Amaranth (*Amaranthus lividus, A. blitum, A. viridis*)

Family: Amaranthaceae: amaranth family

Other Names: blite, pigweed, slender amaranth

Healing Properties: stops bleeding (hemostatic), regulates lung function; helps heal leukorrhea and venereal diseases

Juice: as a tonic for pregnant women, small children and the elderly

Symbolic Meaning: Huitzilopochtli, food for the gods (Native American)

Planetary Affiliation: Saturn, with Venus and Mars

There are many kinds of amaranths. They have been cultivated for at least five thousand years as leaf vegetables—mainly in America—and as "grains." The kind that is indigenous to Europe is called "blite" (from the Greek *bliton*) or "*meyer*" in German. Its stems are often prostrate, radiating from a base and forming a mat. Its dark green, sometimes reddish leaves and can be found in Europe as a garden weed or as a wild plant on pastures, roadsides, and around refuse dumps.

Green amaranth was taken into human culture relatively early in history. In the third century BC, Greek botanist Theophrastus wrote that "*bliton*" was cultivated as a vegetable and pot herb. In the first century AD herbal doctor Pedanius Dioscorides wrote: "The vegetable agrees very well with the body although it has no medicinal properties." (So he thought; others would disagree.) And in the eighth century Charlemagne listed "*Blidas*" in his orders regarding the cultivation of his land holdings. Many other early botanists and herbalists also mention the vegetable. It was not until the worldwide reach of Popeye's spinach came along that green amaranth was forgotten in Europe. Only the Greeks stayed faithful to the pot herb, who know it as "*vlita*"; they cook it and serve it with olive oil, lemon, and salt.

The Americas knew the plant as well. Central and South Americans cultivated amaranth for nearly eight thousand years; for the Aztecs it

Illustration 90. Green amaranth (Joachim Camerarius, Neuw Kreütterbuch, *1586)*

was a staple food. The young leaves are used like spinach and the ripened seeds—each plant has up to half a million shiny seeds like poppy seeds—are dried and threshed out. The seeds are roasted or steamed and/or ground and mixed with cornmeal. They are also mixed in with flat bread, baked into cakes, or cooked as porridge.

Also edible are the leaves and seeds of our garden-variety amaranth, known as foxtail amaranth, or love-lies-bleeding (*A. caudatus*). In their place of origin—Central and South America—they were regarded as sacred plants. For the Pueblo Indians they are the primeval nourishment, brought by their ancestors from the fourth world (under the earth) to the fifth world (here on this earth). The red leaves and blossoms of some kinds of foxtail amaranth are pressed and used as ceremonial body paint. Sacred cornmeal waffles (*hé we*) are also colored with these plants. The gods, the kachinas, who on their visit to earth manifest as masked dancers, carry these waffles with them as they dance and toss them to the spectators.

For the Aztecs amaranth grain was one of the most important "cereals." Ten thousand baskets, each weighing some fifty pounds, were brought each year as tribute to the imperial city, Tenochtitlán. The high priests formed figures of Huitzilopochtli, the "humming bird of the south" and son of the earth goddess, with a red paste made of the ground seeds mixed with blood. These figures, called "*zoale*," were carried ceremoniously to the pyramids. There they were broken into small pieces and distributed among the people to eat as communion, as the flesh and blood of the

gods. The Spanish priests, still under the fresh impression of the Inquisition, saw this as a satanic mockery of the sacred Christian Holy Communion. For this reason, the amaranth plant that produced these seeds
was forbidden.

The Spanish authorities were perplexed that the subjugated natives of
Mexico and Peru repeatedly found the strength to rebel.[1] At some point it
became apparent that the reason must be because ". . . they eat a certain
fruit that is no bigger than a pin head" (from a report to the Spanish
viceroy, 1560). Amaranth, which contains high-quality nutrients, was thus
considered responsible for the vitality of the Indians. (Because it contains
large amounts of lysine, an essential amino acid, it is an ideal supplement
to corn; it also contains a lot of leaf protein, vitamins, and minerals.) To
break the resistance of the Indians for good, the devilish plant was to be
exterminated. This is how it came to be that amaranth—unlike corn,
potato, and tomato, and other Native American plants—did not find its
way into our European food spectrum. At some time, though, probably
thanks to the Portuguese, amaranth found its way to India. It became a
mainstay grain (*tampala*) for quite a few hill tribes in the Mysore area
and in the Himalayas. Among other names the Indians call it "*ramdana*"
(God's gift). The use of this valuable plant as both a green vegetable and
a grain spread to Africa as well.

In India and China closely related kinds of amaranth are cultivated—
as in *chaulai,* Chinese spinach. Contrary to Dioscorides's assertion,
Ayurveda considers amaranth a healing plant; for instance, fresh juice
with honey is given to drink for chronic lung ailments such as asthma,
emphysema, and tuberculosis. It is thought that pregnant women should
enjoy the juice with honey and a pinch of cardamom during their entire
pregnancy in order to ease the birth and increase their milk. The juice is
given to infants and to the elderly, whom it helps keep fit. It is also said
to help for inner bleeding, gum and nose bleeding, excessive menstrual
bleeding, and hemorrhoids. For leukorrhea, gonorrhea, and other venereal diseases it is recommended to boil the grated root in water and drink
the concoction on an empty stomach in the morning (Bakhru 1995, 88;
Dastur 1962, 18). Nicholas Culpeper (1616–1654) also confirmed that

the plant helps to stop bleeding and with venereal diseases; he used the powdered blossoms, however, claiming it takes Saturn to rein in a naughty Venus.

In modern times the seeds of New World amaranth varieties have attracted attention as a possible means of feeding the ever-increasing world population. Indeed, the pseudo-cereal has been called a "crop of the future." We would do well to acknowledge this tasty, nourishing plant and try the leaves as a green vegetable or the delicious seeds in various ways.

Recipe

Warm Vegetable Strudel with Green Amaranth • 4 Servings

½ cup (115 grams) potatoes, peeled or unpeeled, grated
• ½ cup (115 grams) carrots, scrubbed and grated • 1 tablespoon olive oil
• ½ cup (115 grams) green amaranth, finely chopped • 1 pinch ground
nutmeg • herbal salt • pepper • 2 egg yolks, whisked
• 10 ounces (285 grams) pastry dough

FILLING: In a medium pan sauté the potatoes and carrots in the olive oil for 5 minutes. Add the amaranth and continue to sauté for a few more minutes or until tender. Transfer the vegetables to a sieve and let drip into the sink. Season with nutmeg, salt, and pepper to taste. Return the vegetables to the pan to mix in the egg yolks.

STRUDEL: Preheat the oven to 350 °F (175 °C). Grease a baking sheet. Roll out the dough until it is about ¼ inch thick. Transfer to the baking sheet. Spread the vegetables evenly on the dough, leaving a half-inch margin at the edge. Roll into a strudel shape. Brush with water. Bake at 350 °F (175 °C) for 35 minutes. Serve hot.

TIP: This dish pairs nicely with a green salad.

Knotroot or Chinese Artichoke (*Stachys sieboldii, S. tubifera, S. affinis*)

Family: Labiatae or Lamiaceae: mint or deadnettle family

Other Names: artichoke betony, Chinese artichoke, crosne, Japanese potato

Healing Properties:

Taken externally (tea): heals wounds

Taken internally: general health tonic

Symbolic Meaning: wards off witches

Planetary Affiliation: as a vegetable: Sun; as a healing plant: Saturn, Jupiter

Knotroot is a parvenu in Western vegetable gardens. It was planted commercially for the first time in the Western Hemisphere in 1887 by Vilmorin-Andrieux et Cie, a French gardening company in the small town of Crosne. As a result, the root vegetable that originated in Japan (Japanese: *chorogi;* Chinese *ts'ao shih tsan*) became a popular delicacy in France under the name "*crosne,*" or "*crosne du Japon.*" To many it tastes like a mixture of oyster plant, potato, and artichoke; it reminds others of cauliflower. The pearl white tubers grow to about one or two inches long, underground runners that become thick at the root end and look kind of like the marshmallow-like Michelin Man or Bibendum. The tubers are good grated raw into winter salads, cooked as a vegetable with meat dishes, or mixed in with wok vegetables. The skin is very thin and does not need to be peeled. In China, Korea, and Japan, where they've been cultivated for hundreds of years, they are also pickled in vinegar. Instead of starch the tubers have stachyose, a kind of sugar (tetrasaccharide), which is composed of two molecules of galactose and one molecule each of fructose and glucose.

Above ground, this East Asian member of the mint family, which German-Dutch botanist and Japan researcher Phillip Franz von Siebold first described, looks like our mints, especially lemon balm. It is planted similar to potatoes—in rows that have been well composted. Knotroot/Chinese artichoke multiplies very well, especially in a sunny spot. In the late fall one can harvest as needed. They do not keep well once harvested so it is best to harvest fresh for each use.

The use of Chinese artichoke as a vegetable is not entirely foreign to us. Since pre-Christian times a close relative was gathered as a vegetable in Europe: marsh woundwort or marsh betony (*Stachys palustris*), which also has underground runners with thick tubers. John Lightfoot (1735–1788), a British scholar versed in plant lore, mentioned marsh woundwort in 1787 as a plant gathered for food. And in 1850 this kind of betony was experimentally cultivated for its edible root.[1]

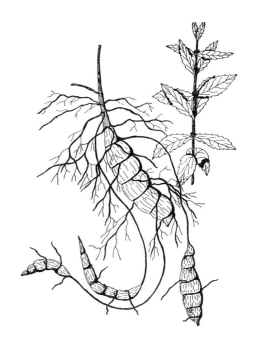

Illustration 91. Knot root

The genera *Stachys,* to which knotroot belongs, contains many formerly important healing plants, including woundwort betony, lamb's ear, and bishop's wort. They are called "*ziest*" plants in German, *ziest* from the Slavic *èist,* meaning "pure." Almost all these plants were considered cleansing and wound healing, as indicated in the name "woundwort." English herbalist John Gerard (~1545–1612) called woundwort "clown's woundwort" because of the many bruises and cuts treated with the plant that fools got from brawling in taverns. Nicholas Culpeper (1616–1654), who put it under the rule of Saturn, made syrup with it to alleviate inner bleeding and coughing blood. Native Americans drank tea made from related betonies for stomach aches and cramps; externally they used it to wash and heal wounds, and for venereal diseases they applied a poultice made with the leaves and roots. For the Germanic tribes such as the Anglo-Saxons, and later for the peasants, the perennial yellow woundwort (*Stachys recta*) was an important heal-all plant—a standard in the apothecaries of earlier times. The herb was used externally as a bath and as a poultice and internally as tea for mucous congestion, stomach cramps, jaundice, kidney and bladder ailments, menstrual ailments, nervousness, epilepsy, and "to improve the fluid balance in the body."

Betonies were also generally used to counter bad magic spells: when an ailing person bathed in a decoction of the plant, the bad magic ended up being tossed out with the bath water. It was also believed that plants from this family could purify the soul, and Anglo-Saxons of old are said to have used them against witchcraft. Presumably knotroot also possesses these qualities, and perhaps it was used similarly in East Asia. But getting to the bottom of that would be a task for ethnobotanists to tackle.

Recipe

Roasted Knotroot and Stinging Nettle • 2 to 4 Servings

4 tablespoons cold-pressed olive oil • 1 teaspoon finely ground coriander seeds • herbal salt • 1 pound (455 grams) knotroot, washed thoroughly or brushed • 1 cup (225 grams) stinging nettle leaves, very finely chopped • ½ teaspoon vanilla powder • ½ cup (115 milliliters) cream (18% fat)

In a medium pan, heat the olive oil; when hot, add the coriander and herbal salt and sauté briefly. Add the knotroot and sauté gently until tender, about 10 minutes Add the nettle leaves and vanilla and continue to sauté for about 1 minute or until nettles are cooked. Add the cream. Serve hot.

Mallow (*Malva* subspecies)

Family: Malvaceae: mallow or hibiscus family

Names of various species: *Malva alcea:* great musk mallow, hollyhock mallow; *M. nelecta:* cheeseweed, button weed, dwarf mallow; *M. sylvestris:* cheeses, fairy cheeses, high mallow, *mauve des bois,* tall mallow, wood mallow; *M. verticillata:* Chinese mallow, cluster mallow, tree mallow; *Althaea officinalis:* marsh-mallow.

Healing Properties: softens abscesses, heals burns, soothes eyes, reduces inflammation (anti-inflammatory), soothes irritation of upper air passages and intestines; as a demulcent it protects mucous membranes

Symbolic Meaning: forgiveness, charitableness, blessing, loyalty; temperance, controlling passion; spiritual vision; St. Simon (Christian); Freya (Germanic tribes)

Planetary Affiliation: Venus

The various perennial mallows, of the hibiscus family, are very rewarding members of a garden. They are easy to care for, needing only some compost and rock flour. Plus, the many different, mostly pinkish blossoming mallows number among the most beautiful wild flowers one can find. But these plants also used to be important vegetables—and should be still.

The mallow deserves much more appreciation than it's been given. For example, in ancient times in the Mediterranean region young mallow shoots were looked down on as merely a vegetable for the poor. In the Bible it is mentioned only in times of hunger: "Hence they were forced to flee into the deserts both for shelter and sustenance, and were put to sorry shifts indeed, when they cut up mallows by the bushes, and were glad to eat them, for want of food that was fit for them" (Job 30:4). In Germany it was also called "St. John's cheese" because, along with locusts, mallow was what the evangelist ate during his time in the desert. (Before the seeds develop completely, the blossoms turn into delicious tight little pods that resemble cheese wheels.) The poor fellaheen—peasant farmers—in Egypt also used to eat mallows.

However, mallows are more than mere food for the needy. The Egyptian national dish *melokhia*—finely chopped mallow leaves cooked in chicken broth with garlic browned in olive oil and cayenne pepper—is a delicacy (Hollerbach 1998, 135). Russians add young mallow leaves to soups, salads, and side dishes and they dry them for seasoning soups and sauces. They also marinate the not-quite-ripened fruits (the "cheese wheels") and add them to *soljanka, rassolnik,* and borscht. When used in salads the cheeses are cooked first; for pierogi and purée they are finely chopped or ground (Koschtschejew 1990, 61). In my experience the delicate flavor of the "cheeses" enrich any vegetable dish. The beautiful

Illustration 92. Mallow

mauve-colored blossoms often decorate my fresh garden salads, along with the also-edible orange nasturtium, blue borage, and white daisy. In China and India various subspecies (*M. sylvestris*) are cultivated for soup vegetables. In fact, the giant, seven-foot-tall Chinese mallow (*M. verticillata*) has been cultivated as a vegetable for so long that no wild varieties remain.

Archeological finds in Lusatia, eastern Germany, indicate that mallows were intensively gathered during the last Ice Age. The Germanic tribal people planted mallows in their "kitchen or leek gardens" alongside various other greens. The taller varieties, such as the *Malva sylvestris,* served as both food and fiber. As with hemp and nettles, bast fibers of mallow were processed into rope and cloth. In some parts of Europe *Malva sylvestris* is still referred to as "hemp mallow." (The mallow Queensland hemp has bast fibers that are even stronger than jute.) As a cloth plant—a "woman's" plant—the Germanic tribes dedicated the mallow to the goddess Freya. Naturally these tribes also used the plant for healing purposes, including for diseases sent by "water elves" that we no longer know today (Wheelwright 1974, 103). Anglo-Saxons are said to have planted common mallow on their gravesites; indeed, in Lower Austria mallow is still included in the selection of obligatory graveyard plants.

For the Greeks and Romans the mallow (from the Greek *malakos* = soft) was a symbol for gentleness, mildness, and control over passion. Galenic doctors describe the mallow as cooling and as an anaphrodisiac. This interpretation predestined the flower to become a Christian symbol, one of forgiveness: just as the muculent plant softens and heals hardened boils, it can also forgive the sins of a hardened soul. And all of the mallows, especially the hollyhock mallow (*M. alcea*), were considered good for the eyes. In the Middle Ages mallow was also called "*Herba Simeonis*" (St. Simon's herb) because the venerable old blind man cleared his dulled eyes by rinsing them with tea made of the roots; he later blessed the plant that had enabled him to recognize the baby Jesus as the Messiah (Luke 2:22–40). Even today country people in Europe dig out mallow roots on St. Simon's Day (October 8) before sunrise to make an amulet against eye disease or for a decoction for eye treatment.

Toward the end of the Middle Ages, the mallow was part of a test for virginity: a mallow on which a girl was made to urinate was kept for three days; if it dried up within that time, she was deemed "no longer a maiden, but had rolled in the clover aplenty." The same process was applied to test a woman's fertility: if the mallow dried up within three days, she was infertile; if the plant remained green, she was deemed able to have children (Baechtold-Staubli 1987, 1559).

Nicholas Culpeper (1616–1654) put the mallow plant under the rule of Venus. He recommended cooking the unripe seed capsules into a decoction to use as both an enema and as a cure for painful urination. In traditional healing lore, mallow poultices were known to have an anti-inflammatory, softening, soothing effect in treating wounds and burns. The plant still has a place of honor in modern phytotherapy, its mucilage used to soothe mucinous tissue in the air passage (nose and throat) and in the digestive tract (stomach, intestines, urinary organs, and rectum). The mucus has also the effect of smothering bacteria.

One of the mallows—the marshmallow (*Althea officinalis*)—has an especially thick, slimy root. Apothecaries in Europe made it into a syrup for coughing, intestinal ailments, and uroliths. But the French took it in a different direction, creating from it a foamy concoction cooked with egg white, sugar, rose water, and spices that was sold in candy stores as "*pâté de gimauve*"—forerunner of the campfire-toasted treat still enjoyed today. However, unfortunately, nowadays the foamy substance is made of sugar, corn starch, whipped gelatin, and artificial flavors and colors.

Toward the end of the nineteenth century the mallow made cultural history once more when its delicate color became fashionable after British "Royals" took a special liking to it. Thereafter, curtains, carpets, table-cloths, clothes, even writing paper were all colored mauve—"*mauve*" being the French word for mallow. And as for the mallow in the language of flowers: to give someone mallows is to say, "I value you as my dearest friend."

Recipes

Mallow Blossoms with Dandelion Salad • 2 Servings

1 cup (225 grams) tender dandelion leaves • 2 tablespoons mallow blossoms • Sauce: 1 tablespoon sesame seeds, roasted and ground • 1 tablespoon sumac • 2 tablespoons hazelnut oil • 4 tablespoons vegetable broth • dab of mustard • sea salt • pepper

In a serving bowl, mix the sesame seeds, sumac, hazelnut oil, and vegetable broth. Add the dandelion leaves and mallow blossoms and toss until evenly covered. Serve.

Mallow Blossom and Onion Cream Cheese Spread • 4 Servings

2 cups (455 grams) onions, finely chopped • 2 tablespoons olive oil • ground coriander • sea salt • 1 cup (225 grams) cream cheese • 4 tablespoons mallow blossoms

In a large pan sauté the onions in the olive oil for about ten minutes or until golden brown. Season with the coriander and salt to taste. Let cool for about 30 minutes. Add the cream cheese and mallow blossoms. Stir until combined.

TIP: This also makes an excellent vegetable dip.

New Zealand Spinach (*Tetragonia tetragonioides, T. expansa*)

Family: Aizoaceae: ice plant family or fig-marigold family

Other Names: Botany Bay spinach, Cook's cabbage, sea spinach, tetragon, warrigal greens

Healing Properties: juice reduces inflammation (anti-inflammatory); heals general ailments and wounds

Planetary Affiliation: Mercury, Saturn

New Zealand spinach belongs to the ice plant family (*Aizoaceae*). These plants, most of which are found in South Africa, are usually succulent. The most well known of this family are lithops, or "living stones." If they are not in blossom and are seen in dried-out streams, they can hardly be distinguished from rounded stones. Herbal astrology puts these plants under the rule of Mercury due to their succulence and their hardy, concentrated life energy; because of their connection to rocky, dry biotopes, they also come under the rule of Saturn.

For a long time New Zealand spinach served as a wild edible plant for the aboriginals in Australia and Tasmania, as well as for the Maori of New Zealand. The latter use the plant as an antiscorbutic, that is, to prevent scurvy, and the red berries as ink or dye. But it was officially "discovered" to the rest of the world in 1770 by Sir Joseph Banks (1743–1820), who was with Captain James Cook in the Queen Charlotte Sound in New Zealand. They brought the plant to England, where it was planted as an exotic vegetable in Kew Gardens. (Incidentally, these gardens were established to showcase all the plants found in the empire "on which the sun never sets.")

This very nutritious vegetable tastes like spinach, but has none of the oxalic acid found in spinach. Very little is known about the healing properties of the plant. One may assume that, like most ice plant family members, the juice is antiseptic. The Zulus in southeast Africa certainly use the juice of these succulents for skin infections and burns, and also as a gargle for tonsillitis.

The New Zealand spinach produces abundantly and likes warmth and good humus. As an ice plant it is specialized to take dry weather, but it grows joyously only when it gets plenty of water. It takes the seeds six weeks to germinate. It is best to sow them in February inside or in a hot bed. Only two to three plants are enough for the needs of one family. They can be planted out after all danger of frost is past (in northern Europe that would be mid-May, the time of the "Frost Saints"). They need plenty of room. Though slow to start, they will grow new shoots continuously until October.

Recipe

New Zealand Spinach Patties with Savory Butter • 2 to 4 Servings

Butter: ½ cup (115 grams) butter, soft • 2 tablespoons herb such as parsley, thyme, or marjoram, finely chopped • Patties: 1 cup (225 grams) chickpeas, soaked and sprouted for two days • ½ cup (115 grams) New Zealand Spinach leaves • 2 ounces (60 grams) oat flakes • 1 white or yellow onion, finely chopped • 4 tablespoons olive oil • herbal salt • pepper • 2 pinches ground coriander seeds

Butter: In a small bowl, stir butter until soft. Add hedge garlic or other savory; season with salt and pepper to taste. Chill in the refrigerator. Patties: In a medium bowl mix the chickpeas, spinach, and oat flakes. In a medium pan, sauté the onion in 2 tablespoons of the olive oil until golden brown. Stir into the chickpea mixture until well combined. Season with salt and pepper to taste. Add the remaining olive oil to the pan. Form the chickpea mixture into patties about ½-inch thick. Fry in the olive oil until brown and crispy, about 15 minutes. Add a dab of hedge garlic butter to each patty and serve hot.

Oyster Plant (*Tragopogon porrifolius*)

Family: Compositae: composite, daisy, or sunflower family

Other Names: common salsify, goat's beard, Jack-go-to-bed-at-noon, Jerusalem star, noon flower, purple salsify, vegetable oyster

Healing Properties: maintains liver functions (tonic)

Symbolic Meaning: loving devotion to the light of life

Planetary Affiliation: Jupiter, moon

The meadow salsify or meadow goat's beard (*T. pratensis*)—which grows wild in Europe and as an invasive plant in the United States—has bright yellow, star-shaped blossoms. As the blooms are only open in the mornings, the English nicknamed them "Jack-go-to-bed-at-noon." The flower heads follow the sun like chicories do, making them "brides of the sun" as well. These plants traditionally symbolize the soul's longing for deliverance, the longing for the "spiritual sun."

A close relative of this early-to-bed flower is the cultivated oyster plant. Although ancient Greeks cultivated the delicate plant, and it was grown in sixteenth-century gardens, few people today are familiar with it; the seeds are only found in rare seed stores. Like its cousin, it also retires at noon. All parts of both the wild and cultivated oyster plant—root, leaf and reddish-purple blossoms—are edible. The roots taste slightly like oysters, which is how the plant got its name. The young leek-shaped leaves are good raw in salads or cooked as a vegetable; the buds are tasty added to mixed vegetables, and the roots can be eaten like salsify. (The wild forbear of this ancient vegetable comes from the Mediterranean area, where the sweet, milky taproot was roasted as a vegetable or added to soups.) The plant is a biennial, its roots harvested at the end of the first year. They store well in sand in a cool space over the winter. Like with so many other vegetables, European settlers brought it with them to North America, where it quickly became a weed.

The oyster plant is very nutritious. In Southern Germany there is a saying: "*Habermark macht d'Bube stark*" (Oyster plant pulp makes boys

Illustration 93. Oyster plant

strong). Nicholas Culpeper (1616–1654) prescribed oyster plant as a liver and gall bladder tonic. (He put it under the rule of Jupiter because this planetary god is responsible for liver functions.) Culpeper wrote: "The roots cooked like parsnips, with butter, are good for cold, watery stomachs." He also recommended it for consumption. Leonhart Fuchs (1501–1566) also mentioned how good the plant is for the liver, noting: "The juice helps greatly for pains in the side."

Over the last century the oyster plant's place in our gardens has been almost entirely supplanted by salsify—and wrongfully so! It's a nutritious vegetable whose lovely blossoms should once again have a place of honor in our soil and at our table. And as seeds are available from organic seed banks and vendors—like Baker Creek Heirloom Seeds—there's no reason why the oyster plant couldn't reign again.

Recipe

Oyster Plant Goulash • 4 Servings

4 tablespoons butter • 2 pounds (905 grams) white or yellow onion, finely chopped • 6 bay leaves • 1 teaspoon caraway seeds • 2 cloves • 1¼ cups (285 milliliters) red wine • 1 quart (945 milliliters) vegetable broth • 3 tablespoons paprika • herbal salt • pepper • fresh marjoram leaves • 3½ cups (800 grams) oyster plant, cubed • ¼ cup (60 grams) chives, finely chopped • ¾ cup (175 grams) sour cream

Warm the butter in a large pan with lid. Add the onions, bay leaves, coriander, and cloves and gently sauté, covered, for about 30 minutes, stirring occasionally. Add red wine and vegetable broth. Season with salt, pepper, paprika, and marjoram to taste. Add the oyster plant and simmer about 25 minutes or until the vegetable is tender. In a separate small bowl, stir the chives into the sour cream. Stir this mixture into the goulash and serve hot.

TIP: This goulash pairs nicely with potatoes.

Parsley Root (*Petroselinum crispum covar. radicosum*)

Family: Apiaceae or Umbelliferae: umbellifer or carrot family

Other Names: common parsley, Dutch parsley, garden parsley, Hamburg parsley, rock parsley

Healing Properties: arouses male desire (aphrodisiac), stimulates menstruation (emmenagogue), promotes urination (diuretic), dissolves uroliths

Symbolic Meaning: prostitution, manly strength, St. Peter, Archemorus

Planetary Affiliation: Mercury

While most everyone knows parsley—with its dark green, aromatic, feathered or crinkled leaves—parsley root is hardly known at all. Romans used the delicious leaves as seasoning but also, like we do nowadays, as attractive garnish. And, since it was believed the plant both neutralizes the smell of wine and counters drunkenness, the Romans also munched on the curly leaves. (There must be something to that: during my boyhood days growing up in Germany, we'd pick parsley to eat after we'd made off with a few bottles of beer from the local brewery—which would have guaranteed us a whipping at home—and no one ever suspected.) In Germany the plant is often called "Hamburg parsley" or "Dutch parsley," names given back in the sixteenth century in Northern Germany. The plant also became quite popular in eighteenth-century England, where it was believed to help with bladder ailments and digestive problems.

Parsley cultivation can be traced back five thousand years to the eastern Mediterranean area. Given this long history, it's not surprising that parsley, like with most old cultigens, has earned countless tales and superstitions. Rock parsley (Gr. *petros* = rock, *selinon* = celery) in particular, as with celery, is associated with death and resurrection—or the victory of overcoming death—as well as with masculine virility. According to Greek legend, the parsley plant sprang up from the blood drops of baby Archemorus. As the story goes, seven wandering warriors asked the child's mother for directions; she left her infant in the grass for a few minutes

312   A Curious History of Vegetables

to show them the way, returning to discover a monstrous snake had devoured the baby. This image—a huge snake eating an innocent—symbolizes the wild power of nature, the power of the chthonic black goddess. This is the power of chaos that rips people out of their normal, everyday lives; it is the power of sexuality and the power of death. According to Greek lore, the true hero (*hérōs*) is the one with the strength and courage to defy both the horrible serpent and the black goddess of death. As such, parsley is not only a symbol of death, and thus appropriate decoration for graves, but it is also a symbol of the victory of life overcoming chaos. It is fitting for a hero like Hercules to wear a crown of parsley foliage. And in Nemea—where Heracles killed a monster lion that was impervious to the weapons of mortals—competitive games were held every two years in honor of the infant Archemorus. Parsley foliage was woven into the horses' manes so they would run faster, and, like Hercules, the winners were decorated with plant's aromatic leaves.

> Parsley helps a man mount his horse, but it helps a woman end up under the ground.

This adage refers to the plant as an aphrodisiac for men, but, interestingly, for women—in strong dosage—it is an abortive. As such we once again encounter, as we did with both the carrot and celery, a gland-activating umbellifer.

When ancient Romans wished to imply that a man was impotent, they'd say, "He needs some parsley," believing parsley could resurrect the "little hero." Throughout the Middle Ages the streets where prostitutes plied their trade were called "parsley lanes." But women during the witch trials in Europe strove to avoid the "parsley spirit," the *Maître persil* or *Peterling*, as he was a horny devil, not to be trusted.

Similarly, traditional lore warned young girls to beware of the irresistible amorous drive of the parsley. A young lady should not give away any parsley, for such "would give away her luck in love"—though the luck lost from accidentally-given parsley could be regained by stealing a sprig from someone else's garden. According to old German folklore, when a young damsel has difficulty finding a dance partner she is deemed to be "picking parsley"; when a young man finally asks her for a dance, she has "gotten rid of her parsley."

A chant on the fulfillment of love, still widely known in Germany, also involves the aromatic herb. It goes something like this:

> *Parsley green for the soup,*
> *grows in my garden,*
> *[Girl's name] is the bride and*
> *she shan't wait much longer.*
> *Behind the elderberry bush*
> *she gave her sweetheart a kiss.*
> *white wine, red wine,*
> *the wedding tomorrow will be very fine.*

As this plant—which can be abortive for women but a "hero-builder" in men—has more than a bit of an uncanny air about it, one should take care using it. In rural England it is advised to not think of one's sweetheart when cutting parsley—else one risks betrayal in love. In Devonshire it was suspected that certain uncanny spirits hover around the parsley bed; for that reason it was taboo to transplant parsley, as such could unleash misfortunes upon the transplanter. Hence the saying, "Transplant parsley, transplant sorrow." And in gardens where parsley flourishes, it is said the missus wears the pants.

When sowing parsley, one should observe the moon's phase: for normal parsley the waxing moon is best, but for the root it should be waning, as then the energy goes downward into the root. The seeds of parsley and parsley root take a very long time to germinate. For that reason it was said they to go to hell and back six or nine times before they could sprout. In Catholic regions it was said they had to go all the way to Rome to ask the pope for permission to germinate—and that would take at least six weeks. In France it was said that the seeds would germinate sooner if notorious liars sowed them, as the seeds would sprout as fast as the lies caught up with the liar. In some places it was advised that urinating in the row before sowing the seeds would speed up the germination process. Also, one should

Illustration 94. St. Peter, patron saint of parsley

never mention anyone's name while sowing without risking that person's death. Of course, traditional folk superstitions considered that particular magical practice one of the best ways to get rid of a rival in love or a brutal husband. On the other hand, if the parsley that eventually comes up is lush and profuse, it was believed there would soon be a baby in the family.

In the Slavic countries parsley generally has a better reputation, as it is believed to keep bad spirits and witches at bay. For this reason in Galicia, Poland, a bride carries bread and parsley under her arm on the way to church. In Moravia in the Czech Republic, it is thought parsley sown on St. John's Day can counter the witchcraft that would harm cows. Parsley and garlic wrapped in a linen cloth can also protect a woman in childbed from witchcraft.

While parsley has been used as a diuretic, too much of it can irritate the kidneys. The leaves, root, and especially the seeds, which are schizocarp fruits, contain an essential oil—"green of parsley oil," or apiol—which stimulates the uterus as well as the kidneys. For that reason it is used to activate a "belated menstruation": in other words, it was used as an abortive for unwanted pregnancies. In the Middle Ages the seeds were used as an abortive. As such, pregnant women shouldn't eat too much parsley. Because parsley seed stimulates the blood circulation in the abdominal organs, causing swelling in erectile tissue, it works for men as a sort of plant Viagra (Van den Toorn 2002, 113).

Parsley has even been suspected of being a psychedelic—in any case hippies used to stretch marijuana with dried parsley leaves. Indeed, the natural organic compound myristicin is toxic to the central nervous system and can cause dizziness. It was used as one of the ingredients for illegal "herbal ecstasy." As modern-day ethnobotanist Christian Rätsch has noted, some kinds of parsley have more myristicin than others (1998, 431). The essential oils, apiol, and myristicin are mainly present in the seeds (≤6 percent) and hardly in the root (0.5 percent). High doses of apiol (contained in the seeds) cause fatty liver disease and hemorrhage of the mucus membranes.

But anyone using parsley root in the kitchen needn't worry about these pharmacological issues—no dangerous dosage can be reached with the amount used in a meal. And this is good news, since the white, carrot-like taproot tastes especially good in stews and mixed vegetable dishes. As for cultivating it, parsley root needs old, ripe compost and the kind of care that its cousin, the parsnip, also needs. And as it is frost-hardy, it can be left in the garden over the winter.

Recipe

Parsley Root with Coriander Sauce • 4 Servings

½ cup (115 milliliters) vegetable broth • 1 cup (225 grams) leeks, finely chopped • 1 tablespoon ground coriander seeds • 1 tablespoon honey • a few drops tamari (or soy sauce) • 1 pound (455 grams) parsley roots • 2 tablespoons olive oil • ½ cup (115 milliliters) cream (18% fat) • 3 tablespoons sesame seeds • sea salt • pepper

Preheat the oven to 380 °F (200 °C). In an oven proof dish, add the vegetable broth, leeks, ground coriander, and honey and mix well. Season with tamari (or soy sauce), salt, and pepper to taste. Bring to a boil. Add the parsley roots and stir. Bake, covered, in the oven at 380 °F (200 °C) for 30 minutes or until roots are cooked but still firm. Stir in the olive oil, cream, and sesame seeds. Bake for another 25 minutes or until well done. Serve hot.

Parsnip Chervil (*Chaerophyllum bulbosum*)

Family: Apiaceae; formerly Umbelliferae: umbellifer or carrot family

Other Names: bulbous chervil, tuberous-rooted chervil, turnip-rooted chervil

Healing Aspects: unknown to date

Symbolic Meaning: elegant indulgence; draws light and air energy into the cold, watery element

Planetary Affiliation: Mercury; root: Jupiter

Parsnip chervil is an almost completely forgotten vegetable. It was popular in the European Middle Ages—before the reign of the potato—because it is both tasty and very nutritious; it contains protein and up to 57 percent starch. The short, thick gray-brown root (botanically speaking the vegetable is a root crown, or hypocotyl) has whitish, yellow flesh that has an aromatic flavor similar to chestnuts—though when eaten raw after a frost it tastes more like hazelnuts. For these reasons the plant was called "earth chestnut" (*Erdkastanie*) and "earth nut" (*Erdnuss*) in German. The flavor improves if the root is left to age after harvesting, during which time much of the starch turns to sugar; indeed, it tastes best around Christmas time.

Parsnip chervil can be found growing in the wild in Austria, the Czech Republic, and eastern Europe, and even into the Ural and Altai Mountains. It is also said to grow in Iran and Turkey. It grows in moist soil between bushes, on the edge of forests, and alongside rivers and streams. As it does not generally grow in western Europe, whenever it is found there it's believed to have either escaped a cultivated garden or to be a relict out of a cloister garden. In 1580 botanist Carolus Clusius incidentally mentioned that it was sold at the market in Vienna as a root vegetable;[1] the plant is also mentioned in herbal books of the time. In the middle of the nineteenth century, after the potato blight had drastically reduced potato harvests and famine was widespread, parsnip chervil enjoyed a brief reprise. For example, in 1846 France reintroduced *cerfeuil tubéreux* as a potato substitute—but in the following decades it was again forgotten. Only some French gourmet cooks held on to it as a delicacy.

The *Jeunes Restaurateurs d'Europe*, famous Michelin-starred chefs, make soups, chutneys, and ravioli with the tangy-sweet tuber; it's said to taste especially good with lamb and red wine. But it can also be prepared very simply and eaten with just salt, pepper, and butter.

Parsnip chervil is an umbellifer member, a family with some 3,500 species, divided up into 300 varieties. The name "Chaerophyllum" (from the Greek *chairein* = to delight, *phyllon* = leaves) leads us to assume that the cataloguing botanists particularly admired these plants' feathery leaves. The umbellifer family has a wide range of opposing characteristics: from tasty vegetables (carrots, parsnips, parsley root, and celery) and seasonings (caraway, parsley, anise, coriander, and chervil)[2] to poisonous plants like poison hemlock and water hemlock.[3] The Chaerophyllum branch also covers the entire spectrum; there are thirty-five kinds in Europe alone. On one side is edible parsnip chervil and Siberian parsnip chervil, and on the other side poisonous varieties like rough chervil (*C. temulum*) and widespread hairy chervil (*C. hirsutum*) that contain the volatile alkaloid chaerophyllin and other lesser-known poisonous substances that attack the nervous and digestive systems. For example, farm animals can go lame from eating the poisonous varieties.

Although the leaves of parsnip chervil also contain traces of this alkaloid, there are no cases of poisoning known among humans since the substance is neutralized when cooked. There are even reports that the young leaves were used in soups in earlier times. But this umbellifer is unknown as a healing plant, even by homeopaths—despite the fact that, generally speaking, umbellifers influence the glandular system, or, as anthroposophic doctors say, they "help the astral body work on the ether body." The signature of the plant tells us that it can bring cosmic warmth down into cold, heavy regions (like water and earth). Parsnip chervil pulls blossom-like influences down into the root, which as a result becomes fruity and aromatic (Pelikan 1975, 69). If the plant can do that in the macrocosm, then it may be similarly able in the human microcosm. There are likely healing properties hidden inside this umbellifer.

My first personal experience with parsnip chervil was rather embarrassing. I was leading a plant excursion near Vienna when we came upon an umbellifer growing on the bank of a creek; it was in full bloom and had feathery leaves. The stems looked similar to those of poison hemlock—with which I am fully familiar—with its spotted reddish purple, slightly frosted stems; the bottom part of the stalks, though, had stiff, coarse, whitish bristles. The stem nodes of the mysterious plant were swollen. When the participants of the excursion asked me what kind of a plant it was, I muttered it must be a local kind of hemlock. (The plant identification book I carried offered no help.) Glancing at me with a look that said, *What kind of a plant expert are you?*, an elder participant went on to explain that the plant was parsnip chervil, not hemlock, and it was very edible.

Parsnip chervil is not as easy to cultivate as other vegetables are, which is likely one of the reasons it's not often found in today's vegetable gardens. It is sown in the fall; like carrots and parsnips, the seeds are light-dependent germinators, so they must be sown right on the surface and only lightly covered with soil, then pressed down gently. The plant is also a frost-germinator, meaning its seeds sprout in the spring only if they've experienced a frost. One can stratify the seeds by sowing them in pots and leaving them, protected in sand, outside over the winter, later sowing them out in March. Parsnip chervil thrives in loamy soil and does not mind a shady, moist location. It grows best in a companion planting situation with onions or leeks; this keeps the carrot flies away. Toward the end of July, when the leaves have died off, one can harvest the roots or even leave them in the ground—as long as no hungry rodents are around. If harvested, they should be kept in a very cool sand pile—best if near freezing—so they can mature in the after-ripening process. When the time comes to eat them they can be prepared as one would cook parsnips.

There is a more productive variety with a bigger tuber: the Siberian parsnip chervil (*C. prescottii*), which is grown in Sweden, Finland, and Siberia. In earlier times this plant was both cultivated and grew wild in potato and grain fields. The yellow root is bigger but is less aromatic, and tastes more like parsnips than like chestnuts. It seems that this variety is relatively unknown in North America and only available in special nurseries and rare seed stores. It also seems not (yet?) to have developed into an invasive weed—but only time will tell.

Shungiku or Garland Chrysanthemum
(*Glebionis coronaria, Chrysanthemum coronarium*)

Family: Compositae:, daisy or aster family

Other Names: chop suey green, crown daisy, edible chrysanthemum, Japanese green, garland-chrysanthemum

Healing Properties: blossoms: reduces high blood pressure, soothes eyes, reduces headaches, heals infections; **leaves:** clears skin ailments and acne, heals abscesses

Symbolic Meaning: queen of flowers, longevity, autumn, reclusiveness, beauty in difficult circumstances, commemoration of the dead (East Asia); nobility, Christ, sun god, oracle flower, St. John (Europe)

Planetary Affiliation: sun, Venus

This garland chrysanthemum that we grow as an ornamental flower is cherished in eastern Asia as an aromatic leaf vegetable. It is part of the Japanese national dish, *sukiyaki,* which is made with tofu, strips of meat, onions, bamboo shoots, and other vegetables cooked in soy sauce, rice wine (*sake*), and sugar. The buds of the chrysanthemum, also known as shungiku, are pickled in vinegar. In China the young leaves are added to chop suey (the Cantonese *shap sui* = mixed together) along with bean sprouts, bamboo sprouts, onions, mushrooms, fish or meat, soy sauce, and water chestnuts.[1]

This plant germinates well and grows quickly, especially when supplied with enough water, sun, and good garden soil. As it grows quite tall, it should be placed where it won't shade other crops. The young sprouts can be eaten raw in salads, soups, and mixed vegetables; they taste especially good with tomato salad. If one does not tear out the shallow roots when harvesting the sprouts, they will continue growing new shoots. Shungiku begins to blossom in the late fall, when the days get shorter, and will continue to flower profusely until the air gets too frosty. (It was a joyful experience for me the first time they bloomed in my garden, as the many bright yellow blossoms transformed my vegetable garden into a flower garden. I also enjoyed the flowers as garnishing for salads.) Shungiku

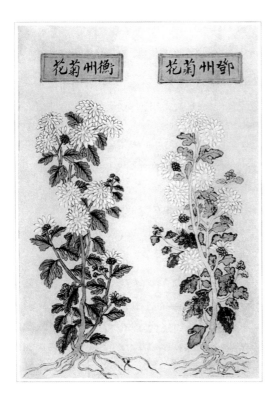

Illustration 95. Chrysanthemums (from the Ben cao gang mu, *an encyclopedia of premodern Chinese pharmaceutical knowledge edited by Li Shizhen, sixteenth century)*

can take quite cold weather. It can be sown fairly early in the year and then in intervals of two weeks. It is easy to keep some seeds for sowing out the next year.

This golden flower belongs to the composite family. In Europe, the most well-known member of the chrysanthemum genus is the oxeye daisy. Children like to put the flowers in their hair, and it's a favorite for the playful "He loves me, he loves me not" pastime. This was the flower poor Gretchen plucked, considering this very question, in Johann Wolfgang von Goethe's 1808 tragic play *Faust*. For the Celts and Germanics of long ago, oxeye was a symbol for the sun; it was the "day's eye" (daisy), that is, Baldur's eye (the pre-Christian sun god); later it came to symbolize Christ's eye. The young shoots of the oxeye are also edible, as modern-day wild food expert François Couplan informs us (Couplan 1997, 40).

The corn marigold, or corn daisy (*C. segetum*), which is also cultivated as a garden vegetable in Southeast Asia, is nearly identical to shungiku, especially its golden yellow blossoms. In the nineteenth century corn marigold was called a "bad flower" because it came to Europe from the

Ukraine as an aggressive invasive plant. It spread like wildfire in the grain fields, and was fought viciously in Germany and Scandinavia. In Germany, names like "*Groschenblume,*" "*Hellerblume,*" and "*Batzenkraut*"—all of which refer to money—remind of the fees that farmers had to pay if government inspectors found even one sample of this alien plant in their fields. Sadly, our modern agricultural practices and herbicides have brought this once-invasive plant to near extinction. Nowadays the pretty flower has become so rare it's been put under nature conservation.

Illustration 96. Chrysanthemum exhibit in old Japan

The Mediterranean costmary, or balsam herb (*Chrysanthemum balsamita*), also belongs to this family. First dedicated to the goddess, it was later attributed to the Holy Mother; churchgoers often used one of the leaves as a bookmark for their Bible. The fresh leaves once seasoned soup, lamb roast, lentils, and herb liquors.

Various chrysanthemums, such as the Dalmatian pyrethrum, have active ingredients that are harmful to insects, fish, and amphibians—but not to warm-blooded mammals. For example, pyrethrum is the active ingredient in mosquito coils used to keep mosquitos out of tents. Since the pyrethrum in the Dalmatian chrysanthemum is an effective insecticide, it is sometimes used by organic gardeners against pest infestation.

Practically all the showy ornamental chrysanthemums or mums originated in East Asia. There, this "queen of flowers" has the same symbolic value as the lotus in Southern Asia or the rose or lily in the West. The plant decorates temples and shrines, and is a motif for artists painting porcelain, embroidering silk, or carving and sculpting in wood and metal. In Japan the sixteen-petaled chrysanthemum is the emperor's flower: it is found on the coat of arms, embroidered on royal kimonos, and engraved on the emperor's sword. In China and Japan the chrysanthemum festival is elaborately celebrated on the ninth day of the ninth month. The twin of the spring festival of cherry and plum blossoms, the fall festival symbolizes the end of the year, the turning from a life of toil back to a simpler life, the blessed time of rest found in winter. Chinese poet Tao Yuanming (365–427) wrote:

> Autumn chrysanthemum in magnificent bloom,
> I picked them in the morning dew
> To take their purity into my soul as
> I sit here alone with my glass of wine.

The golden flower symbolizes beauty maintained in a world full of haste and meanness. It reminds us of friends and ancestors who are gone and whispers gently of the love that transcends death. The flower is also a symbol of longevity (Beuchert 1995, 49). The flower is so noble that the Chinese empress did not find it below her dignity to cultivate the flowers for the palace herself. A court lady wrote: "Every day all of the court ladies and eunuchs accompanied the empress to the western shore of the lake. According to her instructions we cut small branches from the young plants and put them into flowerpots. When there was heavy rain her majesty ordered the eunuchs to shelter the chrysanthemums with delicate straw mats" (Tergit 1963, 130).

At the fall chrysanthemum festival, the Japanese drink a cup of sake with a golden blossom in it. It is a sacred rite that confirms their loyalty and allegiance to the emperor. The custom goes back to when twelfth-century Emperor Go-Toba gave his loyal knight Kusunoki Masashige such a drink as a sign of appreciation. Since those days of old, the Japanese and Chinese have cultivated thousands of wonderful kinds of chrysanthemums, some of which found their way to Europe via a merchant from Marseille during the French Revolution. Chrysanthemums have been cultivated in the royal gardens of Versailles since 1838.

The native European chrysanthemum, the pretty oxeye daisy, was once used as balsam for wounds, and as a diuretic and sudorific tea. Nicholas Culpeper (1616–1654), who put the plant under the rule of Venus, advised using the plant for "swollen and hot testicles." Naturally, in Eastern Asian medicine both the wild and the cultivated plant are also used medicinally. Indeed, the flower was mentioned in *Shennong Bencaojing,* believed to be the oldest herbal book, written

Illustration 97. Chrysanthemum in a basket (Japanese sketch)

by the third-century BC emperor Shennong, venerated as the father of medicine; it underlines the significance of the chrysanthemum that its use is traced to this mythical figure. The carefully dried flowers (in Chinese *ju hua*) are cooling, antibacterial, and detoxifying. In Chinese folk healing the flower is used for headaches, dizziness, and sleeplessness;[2] combined with the blossoms of Japanese honeysuckle (*Lonicera japonica*) it is given for high blood pressure, angina pectoris, and arteriosclerosis (Foster and Chongxi 1992, 194).

In eastern Asia the chrysanthemum has played a role in household medicine for a very long time. It is used for headaches, bad breath, bitter taste in the mouth, and other diseases that come from "cool wind." Cooked, warm blossoms are placed on tired, red eyes—such as after one has spent hours at the computer. Fresh, crushed leaves are applied for skin ailments like acne, boils, and eczema; in the winter dried leaves are scalded with hot water for the same purpose. The Chinese sleep on pillows stuffed with dried, aromatic chrysanthemum blossoms. Wine with chrysanthe-mum blossoms is considered strengthening. In Southern California the plant *Chrysanthemum coronarium* has become what some consider an invasive plant—possibly escaped the garden of Asian immigrants. But is this a problem? With its bright yellow flowers, the bloom can only beau-tify the countryside.

Recipe

Green Asparagus with Fried Shungiku • 2 to 4 Servings

1 pound (455 grams) asparagus, cut in 1-inch pieces • 4 tablespoons olive oil • ½ cup (115 milliliters) white wine • 4 tablespoons (50 grams) cream (18% fat) • sea salt • ¾ cup (175 grams) shungiku • good-quality, neutral-tasting (such as sunflower) oil for deep frying • tamari or soy sauce

Add the olive oil to a medium lidded pan. Sauté the asparagus, covered, for 5 minutes or until tender. Add the white wine and cream. Season with salt to taste. Simmer for 10 minutes. Deep-fry the shungiku. Serve the asparagus with the frittered shungiku alongside the tamari or soy sauce.

Skirret (*Sium sisarum*)

Family: Apiaceae or Umbelliferae: umbellifer or carrot family

Other Names: crummock, sugar root, water parsnip

Healing Properties: cleanses system, increases strength, promotes urination (diuretic); ideal for hepatitis

Symbolic Meaning: joviality, sweetness of life

Planetary Affiliation: Venus, Jupiter

Like the carrot, the parsnip, and parsley, skirret is a member of the umbellifer family. It has its origins in Asia, with wild forms presumably from the Caucasus to Siberia. This root vegetable probably came to central Europe from Russia during the Middle Ages or even during Roman times; from Europe it traveled to America with European settlers. In England tasty skirret or *skirwort* (sugar root) dishes and pies first appeared during the time of King Henry VIII, who was known to live with pomp and grandeur. And though it is generally believed that Roman emperor Tiberius enjoyed the delicate roots, "*siser*"— and had them imported from the Rhine provinces in Germany—this is probably a mix-up; since skirret is not indigenous to Germany, the records most likely refer to parsnips, which we do know Tiberius imported. As mentioned before, there was not much distinction made among the various edible roots, so the same names could refer to many different umbellifers; sadly, sometimes our cultural history leads reach dead-ends.

In any case, skirret was a hit in Shakespeare's time. A tasty recipe for skirret pie says to dredge the cooked roots in egg yolk seasoned with salt, ginger, cinnamon, and nutmeg and then bake them with hard-boiled eggs and peeled chestnuts in a well-buttered, covered baking dish. One can also color the peeled cooked roots with spinach juice and then sauté them in butter, sugar, and orange juice and season with exotic spices. John Evelyn (1620–1706), long-time counselor of the chefs in the British royal palace, raved about "skirret milk"—cooked roots puréed with cream or milk in which ham has been cooked, and then baked with eggs, sugar, nutmeg flower, and other exotic spices (Rohde 1969, 156).

Leonhart Fuchs (1501–1566), German professor of medicine and botany, described "*sisern*" as "delicate and sweet in taste, similar to orange roots," by which he meant carrots. The roots are "delicate to eat, good for the stomach, cause urine to flow, and support a good appetite." The plant also has medicinal value: "The dried, powdered seeds put in wine are good for spasms and stomach cramps. They make married folks interested in each other in bed, strengthen the heart,[1] and are useful for those who have had to vomit very much." The juice of the cultivated plant can also be mixed in goat's milk and taken for "leaking intestines," a condition we know as "diarrhea."

Illustration 98. Skirret (Joachim Camerarius, Neuw Kreütterbuch, 1586)

The astrological doctor Nicholas Culpeper (1616–1654) was also enthusiastic about skirret, which in his opinion has a taste superior to carrots. He considered the plant "diuretic and cleansing" and put it under the rule of Venus, who rules over the urinary organs. "The root . . . frees the bladder from slimy phlegm. It "helps liver disorders and jaundice." With its diuretic, "opening" and gland-stimulating properties, it joins all umbellifers—parsnip, celery, dill, lovage, coriander, etc.—in its influence on body fluids, digestive glands, milk glands, and sexual glands.

Culpeper could just as well have put the sweet root under the rule of Jupiter, as the planetary king rules over the liver and everything that is sweet. The white roots contain up to 8 percent sucrose, which is why in many languages it's called "sugar root" (Dutch: *suikerwortel;* German: *Zuckerwurzel;* French: *racine sucrée*).

Illustration 99. Skirret plant

Sadly, hardly anyone knows skirret anymore, as it has been completely crowded out by the popular orange carrot. But there is no reason to not bring them back to the garden. They like sunny, somewhat-moist soil. As they are perennials, it's best to leave some of the root so it can come back year after year. Like so many umbellifers, skirret can take seemingly forever to sprout; for that reason it's easier to multiply them via their roots. And, as with other umbellifers, they can be left in the garden over the winter or harvested and stored in sand piles.

Recipes

Skirret Burgers • 4 Servings

21 ounces (600 grams) potatoes, peeled or unpeeled, cubed • 21 ounces (600 grams) skirret roots, scrubbed well, cut into ½-inch-thick pieces • ground nutmeg • herbal salt • pepper • lovage leaves • 2 egg yolks, whisked • 1 cup (225 grams) bread crumbs • 2 tablespoons olive oil • 1 cup (225 grams) onions, finely chopped • 2 tablespoons butter • ½ cup (115 milliliters) white wine

Put the potatoes and skirret roots into a large pan with water. (The water can be about 1 inch over the vegetables.) Simmer on medium heat until tender and water is absorbed. Use immersion blender to purée the vegetables. Transfer the blended potatoes to a bowl and let cool. Mix the nutmeg, salt, pepper, and lovage leaves into the potato mixture to taste. Stir in the egg yolks. Put the bread crumbs in a bowl. Form the potato mixture into patties about the size of hamburgers. Dredge each patty in the bread crumbs. Add the olive oil to the pan. Fry the patties until browned, about 5 minutes on either side. Transfer burgers to paper towels and keep warm. Fry the onions in the butter until browned. Add the white wine. Season with pepper to taste. Serve the onions with the burgers.

TIP: This dish pairs nicely with an arugula salad.

Skirret Roots with Herbs from the Grill • 4 Servings

3 cups whole skirret roots, scrubbed well • Optional: 4 to 6 potatoes, peeled or unpeeled, sliced ¼ inch thick • ¾ cup fresh herbs, such as parsley, thyme, or sweet basil • olive oil • 1 cup (225 grams) cream cheese or butter • sea salt • pepper

Preheat the oven to 350 °F (175 °C). Prepare a baking sheet with grease or baking paper. Place skirrets and potatoes (if using) on baking sheet. Bake at 350 °F (175 °C) for 30 to 40 minutes, or until golden brown. In a small serving bowl, mix the herbs with the olive oil and cream cheese or butter. Season with salt and pepper to taste. Serve with skirret and potatoes.

Forgotten, Rare, and Hardly Known Lettuce Greens

There are so many plants that can be added to salads that it's difficult to select only a few. Some of them can be sown directly into the garden, such as various kinds of cress (*Lepidium* genus: peppercress, peppergrass, pepperwort, etc.), common scurvy grass (*Cochlearia officinalis*), buck's horn plantain (*Plantago coronopus*), nasturtium (*Tropaelum majus*), chervil, coriander, cultivated dandelion, and so many more. There are also many vibrant wild plants, which often grow near the garden, that can add interesting culinary notes to a salad and make meals into symphonies of flavor. Many of these are disdained as "weeds," such as ground elder, chickweed, plantain, and even the fresh shiny leaves of smallwort—plants that some cull or even eradicate with poisons. If there is flowing water near the garden, most likely one can find cow cress, watercress, and the very young leaves of meadowsweet (meadowort). Just a few more steps out into the meadows one can find cuckooflowers, young yarrow leaves, burnet saxifrage, sour dock, and many other delicate and tasty greens. If there is a forest nearby, one may find plants such as wood cranesbill, garlic mustard, or common wood sorrel.

In the following section we'll look at some of the many candidates for salad plants that ought to have a place in the kitchen garden.

Miner's Lettuce (*Claytonia perfoliata, Montia perfoliata*)

Family: Portulacaceae: purslane family

Other Names: Indian lettuce, spring beauty, winter purslane

Healing Properties: poultice from the leaves soothes rheumatism, soothes eyes

Symbolic Meaning: survival, new beginning

Planetary Affiliation: Mercury

Miner's lettuce grows wild on the moist mountainsides of the West Coast of the U.S., from California to Alaska. The lettuce got its official name "*Claytonia*," because it was first written about by British-American botanist John Clayton (1685–1773). Miner's lettuce is an annual pioneer plant that can quickly cover ravaged soil with a tender green covering. It's also a light germinator, which means the seeds need direct light to germinate, so if sown in the garden, seeds should not be covered with soil. The lettuce is a typical member of the purslane family: lush, fleshy, fragile and yet incredibly vital. Each plant makes a small bush, which blossoms between April and June. Since it has two opposing leaves that join under the delicate, white blossom that grow together to look like a small plate, in German the plant is called "*tellerkraut*": plate herb.

Gardeners began to notice this green around 1850. With the California Gold Rush in full swing, gold diggers were devastating the mountainsides—leaving broken ground that was immediately overgrown by this prolific pioneer plant. This was fortunate for those with gold fever, for though scores would dig, not all would find, and many remained poor. The Native American Indians showed the miners that the plant could be eaten; indeed, it contains a lot of vitamin C, as well as appreciable amounts of minerals like magnesium, calcium, and iron. And so the plant got its most common name from the fact that it saved more than a few of these miners from starving. The salad herb was a side product of the Gold Rush just like the blue jeans a clever tailor named Levi Strauss sold to the minors.[1]

Soon miner's lettuce was also cultivated on the East Coast as a health-ful winter plant. Apparently it came to Europe via Cuba, for it is known in parts of Europe as "Cuba lettuce" (French: *Claytone de Cuba;* German: *Kubaspinat*). Today it grows wild as an invasive alien plant along the coast of the North Sea, where the moist, mild climate and the sandy soils suit the plant very well. In nurseries in Holland and Northern Germany it has basically become the dominant soil cover and is considered a weed problem.

The Native Americans on the West Coast ate miner's lettuce raw or cooked. To give it a tangy note, they'd put it on an anthill before eating it, taking advantage of the formic acid that the ants squirt in self-defense. The California aboriginals also used it as a healing plant. The Shoshone put freshly crushed leaves on areas afflicted by rheumatic pain. The Thompson Indians in British Columbia used it for eye afflictions. And, long before Yankees lived in California, Mexicans made (and still make) a delicate salad out of miner's lettuce, which they call "*petota,*" and strips of prickly pear cactus seasoned with olive oil, salt, pepper, and vinegar.

Miner's lettuce is sown in August in northern climates. It needs moist soil and can be harvested several times before the winter comes.

Recipe

Miner's Lettuce with Eggplant-Chickpea Balls with Rosemary-Garlic Oil • 4 Servings

Rosemary-Garlic Oil: 4 twigs rosemary, leaves removed from stems and finely chopped • 2 garlic cloves, finely chopped • 5 tablespoons olive oil • 2 tablespoons blueberry vinegar (or other fruit vinegar) • herbal salt • Eggplant-Chickpea Balls: 2 eggplants • 1 cup (225 grams) chickpeas, cooked • 1 teaspoon ground coriander seed • 1 tablespoon paprika • 1 pinch chili powder • herbal salt • pepper • ¾ cup (175 grams) miner's lettuce leaves

ROSEMARY-GARLIC OIL: In a small pan, sauté the rosemary and garlic gently in 1 tablespoon of the olive oil for about 5 minutes or until well done but not brown. Let cool. Put the vinegar and remaining olive oil in a small serving bowl. Add the rosemary and garlic. Season with herbal salt to taste.

EGGPLANT-CHICKPEA BALLS: Preheat the oven to 400 °F (200 °C). Prick the eggplants all around with a fork and bake at 400 °F (200 °C) for 1 hour or until the skin is completely shriveled. Put the chickpeas in a large bowl. Peel the skin off the eggplant and add the flesh to the chickpeas and mix well with a fork. Season with the coriander, paprika, chili powder, salt, and pepper to taste. Spread the miner's lettuce evenly on a plate or clean flat surface. Make small balls (about the size of a golf ball) of the eggplant-chickpea pulp and roll in the miner's lettuce leaves. Arrange the balls on a platter and serve with the rosemary-garlic oil.

Mustard Greens (white mustard: *Sinapis alba*, black mustard: *S. nigra, Brassica nigra*, Indian mustard: *B. juncea*, wild mustard: *S. arvensis*)

Family: Brassicaceae or Cruciferae: crucifer or cabbage family

Other Names: bamboo mustard cabbage, Chinese mustard, Indian mustard, leaf mustard, mizuna, mustard cabbage, sow cabbage

Healing Properties: mustard flour (seeds): *externally:* poultice eases bronchitis, soothes and warms lumbago, sore muscles, rheumatism; soothes inflamed joints; *internally:* stimulates circulation, warms the skin, induces vomiting (emetic); **mustard oil:** *internally:* kills parasites (antiparasitic); *externally:* fights fungal infections, eases eczema and hives, stimulates hair growth

Symbolic Meaning: heaven, spiritual imagination, alchemical lion, drives off demons, matriarchy (petticoat government), idle talk; Agni, Shiva

Planetary Affiliation: Mars, sun, Jupiter

There are several kinds of wild and cultivated mustard greens with similar culinary uses. In northern climates they can be found growing wild along waysides and near dumps or other fallow areas. Mustard, which is closely related to rapeseed and rocket, is an annual with sulfur-yellow flowers and spicy, round seeds that ripen in pods. All mustard plants are edible.

Mustard grew as a weed companion in the flax fields of early Neolithic cultivators; over time it became an important cultivated plant. While Celtic and Germanic tribes knew the leaves as a vegetable, it was not until the Romans came that they learned to use the seeds as seasoning, The Romans macerated ground black and white mustard seeds in cider (called "*mostum*"), using the paste to help digest protein-rich meals. This was the beginning of what we today know as mustard, and today it still helps us digest protein, often in the form of frankfurters, hamburgers, and other grilled meat. It was the western Slavic peoples who came up with the idea of using mustard seeds in pickling brine.

Spiritus
Sulphur.

Illustration 100. Sulfur, the spirit in mustard
(Leonhard Thurneysser, Quinta Essentia. *1574)*

The appetizing young leaves and tender buds are very good in green salads. They are also rich in proteins, provitamin A, vitamin B, and C, as well as mineral salts (Couplan 1997, 30). White mustard leaves are milder, and black mustard is mainly grown for the seed. Indian mustard (*Brassica juncea*) has especially big leaves; it developed a very long time ago in northwestern India out of a cross between wild mustard (*B. arvensis*) and black mustard (*B. nigra*). This variety, commonly sold in markets in China and India, is eaten like spinach. It can also be cultivated very well in northern climates in the West. In order to always have some fresh greens, it's wise to sow them out in two-week intervals in spring and fall. They need to be thinned out well in order to develop to full size.

The leaves also taste good on sandwiches or as Japanese tempura: dredged in beer batter, deep-fried, and seasoned with soy sauce. John Evelyn (1620–1706)—a great English garden enthusiast and green salad fanatic, who wished to guide humanity back to healthful and primal nourishment—persuaded the royal gardener to plant seventy different greens. In his 1699 publication *Acetaria: A Discourse of Sallets,* perhaps our first book on salads, he wrote the following: "Mustard, especially in young seedling plants, is of incomparable effect to quicken and revive the spirits, strengthening the memory, expelling heaviness . . . besides being an approved antiscorbutic."

Mustard has long been an essential ingredient in the kitchens of India, where it is called "*rái.*" It was mentioned in as early as 500 BC as a spice and vegetable in the *Acaranga Sutra.* Mustard, regarded as "hot," is thought to strengthen the inner fire (*agní*) and open and cleanse the subtle "canals" (*srota*). For these warming and strengthening effects a lot of mustard is eaten in the winter months. And the poor fry food in mustard oil instead of the more expensive *ghee,* clarified butter; since mainly the poor use it, mustard falls into the *tamasic* category. As such, the offerings made for the dark (*tamasic*) god Shiva and his cohorts are prepared in mustard oil and seasoned with bitter neem leaves. This is because, according to the Indian mindset, one cannot detach the food one eats from mood and character. By contrast, offerings to Vishnu are made with butter and are sweet, as the god is full of light and has a *sattvic* character (Achaya 1998, 131).

But in Western esotericism and alchemy, mustard was seen as anything but dark and lowly. With its deep-yellow blossoms it was regarded as a bearer of light and fire, as sulfur in plant form and as a "sun bearer" (from the Latin *sol* = sun, *ferre* = carry). For these mystics sulfur is "fire of the earth" (*ignis terrae*), it is the saving light of Christ that descended down into matter. Even Jesus likened the kingdom of heaven to a mustard seed:

> The kingdom of heaven is like a mustard seed which a man took and
> sowed in his field; it is the smallest of all seeds, but when it has grown
> it is the greatest of all shrubs and becomes a tree, so that the birds of
> the air come and make nests in its branches (Matthew 13:31–32)

Mustard was the last of the thirty-eight flower essences discovered by Edward Bach (1886–1936). He recommended it for psychic distress that comes from the deepest parts of the soul, when depression and sadness well up from the depth of the unconscious. Bach wrote that mustard drives off depression and restores the joy of life. Without this sulfur power, without the inner sun, people can easily sink into black depths.

Because of its sharpness, Nicholas Culpeper (1616–1654) put mustard under the rule of Mars. He prescribed ground mustard seeds mixed with honey and rolled into small pills taken on an empty stomach in the morning, or rubbed into the temples and under the nose to "warm and enliven the spirit." Other astrological herbal healers saw the sun as the ruler of the yellow blossoming, spicy plant; but, due to its effect on the digestion, it is from a Jupiter-influenced sun.

In both European and Asian healing lore, the seeds are a very important healing agent, especially when ground into mustard flour. The plant contains mustard glycosides that when mixed with warm water separate and develop both extreme pungency and an antibacterial effect. Apparently Hippocrates (460–370 BC), the "father of natural healing," used the pungent black mustard in this way. A poultice of mustard flour draws the blood to the skin's surface to deeply heat the tissue. (It can even burn the skin if not correctly applied.) Freshly ground seeds are mixed with water and made into a poultice (rye flour is added to make it milder), then applied to the ailing area. Mustard poultices are used for acute inflammation in the joints, rheumatism, sciatica, muscle pain, pneumonia, pleurisy, and lumbago. A mustard flour poultice can also be placed on the lower abdomen for chronic constipation. To induce vomiting, one teaspoon of mustard flour mixed with water is useful in cases of poisoning and intoxication. Mustard oil can be rubbed into the skin as an antiparasitic for fungi infections, hives, and eczema.

Mustard was also used magically. It was thought that whoever eats mustard seeds on an empty stomach in the morning ensures against suffering a stroke. And whichever woman wants to rule the roost in marriage is advised to secretly carry mustard seeds and dill to the wedding ceremony. While the servant of God speaks the solemn words, she should quietly whisper: "I have mustard and dill; man, when I talk, you remain still!"

In Indian lore, mustard, and especially mustard seeds, play a major role as demon expellers. Mustard seeds and other plants are censed (ritually burned) for the protection of newborns; the mother's first bath after giving birth is prepared with some mustard seeds. During funerals or *shraddha*—ceremonies for feeding the spirits of the dead—participants rub mustard oil into the palms and soles of their feet. Mustard oil cooked in henna leaves is a favored hair oil; massaged into the scalp, it is believed to encourage hair growth.

There are a lot of expressions in northern Europe involving mustard. In Germany, to give one's two cents' worth is called "to give one's mustard" (*seinen Senf dazugeben*); if someone is told to not dramatize a situation, one says, "Don't make mustard out of it" (*Mach keinen Senf daraus*). In Germany, Holland, and France, when things get out of hand and the jokes get too coarse, one says, "This mustard bites the nose." In Holland mothers sometimes wean their babies by putting some mustard on their nipples—therefore, when someone wants to ruin something for someone else, they "put some mustard on the teat." And of course there are some English expressions too, such as "as keen as mustard," "the proper mustard" (the genuine article), and "doesn't cut the mustard."

Recipe

Mustard Greens Lasagna with Sauerkraut and Horseradish • 4 Servings

Filling: ½ cup (115 grams) white or yellow onion, chopped • 1 tablespoon olive oil • 1 teaspoon honey • 1 heaping cup (250 grams) sauerkraut, finely chopped • herbal salt • Sauce: 3½ cups (800 milliliters) vegetable broth • 1 cup (225 milliliters) white wine • 4 bay leaves • ½ cup (115 milliliters) cream (18%) • 5 tablespoons lentil flour • ground nutmeg • Lasagna: 12 fresh green lasagna noodles • ½ cup (115 grams) mustard greens • 2 tablespoons (40 grams) pine needles, finely chopped or 20 juniper seeds • 1 tablespoon horseradish • ½ cup (115 grams) cheddar cheese, grated

FILLING: In a medium pan, gently sauté the onions in the olive oil until glassy, about 10 minutes. Add the honey, sauerkraut and horseradish and sauté another 5 minutes until very well blended. Remove from the heat and let cool. Season with salt to taste.

SAUCE: Pour the vegetable broth and white wine into a large pot. Bring to a boil. Add the bay leaves and cook for 10 minutes. Add the cream and lentil flour to bind slightly. Season with nutmeg to taste and set aside.

LASAGNA: Preheat the oven to 350 °F (175 °C). Put 1 layer of lasagna noodles into a large ovenproof dish. Arrange one-third of the mustard greens in an even layer on the noodles. Arrange one-third of the sauerkraut in an even layer on the greens. Add one-third of the sauce in an even layer on the sauerkraut. Repeat with the remaining quantities of noodles, greens, sauerkraut, and sauce. Arrange the pine needles on the last layer of sauerkraut. Finish with the last bit of sauce and the grated cheese. Bake at 350 °F (175 °C) for 1 hour. Serve warm.

Opium Poppy (*Papaver somniferum*)

Family: Papaveraceae: poppy family

Other Names: garden poppy, mawseed, plant of joy, tears of Aphrodite (term also applied to other flowers); the latex is also called "plant of forgetting," "tears of the moon"

Healing Properties: reduces or stops coughing; eases cramps; increases desire (aphrodisiac); eases diarrhea, dysentery, and stomach cramps; reduces or stops pain; induces sleep

Symbolic Meaning: fertility, sleep, forgetfulness, death, comfort; Demeter/Ceres, Aphrodite, Cybele, Morpheus, Hypnos

Planetary Affiliation: moon

Most of us know poppy seed buns, bagels, and cakes. But who knows about young, tender poppy leaves as an addition to a green salad? Most would wonder if the bluish-green leaves are really edible; after all, the plant is known to produce opium—which can lead to madness or even death. But the young leaves have no nasty addictive alkaloids, and make for tasty additions to salads. The seeds—also tasty, nutritious, and devoid of opium—are harvested like other capsule seeds: by bending the ripe capsules into a paper bag and shaking them out. The seeds that fall on the ground in the process will sprout the following spring, and can be harvested once they form tender green rosettes, which the French traditionally enjoy in salads. François Couplan, a French expert on edible wild plants, confirms that neither the common poppy (*Papaver rhoeas*) nor the opium poppy (*P. somniferum*) contains psychotropic juice at the tender, rosette stage in their development (Couplan 1997, 73).

Poppy is one of the oldest cultivated plants. In northern Europe it's been cultivated for so long it would appear to be an indigenous plant, but it arrived there with the first sedentary farmers (Linear Pottery culture) from the Fertile Crescent region. The oldest archeological findings in Europe are from New Stone Age peasant cultures that settled in the Rhine river area some 6500 years ago. Many poppy seeds and capsules were also found in lake dweller settlements (3000–2000

BC) such as at Pfäffikersee, a lake near Zurich, Switzerland. Poppies were most likely grown for their seeds, which contain lots of protein and some 40 percent nutritional oil, which has a high percentage of unsaturated essential linoleic acids. It's also possible that the Stone Age peoples used the rosette as a vegetable and the sap for healing. We know through comparisons with other cultures that simple agricultural peoples seldom distinguished between edible and healing plants.

The milky juice of the poppy contains some twenty different alkaloids, many with exceptional healing qualities. For one thing, opium happens to be the best remedy for dysentery—as many

Illustration 101. Poppy, an important edible plant

a traveler in the tropics may have experienced. The bitter narcotic sap, which the Greeks called "*opos*" (juice), is also one of the most effective painkillers. Depending on the dose, it can have a euphoric and extremely relaxing effect; at higher doses it can lead to hallucinations, labored breathing, reduced heart rate, coma, and even death. Opium's many alkaloids, some in very low concentration, often combine with inactive components that delay their release in the intestinal tract. The danger of narcotic poisoning or addiction arises when chemically individual constituents are isolated and purified before being smoked or injected in large amounts (Weil 1983 125).[1]

Note that it cannot be assumed that the lake dwellers became addicted to the use of poppy juice. The mountain tribes in India—the Miao in Vietnam, Thailand, and Myanmar (formerly known as Burma), who cultivated opium poppy and even used it recreationally—did not develop any physical or psychic dependency.[2]

The poppy was a sacred cult plant in late Minoan Crete and Cyprus (1600–1100 BC). Several clay statues of goddesses from this time have been found, depicted with poppy seed capsules in their hands or in their hair bands. These capsules have slits in them, indicating that raw opium was extracted from them. In ancient Greece the poppy was associated with several goddesses: Demeter, the goddess of grain; Hera, the protector of women and marriage; the mother goddess Cybele, and Aphrodite, the goddess of love. The Greeks also dedicated the beautiful flower to both Morpheus, the god of dreams, and his father, Hypnos, the god of sleep. Many Classical scholars consider nepenthe—used by Greek physicians as a "medicine that lets one forget emotional distress and worries"—to have been a concoction containing opium. Homer (800 BC) is thought to have referred to nepenthe in book 4 of *The Odyssey:*

> *Then Helen, daughter of Zeus, took other counsel.*
> *Straightway she cast into the wine of which they were drinking*
>   *a drug*
> *to quiet all pain and strife, and bring forgetfulness of every ill.*

Dioscorides (~40–90 AD) reported that the seeds could be eaten baked into bread or mixed with honey, and that one could make a sleeping medicine out of boiled poppy pods; in addition, just a small portion of the plant juice—the size of a small lentil—could be taken to calm digestion, but a larger dose could lead to somnolence and even to death. (An overdose of poppy paralyses the central nervous system.)

In medieval Europe poppies were mainly cultivated for their nourishing seeds and oil.[3] However, doctors did use opium and henbane to prepare an anesthetic for surgical intervention. A tiny bit of the juice was also stirred into the porridge of children who could not sleep—the generic name "*Papaver*" (from the Latin *papa* = porridge, meal) is derived from this practice.

The plant has been used as an intoxicant since the Neolithic era. The modern, accelerated kind of use first appeared in the Middle East in Islamic circles; after the Koran forbad wine as an intoxicant, opium became a substitute inebriant, used to tranquilize harem ladies and as a mystical drug for Sufis. From there it spread to India and China, where it was known as a love potion. In the seventeenth century, after the Chinese emperor forbade the smoking of American tobacco, the Chinese began to smoke opium—sold at exorbitant prices by the British, who grew opium poppies on their plantations in colonial India. Masses of Chinese became addicted to opium smoking, to the point that the gold and silver reserves of China were nearly emptied. Then, when the emperor tried to prevent the lucrative trade of opium in the mid nineteenth century, the infamous Opium Wars ensued. Previously, the self-sufficient Chinese economy had not been dependent on any foreign trade at all, but opium had drastically changed that—as the British had hoped it would. The Brits then made a show of their might in the name of "free trade," ending in humiliating defeat for the Chinese.

In North America during the Civil War opium was widely used to treat wounded soldiers, who often developed an addiction. Presumably the plant came to America with the European settlers. Sadly, even today opium still factors in world economics and global power politics, involving criminal syndicates as well as giant pharmaceutical corporations. Currently 95 percent of the world's opium and heroin comes from Afghanistan—part of the reason for the wars waged there. There is, thus, a great tragedy surrounding this plant. According to a clairvoyant woman's vision, the very friendly poppy-deva—who gives people food and healing—is deeply saddened by its misuse. According to her vision, some people get addicted in multiple lifetimes; as such, to start could be to never stop.

Despite all that, in eastern Europe the poppy has not lost its status as a quasi-sacred food plant. Poppy seeds are baked into treats the year around—especially at Christmas, New Year's, Easter, and Pentecost. In Silesia it was a tradition to give the farm dog three poppy dumplings on

Christmas Eve so that it would stay strong. The bowl used to make the poppy dumplings was filled with water—the number of seeds that floated to the surface determined how rich the next harvest would be. In Slavic regions the chickens were given poppy seeds on Christmas Eve—as many seeds as they pick, so many eggs would they produce. Another belief was those who eat enough poppy seeds during the Christmas days would not run out of money. On St. Andreas evening (November 30) girls would toss poppy seeds over themselves so as to dream about whom they would marry. In a tradition similar to one we learned about in the fennel chapter, farmers in Bohemia strew poppy seeds on a freshly dug up piece of turf in front of the barn door; as any wicked witch passing by would have to stop and count them—and of course, she would lose count again and again—she'd never manage any mischief. A similar belief could be found in western Prussia, where poppy seeds were strewn into the coffin of the deceased so as to thwart vampires. It's a benefit to civilization indeed that evil beings can be so easily distracted from their evil doings!

Recipe

Opium Poppy Leaves on Dandelion Leaves • 2 Servings

½ cup (115 grams) young, tender poppy leaves • ½ cup (115 grams) young dandelion leaves • 1 tablespoon sesame seeds • 1 tablespoon pumpkin seeds • 2 tablespoons chopped almonds • Dressing: 1 tablespoon balsamic vinegar • 3 tablespoons hazelnut oil • ¼ cup (60 grams) chives, finely chopped • herbal salt • 1 teaspoon caraway seeds • pepper

Mix the poppy and dandelion leaves in a serving bowl. Sprinkle with the sesame seeds, pumpkin seeds, and almonds. In a separate small bowl, mix the balsamic vinegar, hazelnut oil, chives, and caraway seeds. Season with salt and pepper. Drizzle over salad and toss gently.

Purslane (*Portulaca oleracea*)

Family: Portulacaceae: purslane family

Other Names: little hogweed, moss rose, little pigweed, pursley, pressley, red root, verdolaga

Healing Properties: cools fever and inflammation, stimulates circulation and regulates heart function, strengthens immune system

Symbolic Meaning: marriage, bonding of opposites (language of flowers)

Planetary Affiliation: moon, Mercury

The hot continental summer climate such as is found in the American Midwest—where I spent most of my childhood—is a perfect place for purslane to grow wild. Indeed, the delicate but extremely vital plant used to overgrow the ground in the cornfields to the extent that the farmers scornfully called it "pigweed." The Amish who live in that same area called it "*meisdreck*" (mouse filth). In those preherbicide days, kids could earn some pocket money by helping hoe the cornfields in order to hopefully rid them of this competing vegetation. No one seemed to know back then that the plant is edible and that it is actually a humus-protecting natural ground cover. No one seemed to know, either, that the seeds of the hacked-off plants continue to ripen and can go on to germinate despite the disruption.

Many years later I had the pleasure of enjoying a vacation in Greece. One day I ordered a salad and was astonished to see a plate of nicely chopped purslane with tomatoes and onions—dressed with olive oil, lemon juice, and sweet basil. It was absolutely delicious. Somewhat later, I was even more surprised to find cultivated purslane (considerably larger than the wild plant) in a French garden. It was called "*pourpier doré*," and the gardener told me that it's popular in soups and salads; purslane and sorrel (*oreille*) are ingredients in a soup called "*bonne femme*" (good woman) in France. Eventually I realized that purslane is very much liked as a vegetable all over the world.

This juicy plant, with its succulent, round leaves and thick, fleshy stems, is a true cosmopolitan. It blossoms modestly with small yellow flowers and has black seeds that ants carry away, thus distributing the plant. It grows wild in South Africa, where it is called "women's food," as well as in Southern Asia, where it is cultivated and sold in markets. In the Near East it is an ingredient in a mixed salad called "*fattoush*." In Mexico it is called "*verdolaga*," and is used in salads and soups; in China it is sautéed in sesame oil

Illustration 102. Tender purslane leaves

with bean sprouts in a wok. Purslane is generally recognized as cooling and thirst quenching, and thus helpful in calming a hot temper. Ancient Greeks and Romans knew it as both an edible plant and a healing one. Dioscorides (~40–90 AD), who called the plant "*andrachni*," recommended the leaves for headache, heartburn, and kidney and bladder ailments; he noted the juice soothes the eyes. Pliny the Elder (23–79 AD) derived forty-five remedies from purslane; Galen (129–~216 AD) considered it nearly a heal-all plant. Pliny wrote that just wearing an amulet with the plant would ward off all kinds of evil. Purslane's generic name "*portulaca*" comes from the Romans, derived from the Latin *portula*, meaning "small door"—likely a reference to how the seed capsule opens like a door when the seeds are ripe.

Purslane came to northern Europe with the Romans. The earliest seed findings in northern Europe were discovered in Neuss on the Rhine. The plant can still be found growing wild in the Rhine region in gardens, potato fields, and asparagus fields (Koeber-Grohe 1987, 296). Hildegard von Bingen (1098–1179) was the first to write about it, as "*burtel*" or "Portulaca," though she saw little virtue in this "cold and slimy" plant. Wolfram von Eschenbach, the twelfth-century troubadour, wrote that the

Illustration 103. The Romans brought purslane to all their colonies

knight Gawain liked to eat it. But, in general, it seems that the northern Europeans did not find the plant very interesting. This changed, however, in the sixteenth century, when it became popular in salads.

Famous German physician and botanist Leonhart Fuchs (1501–1566) elaborated on the plant: "It is moist to the third degree; mixed with barley flour and used as a poultice on the head, it reduces heat and also helps inflamed, red eyes; it can be chewed to help with a toothache; it helps damaged bladders and kidneys; to alleviate a sunstroke, one can mix the juice with rose oil and rub it into the head." He also mentioned that purslane can be pickled (like olives or capers) and that, added as a green to salads, "it strengthens the stomach." A century later, Nicholas Culpeper put it under the rule of the moon because of its "cooling properties"— countering the damaging hot, negative aspect of Mars. He prescribed drinking the juice for a dry cough and applying it topically for fever and inflammations.

As mentioned earlier, Americans did not show much enthusiasm for the plant. For example, in his 1821 publication *American Gardener,* farmer and journalist William Cobbett described it as "a mischievous weed that Frenchmen and pigs eat when they can get nothing else. Both use it in salad, that is to say, raw" (Cobbett 1856, 157). But, fortunately for purslane, times change. In the 1980s it gained notoriety—alongside mineral water, muesli, and yogurt—as part of fresh, healthy approach to life.

Purslane presumably originated in South Asia; later it spanned the globe. Research shows that the plant (called "*khursa*" in Hindi) has been cultivated in India for thousands of years, where it is also used as a healing plant for liver, spleen, kidney, and bladder ailments. It remains unclear how the plant reached America. Samuel Champlain, who was active in the French colonization of Canada, reported from a trip to Maine (1604–1610) that purslane grew under the corn but that the natives didn't use it. But ethnobotanists disagree, noting that the Native Americans used purslane as both a vegetable and as a healing plant; they gathered the edible seeds and dried the leaves for winter use. (I posit that perhaps Champlain did not correctly identify the weed on the corn mounds.) The Cherokee used fresh purslane juice for earaches. The Iroquois put fresh juice on burns and bruises, and drank it as an antidote to "bad medicine." For the Navaho the plant is basically a heal-all for just about any sickness; for scarlet fever, they rub the whole body with the juice (Moerman 1999, 434).

Purslane abounds with vitality; it contains many minerals (magnesium, potassium, phosphor, and iron) and vitamins, especially vitamin C (18–25 mg), vitamins B1 and B6, and carotene. The leaves' refreshing flavor comes from omega-3 alpha-linolenic acids, which are also present in fish oil and cod liver oil; in purslane, however, they also taste good. It has a positive effect on the heart and circulatory system, and strengthens the immune system.

The seeds are also edible. They can be cooked in mush or added to bread flour or mixed in with cereals. A good way to harvest the seeds is to cut the capsules from the plant and let them dry in a paper bag; when they are dry, shake the bag until the seeds all fall out of the capsules. The fleshy stems and leaves are good in soups and salads, and can also be preserved in vinegar like capers.

Very little is known about the symbolism of the plant. An old German herbal book reads: "Even though purslane is cold and moist, it is a real summer plant and does not like the cold. There is a saying that in marriage it is always good when two different temperaments join together. The good Lord alone knows what is best and for that reason sometimes two very different personalities join together in marriage" (Axtelmeier 1715). Accordingly, purslane is a good symbol of marriage.

Recipe

Purslane Salad with Red Currants • 2 Servings

1 cup (225 grams) purslane • ½ cup (115 grams) red currants • ¼ cup (50 grams) parsley, finely chopped • Dressing: 2 tablespoons vinegar (red currant, red wine, or balsamic) • 4 tablespoons sesame oil • 1 pinch cinnamon • 1 teaspoon turmeric • 2 tablespoons Parmesan cheese, grated • herbal salt • white pepper

Gently combine the purslane and berries in a serving bowl. In a separate small bowl, mix the vinegar, sesame oil, cinnamon, turmeric, and grated Parmesan. Season with salt and pepper to taste. Drizzle the dressing over the salad and toss gently.

ACKERGLOCKENBLUME
CAMPANULA RAPUNCULOIDES

Rampion (*Campanula rapunculus*)

Family: Campanulaceae: bellflower family

Other Names: bellflower, Genevieve's root,[1] rover bellflower

Healing Properties: taken externally: cleanses and smooths skin; taken internally: stimulates appetite, cleanses system, soothes throat and tonsil inflammation

Symbolic Meaning: loyalty, atavistic primeval knowledge, wisdom and vitality of the earth, world of elves and dwarves; flowers associated with the ancient wise women and visionaries Veleda and Wala; quarrel (Italy)

Planetary Affiliation: Saturn

Rampion is a beautiful, blue-violet bellflower that blooms from June to August. Today it can be found across Europe—in dry pastures, at the edge of forests, and in the occasional flowerbed. It grows wild from Europe to Siberia and as far south as northern Africa. Though hardly anyone knows the plant anymore, it was once a desirable edible plant, found in most vegetable gardens well into the seventeenth century. It prevailed in Switzerland and Alsace into the twentieth century.

The plant has a thick, fleshy root about three inches long that can be harvested in fall, winter, or spring. The smaller roots can be added to salads. The larger roots can be eaten as a vegetable; they have a pleasant, sweetish flavor that some liken to walnut. In the fall rampion has small rosettes that look very much like lamb's lettuce—they are often mistaken for one another. The young shoots that come in the spring can be prepared like asparagus.

Rampion symbolically partakes of the "blue flower" mystique of the Age of Romanticism. It is the far-away blue of heaven—of longing, loyalty, profound wisdom, and so on. In Christian iconology this mystical blue is symbolized by Virgin Mary's blue cloak, full of golden stars. Of course, the color blue also relates to the American "blues," the style of music that expresses the suffering and pain of millions of African slaves torn from their families and stripped of their culture.

In the Celtic-based British language of flowers bellflowers symbolize the "other world," the world of elves and nature spirits. Whoever has entered that realm knows that bellflowers are not silent; like gentle silver bells, they ring in the nightly dance of the elves, as Cicely Mary Barker described in her 1923 book *The Complete Book of the Flower Fairies:*

> *They tinkle while the fairies play*
> *with song and dance the whole night long*
> *Till daybreak wakens, cold and gray,*
> *and elfin music fades away.*

Indeed, a fairy tale in Calabria, Italy, declares that whoever pulls a rampion plant out of the soil will find a doorway and steps leading to the realm of the fairies.

Blue is also the color of the Saturn sphere, the border between the created world and the eternal world. The wise women and prophetesses of the old Germanics and Celts, who were known by the title "Wala" or "Veleda" [from the Proto-Celtic *welet* = seer, a derivative of the root *wel* = to see]), took seats on towers in order to see, while in trance, far into the other world—to get into contact with its deep wisdom. The radiant wisdom of these women, the very rays of the sun, was symbolized by long, flowing golden hair. The Rapunzel story, as mentioned earlier in relation to lamb's lettuce, reflects this ancient imagery; indeed, rampion lent its name to Rapunzel. The goddess—in

Illustration 104. Rampion, a popular edible plant in the Middle Ages (illustration by David Kandel, from Hieronymus Bock, Das Kreütterbuch. *1546)*

Illustration 105. The woman looked down into the garden, where luscious lamb's lettuce Rampion grew (illustration by Otto Ubbelohde in Grimms Märchen, *1922)*

this case the young maiden Rapunzel, who is beautiful, full of light—lives in a tower, far removed from the earthly realm. As such Rapunzel represents both the archaic sun goddess imprisoned by the winter witch and a captive in the isolated puberty tower, into which young maidens were separated from their kin so elder women could initiate and educate them. Therefore rampion, the Rapunzel plant, represents not only the resplendent wisdom of the heavens but also, with its taproot, the earthly wisdom of the soil. The maiden needs this root, this connection to the fertile earth—she needed it when still in her mother's womb. That is why, as the tale tells us, her pregnant mother could not resist the *rapunculus* plants growing in the sorceress' garden next door,[2] and why she enlisted her husband to steal some for her. Such was the unborn child's undoing, for the angry sorceress demanded she be given the newborn in repayment; the witch later named her Rapunzel, after the plants for which she'd been exchanged. The sorceress plays an important part in the constellation: she knows the secrets of the earth, its vitality and strength. United harmoniously, heavenly wisdom and earthly strength allow the human being—ultimately a divine being—to fulfill all it needs to achieve. Such is what this bellflower plant symbolizes.

Leonhart Fuchs (1501–1566) categorized rampion as a beet; indeed, *rapum* is Latin for "beet." He noted that the appetizing root can be eaten raw with salt and vinegar as a diuretic. When the root is mixed with wheat flour, ground lupine seeds, and ground corn cockle seeds, it makes an ideal skin cleanser.[3] He also suggested that the plant juice gathered at harvest time and mixed with a woman's breast milk is beneficial as an external tonic for eyesight. Incidentally, Native American healers have also used a rampion decoction as a rinse for painful eyes (Moerman 1999, 135). The sixteenth-century English herbal doctor John Gerard used a decoction of the root for sore throat and tonsillitis. And an old recipe recommends the distilled water of the whole plant for clear and smooth skin.

A few tips for gardeners: rampion has tiny seeds, like tobacco, which makes sowing difficult. It is best to mix them with sand at about a 20:1 sand:seed ratio in rows one and a half feet apart. The seeds should not be covered with soil, as they are light-dependent germinators. The vegetable can grow in a fairly shady place and must be kept moist. Be sure to repeatedly thin out the young plants so they don't crowd each other. Plant out in May; the roots and rosettes will be ready for harvest in late fall.

Recipe

Rampion Salad on Alfalfa Sprouts with Caraway Dressing • 2 Servings

1 cup (225 grams) rampion leaves and buds • 1 cup (225 grams) alfalfa sprouts • ¼ cup (60 milliliters) apple vinegar (or other fruit vinegar) • ¾ cup (175 grams) hazelnut oil • 1 teaspoon ground caraway seeds • sea salt • pepper

Put the alfalfa sprouts in a serving bowl. Arrange the rampion leaves and buds over top. In a separate small bowl, mix the vinegar and hazelnut oil. Season with caraway powder, salt, and pepper to taste. Drizzle the dressing over the salad.

TIP: This salad pairs nicely with fresh olive bread.

Rocket or Rucola (*Eruca sativa*)

Family: Brassicaceae or Cruciferae: mustard family

Other Names: arugula, colewort, rucola, rucoli, rugula, roquette, salad rocket

Healing Properties: increases desire (aphrodisiac), prevents scurvy (antiscorbutic), promotes urination (diuretic), induces vomiting in large doses (emetic)

Symbolic Meaning: betrayal (language of flowers)

Planetary Affiliation: Mars

Rocket is a cruciferous vegetable like cabbage, horseradish, and mustard. As the glucosinolates in crucifers have a pungent flavor—which can be very strong, as in horseradish—they give a peppy note to salads, sauces, soups, spreads, and sandwiches. Rocket can basically be used like parsley. Forgotten for many years, it was fortunately rediscovered in the last few decades as another very tasty, vitamin-rich green.

The annual plant grows wild from central Asia to the Mediterranean and south to Morocco. Originally the pioneer plant appeared as a weed in flax fields, but in Asia it was soon appreciated as a valuable culinary herb. In central Asia it is still cultivated as a companion plant in flax fields, and in India in cotton fields. In these two countries it is not only valued as a green but also for its seeds, which have a high oil content (about 32 percent). The golden-yellow oil, known in India as "*jamba*" or "*taramira*" oil, is used for cooking and to conserve vegetables, as a lamp oil and hair oil, and for medical purposes as a diuretic, aphrodisiac, and stimulant. In higher doses it is an emetic.

Though the Romans and Greeks of antiquity cultivated rocket, in northern Europe the plant was unknown until the sixteenth century. The physician and botanist Leonhart Fuchs was one of the first to mention it, writing in 1543 how this "white mustard" that was "new in our area" arouses unchaste desires if eaten in quantity. It also "forces urine" and strengthens digestion, and should be eaten with lettuce leaves—else one can get a headache. Furthermore, Fuchs noted that the seeds can

Illustration 106. Nicholas Culpeper, astrological herbal doctor (1650)

counter snake bite and scorpion poisoning and drive off parasites such as lice, mites, fleas, etc. The ground seeds, mixed with honey, can remove all kinds of facial blemishes; mixed with ox gall, it can remove black spots on the face; with vinegar, it can remove freckles. Most of these statements derive from the famous Roman doctor Galen rather than Fuchs's own experiments.

A century later, Nicholas Culpeper described rocket in almost the same terms. He wrote in 1649 how one should not eat the leaves "alone, in regard their sharpness fumes which go into the head, causing aches and pains therein." At most, hot heads and choleric types might be able to take it, "for angry Mars rules them, and he will sometimes be restrictive when he meets with fools." In addition, rocket seeds increase sperm and "venerous [libidinous] qualities," aid digestion, "provoke urine exceedingly," drive out intestinal worms, and counter snake, scorpion, and shrew poison. He advised boiling the plant with some sugar and giving it by the spoonful to cure children from coughing; he noted that ingesting ground seeds added to a beverage lessens underarm smell. Mixed with honey it cleanses the skin from blemishes and pox. Culpeper's predecessor, the herbal doctor John Gerard, also advised eating rocket seeds to better stand torture, as one would not feel the whipping as much.

In the flower language of the time the whitish-yellow blossom was a symbol for betrayal: in the evening it smells sweet, but in the day it has no smell at all.

For gardeners: sowing rocket in intervals of two to three weeks ensures tender fresh leaves are always available. And the blooms, which make a floral haven for bees, can also be used to garnish salads.

Recipe

Onion-Grape Salad on Arugula (Rocket) with Goat Cheese • 4 Servings

1¼ cups (285 grams) onions, finely chopped • ½ cup (115 grams)
grapes, halved • 2 tablespoon wine vinegar • 3 tablespoons olive oil
• 1 tablespoon honey • 1 teaspoon ground caraway seed • 1 teaspoon
turmeric • sea salt • pepper • 4 small goat cheeses, each about
8 ounces (225 grams) • ¾ cups (175 grams) arugula (rocket)

In a large bowl, mix the onions with the grapes, vinegar, and olive oil.
Season with honey, caraway powder, turmeric, salt, and pepper to taste.
Place the cheeses into the sauce. Marinate, covered, at room temperature
for 6 hours. Arrange the arugula (rocket) in a serving bowl. Arrange the
cheeses on the arugula. Pour the marinade over top and serve.

Illustration 107. The seven planets as rulers of the weekdays, from Guy Marchant's The Kalendar of Shepherds, 1503.

Cosmic Cooking: the Planetary Cuisine of Arthur Hermes

Until he was ninety-six years old, Arthur Hermes walked several times a month down a steep path through a forest of beech and pine trees to the train station near his home in Canton of Vaud, Switzerland. He looked like the wise old wizard out of fairy tales, with his wide coat and snow-white hair fluttering from under his worn, wide-brimmed hat—except that he usually had a briefcase with old, obscure notes clamped under his arm. With each such journey he was answering calls for help. He believed that the knowledge that had been imparted to him by his spiritual guide was intended for everyone, and so to those who called he would go. People in the entire area of Canton of Vaud turned to him for advice, including doctors and nurses, teachers and students. But mainly it was farmers and gardeners who sought his advice, which they then often applied in their professions—without necessarily crediting the source.

When Hermes spoke, he talked about Mother Earth, about helpful elemental beings, the spirits of the planets, or the influence of the dead upon the vegetation. He told inquiring farmers and gardeners about biodynamic herbal preparations, companion planting, and the cosmic rhythm involved in plowing, planting, and harvesting. He seemed to know everything about animals as well—and to many it was as though he could communicate with them. He told inquiring doctors and healers about the therapeutic effects of color, music, plants, and rocks, as well as about prophylactic herbal teas and healing meditation. And even though the academicians and scientists who sought him, convinced of their world view, were inevitably skeptical of some of his beliefs; nonetheless, they were impressed by his vitality and conviction—and usually left in a reflective mood. The people admired him as if he were a resurrected Paracelsus or, better yet, a reborn druid. Indeed, his farmstead, in a forest clearing way up in the Jura Mountains, had huge stones left by the ancient megalithic peoples, stones later used by actual druids in ceremonial rituals. Incidentally, Arthur's last name, "Hermes," does not concern the Greek god of the same name but is derived from "*Irm*" or "*Irmin*," the old Germanic name for megaliths or menhirs. Indeed, *nomen est omen:* the name speaks for itself.

Given how visibly healthy, strong, and active Hermes was, people could hardly believe his age when they learned it. He would answer, "My daily meditations draw on primal sources, and my nutrition gives my spirit the strength for these meditations."

Hermes avoided alcohol, saying: "Alcohol conserves and mummifies worn-out thoughts. It obstructs all fine and tender impulses that come to us from the etheric dimension." He was a vegetarian as well, though not a vegan; he accepted milk and cheese as "innocent, moonlike substances, full of fresh, lively energy." He could even accept that someone might eat meat: in order to gain the necessary strength needed in times of crisis, in order to become "strong as a bull." But, he felt, "whoever eats meat should realize that—karmically speaking—he or she owes the animal spirit appropriate thanks, and will have to pay back the debt incurred."

When he was asked by a large organic garden community to do a series of talks on food preparation, he shared his thoughts on the sacred act of eating. "We eat the cosmos," he declared, explaining that plants are made up of over 90 percent water and air, and how the mineral that is part of the plant makeup is actually very small. Both the alchemists of old and the homeopaths of today know that water and air are very sensitive elements, receptive to a multitude of vibrations and diverse radiation. Watery plant organs are, therefore, very adapted to receive the rhythmic and cyclic impulses that radiate from the sun (photosynthesis), the moon (germination, growth), and the planets and stars. The minerals in this watery milieu can be seen as "bait," amplifiers for certain cosmic vibrations.

The relationships between planets and earthly matter have been observed and studied since ancient times. But Hermes would not accept older traditions just for their own sake; his conclusions that the planets do influence as formative forces derived too from his own observation and experience. He concurred with the Renaissance concept that lunar forces are in resonance with silver, that solar forces are in resonance with gold—and iron with Mars, tin with Jupiter, lead with Saturn, copper with

Venus, and mercury with Mercury. In addition, he postulated that the nearer planets—the moon (as satellite rather than planet), Mercury, and Venus—working with the calcium in the soil, stimulate the metabolism and the building up of substance and mass in our planet's vegetation. In comparison, the more distant planets (Mars, Jupiter, Saturn), working via silicon—quartz, flint—bring forth qualities in plants that our senses perceive as aroma, color, durability, and taste. It's not just the manufacturers of silicon chips who know of the power of silicon crystals to transmit information; those known as "sensitives" believe that silicon can also transport subtle etheric or spiritual vibrations. Perhaps that is why—as anthropologists have noticed—shamans often wear quartz crystals.

"With the help of these mineral elements, the plants become the antennas or senses of our Mother Earth," said Arthur Hermes. "They take up the cosmic vibrations and transform them into living substance, so that they become nourishing for humans and animals. Healthy, nutritious plants—especially siliceous grains [that are] naturally fertilized and sown at the right times, according to the stars—are saturated with cosmic energy. Such food plants are fundamental to our life; they open us up to true spiritual inspiration and give us the strength to do our work here in the physical realm. Plants that have been pepped up with artificial fertilizer and treated with poisons can hardly do this. [Though] they swell up like sponges and weigh more, the high qualities, . . . which cannot be weighed, they are not able convey."

"Unfortunately," the wise man continued, "with our wrong cooking and bad eating habits," "we often destroy what organic farmers have worked so hard to establish. Here too, we should work together with the planets and stars."

In such working together, Arthur Hermes didn't just advocate the correct time for harvesting plants. He also paid much attention to the correct time for preparing the harvested food, and explained extensively how cosmic rhythms are mirrored in plant growth. As they germinate and grow, blossom and fruit, plants follow the yearly cycle of the sun. Each full moon provides a new stimulus in growth, and these lunar impulses are different depending on which sign the moon is in. "The main lunar rhythm, next to the sidereal rhythm [that is, the twenty-eight day course through the twelve zodiac signs], is the synodic rhythm of the waxing and waning moon. These cycles are the bases for the four seven-day weeks of the month. Indeed, the seven-day week isn't just a convenient compartmentation of time we made up—it's based on cosmic occurrences. According to Arthur Hermes, primeval powers are reflected in these seven days; they've been named after seven major gods, whose energies pulse through our earthly world and manifest in the seven visible planets, the seven metals, the seven notes in an octave, the seven colors of the rainbow, the seven chakras in the body, and even in the seven dwarves (elemental powers) that accompany Snow White (who could be interpreted as symbolizing the soul of the earth)."

It follows that seven different qualities are expressed in each of the seven days of the week. Hermes also categorized the herbs, vegetables, and trees into seven categories, according to which characteristics were dominant in each:

- *On a Monday (day of the moon),* he harvested "moon" vegetables for the main meal of the day; these are watery, succulently bloated, climbing plants, such as cucumbers or melons; or juicy ones with milky sap, such as oyster plant, poppy leaves, or lettuce. On Mondays he gathered herbs that are sedative—like lettuce—or, for mothers, herbs that induce lactation.

- *On a Tuesday* (Tiw's Day, the day of Tiw or Týr, the Norse god of war equated with Mars), he looked for "Mars plants"; these are reddish-colored flora that may have thorns or stickers, may have deep taproots or be spicy or hot in flavor, such as carrots, radishes, nettle, hot peppers, or leeks. And as Tuesday is Mars's day, he also gathered the plants for healing wounds.

- *On a Wednesday* (Woden's day, the day of Odin, the Norse god of shamanism, healing, and death equated with Mercury), he looked for "Mercury plants." These are quickly sprouting, slimy, or especially powerful healing plants, such as purslane, fennel, onion, okra, or mallow. Because Mercury rules over the lungs, he also gathered his healing herbs for lung ailments on this day.

- *On a Thursday* (Thor's day, the day of Thor, the Germanic god of sky and thunder equated with Jupiter), the main meal was made with aromatic, tasty, or sweet "Jupiter plants," such as parsnips, burdock root, or salsify; or yellow-orange vegetables, such as pumpkin or other kinds of squash. Healing plants for liver ailments were also picked on this day.

- *On a Friday,* (Frige's day, the day of Frigg, the Old English goddess equated with Venus), he'd select tender green, cool, and soothing plants, such as peas, green beans, or asparagus. And, as Venus rules over urinary and sexual organs, he also gathered healing plants for venereal issues, bladder ailments, etc.

- *On a Saturday* (Saturn's day), Hermes prepared bitter or salty Saturn vegetables, such as celeriac, Swiss chard, or orache. Dark vegetables like purple cabbage were also considered for this day, in addition to the herbs that affect the spleen, the organ of Saturn, or those that heal broken bones, such as horsetail or comfrey.

- *On a Sunday* (day of the sun), he selected fine, white, delicate vegetables, such as cauliflower or evening primrose; or ones with sunny yellow blossoms, such as sunchokes. And since the sun is the heart of the planetary system, he would also collect healing plants such as hawthorn leaves and flowers on this day.

To Arthur Hermes, it wasn't only important to observe the qualitative difference of each day; we must also live in harmony with the yearly cycle—and cook accordingly. By eating what nature has to offer over the seasons, one follows the sun through its cycle. And in the spring it's important to both purge and nurture the body after the winter's lack of sunlight and fresh greens. So Hermes picked various edible wild springtime herbs as soon as they began to sprout after the long winter. These plants activate the glands and clear out the slack—the ureic acid built up over the winter. Later in the year, of course, leafy vegetables and lettuces follow. As the year progresses, sweet fruits and root crops enable us to load up on vitamins and to strengthen our immune systems in preparation for the wet, cold winter. In late fall, Arthur Hermes always made an elderberry soup, a "gift from Frau Holle (Mother Hulda, the ancient earth goddess)," he'd say, smiling. He also gathered many various edible mushrooms in the fall, because they connect our spirits with the depth of the earth. In anticipation of the cold winter days, he'd stored many nuts and vegetables in his root cellar. Herme firmly believed that bringing one's eating habits into full harmony with the cycle of the year opens one's soul to nature's inspirations.

For this reason, he felt that lettuce, cucumbers, and strawberries were not to be eaten in the winter; to eat them then was a sign of typical modern estrangement from nature. As he phrased it: "To eat in such an estranged way confuses our finer inner senses that are tuned into the cosmic rhythm of nature. Besides, it is irresponsible if you consider how much of fossil fuel energy is necessary to raise and transport these things in the wintertime. It always takes an immense effort, because nature resists such unnatural ways."

He also taught that every day we should eat all the various parts that make up plants, that is: some root, some leaf—some stem, fruit, and seed. This is because the threefold archetypical plant corresponds to the threefold human being:

- The head and nervous system need the salts that are contained in roots; involved is the alchemical *sal*-principle of concentration, of centrifugal energy.
- Our lungs and circulatory system need green leaves, which are the plant mirror of red hemoglobin; involved is the rhythmic, balancing *mercurius*-principle.
- Adding blossoms and seeds to our meal benefits our digestive and reproductive systems; involved is the *sufur*-principle of dissipation.

An example of such a balanced meal would be red beets or carrots, grains, and a lettuce with a dessert of some fruit.

But carefully choosing our ingredients is just the beginning of the process. "Planetary cooking is pure alchemy; it involves metamorphosis and ennoblement of the substances. In alchemy the sun and moon play a major role, just like in nature, in the climate, in the seasons and biological processes. The sun warms, dries, ripens, and consumes. By contrast the moon is cooling, expanding, and moistening."

This thinking, based on cosmic rhythms and cycles, is similarly found in many traditional cultures. For example, in East Asia it is expressed through the yin-yang dynamic; in America and India, it's found in the symbolism of the snake and the eagle. For Hermes, any heating—cooking, baking, roasting, drying—constituted a "sun process"; a continuation of the ripening process in nature. Everything having to do with water—soaking, pickling, fermenting, marinating—is a "moon process." By surrounding the food with water, it is protected from a too-strong sun influence (burning, charcoaling, wilting).

Arthur's planetary cooking system also attended to the source of heat in food preparation. Wood, gas, or coals are actually stored sun energy, and each kind of heat has its own quality. As he explained:

> It is very primitive to reduce heat to the temperature measured by the thermometer. I have researched the subject. I have made Capillary Dynamolysis[1] experiments with various heat sources. Gas and coal fires show relatively harmonious patterns, but electrical heat results in disharmonious flat lines. However, the most harmonious patterns are shown with wood fire heat. Each kind of wood has its typical pattern. One can actually put them into a sevenfold order because trees also belong to the seven planets. Beech wood burns slowly and hot, pinewood burns hot but a little bit faster. Whoever wants "Saturn warmth" in the soup should make a fire with wood from beech or pine trees. One finds "Jupiter warmth" in maple wood and oak wood. The wood from ash trees burns to pure, white ashes, and radiates sun energy with some Mercury involved. Mercury rules

elm wood and hazel wood. Cherry, cottonwood, and willow give a relatively cool and pleasant "moon warmth." Birch and linden wood contain wholesome "Venus warmth." I am lucky to live in a mixed forest and not in some tree monoculture; I can choose my "planets in the fire" as I please. Whoever lives in the city cannot do this. But still it is good for city folks to know that different kinds of wood have different healing properties. Occasionally city people can have a fire if they go camping; they can try the different woods and observe the different qualities, the different smells or how the heat feels. We all know how relaxing it is to look into a living fire, and to capture some of its radiance in the cooking pot makes it even better.

Water, as a medium for "moon processes," cannot be reduced to the simple chemical formula H_2O. The water of each well, pond, stream, or spring has its own special quality. Soft, living rainwater, especially that of the full moon, is full of ethereal vitality; "it makes seeds sprout," Arthur Hermes would note, with a twinkle in his eyes. The water from melted snow or ice, he claimed, contains crystal vitality transmitted from faraway starry regions. Fresh spring water is the best water, and chlorinated pipe water is the worst. (He himself had to use water from a cistern in dry summers.)

In the "planetary" cooking of Hermes, a whole, sun-filled grain—wheat, rye or oats—is, or should be, the mainstay of each meal; like planetary satellites, vegetables, milk products, and salads orbit the "sunny" grains. Only meat is missing. Cooking begins with the moon process: the grain is soaked in water the evening before it will be cooked. The vegetables can also go through the moon process. The next morning, the sun process begins. The soaked grains are slowly cooked on low heat, like a continuing ripening process. The unpeeled vegetables are cut into mouth-sized pieces—they are never grated or mashed. According to Hermes, such would diminish the nutritional value. One-third of the vegetables is quick fried, wok-style; the other two-thirds are slowly cooked in the same water they were soaked in.

Now, imagine taking a seat at a hand-carved wooden table to eat a planetary meal with the old wizard. A beautiful Sistine Madonna hangs on the wall at one end of the table, smiling graciously; a burning bees-wax candle offers a golden glow, and a small bouquet of wild flowers offer their fragrance to the table. None of the meals here begins without appropriate thanks to the goodness of Mother Earth and the sun. Once the gratitude has been expressed, some of the vegetable of the day is eaten raw as an appetizer. Then comes the soup to warm one up from inside: the water the vegetables were cooked in to which has been added grated cheese and fresh wild herbs. Then comes the main dish: cooked grains with the vegetable of the day (about two-thirds cooked and one-third quick fried) served with cream cheese. In addition there is home-baked bread, but it is more than just home-*baked;* Arthur Hermes grew his own grain, sowing it at the fall equinox, on the day of St. Michael. It is thus "St. Michael's grain."

All of the herbs for seasoning came out of his garden or the nearby meadows or forest. According to Hermes, the bitters and aromatic essential oils belong to the outer planets: sharp seasonings to Mars, aromatic to Jupiter, and bitter to Saturn. These help balance the heavier carbohydrates that are connected to the inner planets: the moon, Mercury, Venus.

There is no salt on the table. "Salt is important for our incarnation on earth, but too much damages the kidneys, raises blood pressure, and hardens out our thinking. It is better to get salts needed from the root vegetables." And the same goes for sugar. Roots and fruits can easily cover the human need for sweets. But such isn't to say that if, for example, a visitor brought a cake, the old master wouldn't accept it; he would, and graciously. "You'll surely go to heaven for that!," he'd say. He also enjoyed one daily cup of strong coffee—"poison," he jestingly called it. "It should be as hot as hell and as black as the soul, but not necessarily sweet as sin," he would say. "Coffee drives off our vegetative slumber and shakes our thinking awake." But, he'd specify, "one should only drink coffee after the midday meal. In the morning one should have brought enough cosmic energy from sleep so as to not need coffee." He'd also then mention the Lady of Noon, a beautiful elfish being who appeared to the peasant taking a midday nap and begged him to save her. The farmer then woke up and took a drink of coffee, and the spooky apparition disappeared.

Animated by coffee, Hermes might make an excursion into the nutritional development of humanity. "In the golden ages human beings lived from milk and honey and sweet fruit. As people became more enmeshed in material existence, energy-spending cereal grains became more important. High spiritual beings manifested in grains, Christ in wheat, Indian goddesses in corn, Freya in millet, Thor in oats, Buddha in rice. . . . The planetary powers also revealed themselves in the various cereals. Is rice that grows in water not moon-like, barley that is used to brew beer not Jupiter-like, and wheat not sun-like? Don't oats, which horses love so much, have a Mars-like nature, and corn a Saturn-like nature? But now in Kali Yuga times humans need more: the power of roots that can pierce into the dark depths of the earth."

Hermes did not think in terms of vitamins, amino acids, or other molecular structures. Instead he thought about whether he had enough Mars, Venus, or Jupiter in our organisms. He once advised a pale, anemic young lady to go on a Mars-Venus diet, and a phlegmatic person a Mars-Mercury diet. He explained that "narrow-minded establishment science crawls into a microscope and cuts people off from their cosmic roots." To which he added: "The experts' opinions change constantly!"

Hermes is aware of how stressed some people feel about the food they eat, how stringently some will first weigh and measure and calculate the calories and essential nutrients of anything they dare to consume. To this he'd say: "It's better to trust one's instinct, or to get to know the eternal cosmic principles and live by them." In this way, Hermes stayed true to his basic philosophy of life: "Stay close to Nature and trust her wisdom. Follow the rhythms of the greater cosmos—the daily and seasonal cycles—and the natural rhythms of the microcosm that is your body. There is a deeper intelligence in Nature than our limited rational mind realizes."

Whether or not a nutritional expert would appreciate the cosmic background of Hermes's cosmic cooking, it must be said that his meals, and the concepts behind them, are well balanced. Many Hermes devotees attest to the good health they feel from following Arthur's planetary guidelines. As he would say: "An idea is only a good one when it is practically applied."

Notes

INTRODUCTION

1. Tacitus's biased observation should be taken with a grain of salt, given that the Romans weren't enthused about hard work in gardens either. As in many other highly organized civilizations, it was slaves who did such manual labor.

2. Archeological discoveries in Danish moors and swamps uncovered perfectly conserved corpses that were two thousand year old. The intestinal contents of these bodies, which had been sacrificed to the god Odin, revealed their last meal: barley porridge with linseeds (flax seeds) and hemp seeds, as well as knotweed, burdock, wild asparagus, lamb's quarters, violets, and hemp nettle (Glob 1969, 30).

3. From Sanskrit, etymologically related to the Latin *divus* = godly; old Latin *deivos* = God; Celtic *devos* = a god. A deva is, thus, a heavenly being of light.

BEANS

1. Curare is a mixture of various plant juices that kills monkeys and other tree dwellers without making the meat toxic. It is a muscle relaxant that loosens the animals' grip, after which they can be easily overtaken.

2. Several commonly cultivated types of beans may cause poisoning, including the French bean, pole bean, Kentucky wonder pole bean, bush bean, and the common kidney bean (*Phaseolus vulgaris*) and its associated varieties. The raw beans and bean pods of such beans can contain small amounts of cyanogenic glycosides, which once eaten break down to produce cyanide. Cooking destroys the glycoside molecule, making the food safe to eat. However, eating large amounts of raw beans can lead to vomiting, diarrhea, and stomach pains. Similar symptoms can arise from eating the raw bean pods of the scarlet runner bean (*P. coccineus*), which is grown both as an annual ornamental vine and for its edible seeds. (Levy 1984, 60).

BELL PEPPER AND CHILI PEPPER

1. A special Indian condiment made of conserved chilies is called "*achar*" in Hindi. Linguists assume that the word came originally from "*ají*," the Arawak/Taino Indian term for the chili pepper. The word "*achar*" (which is

also used for other conserved foods, such as green mangos) came with the red pepper when it was imported in the sixteenth century.

CARROT

1. The first descriptions and illustrations of the orange colored garden carrot were from the sixteenth and seventeenth centuries. In 1546 Hieronymus Bock wrote about "*geel*" (yellow) turnips, and in 1586 Joachim Camerarius was the first to mention "*carota*." Though some assert the orange carrot was bred in honor of the Dutch Royal House of Orange, there is no evidence to back up this claim. (The World Carrot Museum. "Carrots: The Road to Domestication." Accessed 6 February 2016. www.carrotmuseum.co.uk /history5.html.)

2. The FAO (Food and Agriculture Organization of the United Nations) reports that carrots are the third most widely produced agriculture product, with a worldwide annual production of six million tons.

3. I knew a smoker who ate a carrot each time she wanted to smoke a cigarette. She ate so many carrots that her skin took on an orange tinge.

CELERY

1. "*Si la femme savait ce que le céleri fait à l'homme, elle irait en chercher de Paris jusqu'à Rome.*" "*Si l'homme savait l'effet du celery, il en remplirait son courtil.*"

CHICORY

1. "*O Wegwart an des Pfades Rand / Es pflückt um Glück dich meine Hand / Schenk mir den Liebsten Wegwart // Auf den Du hast umsonst geharrt!*"

2. "*Gott grüß Euch, ihr lieben Wegwarten allzumal, die ihr hint' und vor mir seid. Stillt Blut und heilt Wunden und alles insgesamt und behaltet Eure Kraft, die Euch Gott und die heilige Maria gegeben hat!*"

CORN

1. In the early sixteenth century, southern Europeans began preparing cornmeal as their daily fare in the same manner as they had always prepared wheat meal—that is, without adding ashes; thereafter, they began to suffer from vitamin deficiency. Especially pellagra became a problem, with

symptoms such as headache, intestinal infections, disorientation, agitation, rough skin, and blotches on the neck, hands, and feet.

2. In the beginning of the eighteenth century, planter John Brickell reported how an Indian medicine man saved his gangrenous leg: "The Indian doctor ground the dry, rotten corn kernels to a powder and dried the abscess with it" (Vogel 1970, 79, 145).

3. Due to the new field crop, the population in Italy in the eighteenth century rose from eleven million to eighteen million; in Spain and Turkey, the population doubled (Farb/Armelagos 1983, 76).

4. According to newer systems, it is assigned to Pluto.

CUCUMBER

1. The exact date each year is the sixth day of the second fortnight in the lunar month of Bhadrapada—which corresponds to our late August/early September.

2. The Greeks learned about cucumbers from the Egyptians. They called the plant "*ágourus*," from *áoros*, (unripe) because the fruits are harvested before they are ripe. The Slavic names derive from this word because cultivated cucumber gardens came to the western Slavs from Greece in the early Middle Ages.

EGGPLANT

1. The Sanskrit name for eggplant is "*vrintaka.*"

EVENING PRIMROSE

1. This is the case, for example, with the plant hemp, which is used for its fiber and oil. In order to prevent illegal use—hemp and marijuana come from the same cannabis species—in the process of breeding hemp the THC content was drastically reduced, to less than 1 percent, rendering it nonpsychoactive. Unfortunately, this manipulation made the plant more susceptible to mold and pests.

JERUSALEM ARTICHOKE

1. The sweet potato belongs to a completely different family, namely that of the morning glory family.

2. Chinese water chestnut (*Eleocharis dulcis*), or "*Pi tsi*," the sprouting tuber of a swamp rush, is a tasty, crispy vegetable used in Chinese cooking. It is often mistaken for water nut (*Trapa bicornis*), which is also often called "water chestnut." Water nut used to be eaten raw or cooked as a delicacy in northern Europe, but now it's a protected species. In Asia one can buy the seeds, which are rich in starches. Water nut is a water plant with a floating leaf rosette that can be easily grown in a swamp or pond.

3. This prominent anthropological sourcebook was published in German in 1576 with the title: *True History: An Account of Cannibal Captivity in Brazil* (*Wahrhaftige Historie und Beschreibung einer Landschaft der Wilden Grimmigen Menschenfresser*).

LEEK

1   Even into the Middle Ages, Hildegard von Bingen spoke of *viriditas* (greenness, fecundity)—"There is a power of eternity and this power is green"—a statement that was still very much in accordance with the old folk spirit of the region.

OKRA

1. The seeds of closely related abelmosk (*Abelmoschus moschatus*) are indeed cultivated for use for incense and fragrance. This variety of okra is also used as a vegetable and fiber plant.

2. Literature about Africanisms in the New World: William E. Grimé, ed., *Ethno-Botany of the Black Americans* (Algonac, MI: PUB, 1979); Melville Herskovits, *The Myth of the Negro Past: The Classic Work on African Heritage in the New World* (Boston: Beacon Press, 1958); Wolf D. Storl, "Afrikanism im Amerkinischen Großstadtghettos," in *Wiener Ethnohistorische Blätter*, 2, Vienna, 1971.

ONION

1. Interestingly, in modern Western countries nursing mothers usually avoid eating onions because it causes flatulence for the babies.

POTATO

1. Indeed, potatoes produce 7,500,000 kilocalories per hectare, whereas grains produce only some 4,200,000 kilocalories. Potatoes also require less agricultural time and energy than do grains.

2. The word "potato" comes from the Spanish *batata,* which in turn derived from the Caribbean Taino Indians term for the sweet potato: "*Ipomea batatas.*"

RADISH

1. Large radishes and small garden radishes are the result of hybridization with the common wild radish, jointed charlock (*Raphanus raphanistrum*), a common field weed.

SALSIFY

1. Inulin is a storage carbohydrate that is typical of the composite family. It is made of fructose instead of starch.

TOMATO

1. Since then agribusiness's manipulation of the tomato, including genetic standardization, has taken on vast dimensions. The "Flavr Savr tomato" (also known as CGN-89564-2) was genetically modified to have a longer shelf life. With such unnaturally grown plants, one cannot expect the same kind of healing strength that naturally, organically grown tomatoes possess. See Wolf D. Storl, *Culture and Horticulture*, Berkeley, CA: North Atlantic Books, 2013.

2. Ketchup, originally "tomato catsup," was developed in the middle of the nineteenth century. The word comes from the Chinese, and originally meant a spicy seasoning made of salted fish, mussels, and spicy herbs. In 1876 the German American H. J. Heinz debuted ketchup as one of America's first packaged foods.

BURDOCK

1. Burdock oil is easy to make: Fill a glass jar with scrubbed, finely chopped roots and pour good-quality oil (olive oil, wheat germ oil) over them until completely covered. Let stand in a warm, dark place for three weeks and pour through a sieve.

GOOD KING HENRY

1. The plant is known in many languages as Good King Henry: Dutch: *Goede Hendrik*, Danish: *Goder Henrik*, Swedish: *God Hindrich*, French: *Bon Henri*,

Italian: *Bono Enrico*, Polish: *Dobry Henryczek*, Finnish: *Hyvaen Heiken savikka*, etc.

2. *Schmotzenheiner*, "dirty Henry," refers to the fact that the leaves look and feel dusty. Elves and other magical beings who follow in the retinue of the great goddess Holle (Hulda) were also often connected to plants of the goosefoot family in the entire northern European area. The goose is a symbol of the magical flight that brings a being close to or into the "other world," to which the kobolds and dwarves also belong.

GREEN AMARANTH

1. The viceroy in Lima, the Marquis of Cañete, is supposed to have said: "Why do these dirty Indian women continue to bear healthy and robust children even though we hit them on their bellies and heads?" The priests finally solved the riddle. They discovered that the natives ate a "sacred" plant that they cultivated on small, hidden mountain fields.

KNOT ROOT, OR CHINESE ARTICHOKE

1. "Livingstone potatoes" (*Plectranthus esculentus*) (Africaans: *aartappel*, Zulu: *umbondive*) from South Africa are similar to knotroot and belong to the same family. This productive vegetable grows in just about any climate zone.

PARSNIP CHERVIL

1. The Dutch botanist and protestant humanist, Carolus Clusius (Charles de l'Écluse) made a name for himself by introducing to Vienna the potato, the tulip, the crown imperial, and the buckeye.

2. Though chervil (*Anthriscus cerefolium*) is also an umbellifer, it belongs to the Anthriscus genus. Chervil is good for seasoning meat and fish, and chervil soup is a delicacy. It should not be mistaken for cow parsley, or wild chervil, which has practically no essential oils.

3. Water hemlock (*Cicuta virosa*), which can be deadly poisonous, grows, just as parsnip chervil, in moist areas, on riverbanks and meadows that are occasionally flooded. This plant also has a bulbous tuber. One must be very careful while looking for the plant growing wild and be sure one has it correctly identified.

SHUNGIKU

1. The water chestnut (*Trapa natens*), a water plant with edible fruits, used to grow in Europe; it is one of the best "forgotten" vegetables. It is also a wild plant in the northeastern United States.

2. Clinical tests by Western researchers have shown that feverfew (*Chrysanthemum parthenium*) has a similar effect with migraines and giddy spells.

SKIRRET

1. Doctors in those days did not see the heart as a circulatory pump as we do, but more as "the seat of the soul," the source of courage and cordiality.

MINER'S LETTUCE

1. A Jewish tailor named Levi Strauss, who had emigrated from Bavaria, planned to earn some money by sewing canvas for tents and covered wagons and selling them to the Gold Rush hopefuls. But when he noticed that they needed sturdy pants even more he decided to sew his heavy-duty cloth into more rugged gear worthy of the back-breaking work of panning for gold. Once he dyed them blue, the first jeans were born.

OPIUM POPPY

1. Addicting alkaloids isolated from poppies include: morphine, which kills pain and induces sleep; codeine, which calms coughing and eases pain; papervine, which relaxes intestinal and urinary tract cramps; as well as thebaine (paramorphine), rhoeadine (rheadine), and others.

2. I was told this personally by Viennese anthropologist Graf Hans Manndorff, director of the Museum of Ethnology (Vienna), who did several years of fieldwork with the Miao tribes.

3. The first pressing of the seeds provides an excellent cooking oil. The second pressing results in a drier oil that can be used for soaps or paints.

RAMPION

1. Named after a duke's daughter who was forced to hide in the Ardennes Forest and had to eat wild roots in order to survive.

2. Today we know that embryos, needing certain substances for their development, indeed guide the strange cravings of their pregnant mothers (Farb/Armelagos 1983, 88).

3. Red flowering corn cockle (*Agrostemma githago*) used to be a common weed in grain fields; it has unfortunately become rare in our time.

PLANETARY COOKING

1. Capillary Dynamolysis is a method developed by anthroposophic researcher Dr. Lili Kolisko. It claims to make visible the formative forces working in, for example, plants. The plant juice—or whatever is being examined—is put in a petri dish; blotter paper is placed upright in the dish so that the paper absorbs the fluid. When the paper is dry, the process is repeated with a metal-salt solution. From this forms and patterns appear on the paper that make visible the formative forces involved (Kolisko 1939).

Bibliography

Achaya, K. T. *Indian Food: A Historical Companion*. Delhi: Oxford India Paperbacks, 1998.

Andresen, Astri, and Kari Tove Elvbakken. "From Poor Law Society to Welfare State: School Meals in Norway 1890s–1950s." *Journal of Epidemiology & Community Health* 61, no. 5 (2007): 374-377. Accessed 7 February 2016, doi:10.1136/jech.2006.048132.

Axtelmeier, Stanislaus Reinhardo. *Ebenbild der Natur (The Self-Image of Nature)*. Augsburg: Caspar Brechenmacher, 1715.

Bächtold-Stäubli, Hanns, and Eduard Hoffmann-Krayer, eds. *Handwörterbuch des deutschen Aberglaubens (Lexicon of German Folk-Superstitions)* vols. 1–10. Berlin: Walter de Gruyter Verlag, 1987.

Bakhru, H. K. *Foods that Heal*. New Delhi: Orient Paperbacks, 1995.

———. *Herbs That Heal*. New Delhi: Orient Paperbacks, 1993.

Bankhofer, Hademar. Die Naturheilkunde der Seefahrer: Rezepte und Heilmethoden aus aller Welt (The Naturopathy the Sailor: Recipes and Healing Techniques from Around the World). Düsseldorf: Albatross, 2001.

Barker, Cicely Mary. *The Complete Book of the Flower Fairies*. London: Blackie & Son Limited, 1923.

Basham, A. L. *The Wonder That Was India*. Calcutta: Fontana Books, Rupa & Co., 1982.

Baum der Erkenntnis. Frankfurt: Buchsignet, 1531.

Bellinger, Gerhard. *Knaurs Lexikon der Mythologie*. Augsburg: Weltbild Verlag, 1989.

Beuchert, Marianne. *Symbolik der Pflanzen: Von Akelei bis Zypresse (Symbolism of Plants: From Columbine to Cypress)*. Frankfurt: Insel, 1995.

Bock, Hieronymus. *Das Keütterbuch: Darin Vnterscheidt nammen vnnd Würkung der Kreutter . . . (The Herbal: The Names of Herbs and their Medical Effects . . .)*. Strasbourg: Josias Rihel, 1546.

Borneman, Ernest. *Sex im Volksmund: Die Sexuelle Umgangssprache des Deutschen Volkes (Sex in the Vernacular: The Sexual Slang of the German People)*. Reinbek: Rowohlt Taschenbuch Verlag, 1991.

Brill, Steve, and Evelyn Dean. Identifying and Harvesting Edible and Medicinal Plants in Wild (and Not So Wild) Places. New York: Quill/William Morrow, 1994.

Brosse, Jacques. *La Magie des Plantes.* Paris: Albin Michel, 2005.

Brunfels, Otto. *Herbarum Vivae Eicones ad Naturae Imitatione (Herbal with Images True to Nature).* Strasbourg: Johann Schott, 1532.

Bürger, C. F. *Die Blumensprache: Ein Buch der Liebe und Freundschaft (The Language of Flowers: A Book of Love and Friendship).* Würzburg: Stürtz Verlag, 1995.

Camerarius, Joachim. *Neuw Kreütterbuch Deß Hochgelehrten vnnd weitberühmten Herrn Doctor Pietro Andrea Mattioli . . . (The New Herbal of the Highly Learned and Widely Famous Doctor Pietro Andrea Mattioli . . .).* Frankfurt: Sigmund Feyerabend, 1586.

Carper, Jean. *The Food Pharmacy: Dramatic New Evidence That Food Is Your Best Medicine.* New York: Bantam Books, 1988.

Clause, L. *Guide Clause: Traité Pratique du Jardinage.* Brétigny-sur-Orge: Socieété Anonyme pour la Culture des Grains d'ÉLITE, 1979.

Clusius, Carolus. *Rariorum Plantarum Historia (The History of Rare Plants).* Antwerp: J. Moretus, 1601.

Cobbett, William. *The American Gardener: A Treatise on the Situation, Soil, and Laying Out of Gardens.* New York: C. M. Saxton & Company, 1856; New York: Modern Library, 2003.

Couplan, François. *Wildpflanzen für die Küche: Botanik, Sammeltips und Rezepte (Wild Plants for the Kitchen: Botany, Collecting Tips, and Recipes).* Aarau: AT Verlag, 1997.

Culpeper, Nicholas. *The Complete Herbal and English Physican.* Delhi: Sri Satguru Publications, 1999.

Dastur, J. F. *Medicinal Plants of India and Pakistan.* Bombay: D. B. Taraporevala Sons & Co., 1962.

Dayton, Leigh. "Spicy food Eaters Are Addicted to Pain." *New Scientist,* no. 1817 (1992), accessed 5 February 2016, www.taste-matters.org/styled-6/styled-14/index.html.

De Vries, Herman. *Natural Relations: Eine Skizze (Natural Relations: A Sketch).* Nuremberg: Verlag für moderne Kunst, 1989.

Engel, Fritz-Martin. *Zauberpflanzen, Pflanzenzauber (Magic Plants, Plant Magic)*. Hanover: Landbuch Verlag, 1978.

Farb, Peter, and George Armelagos. *Consuming Passions: The Anthropology of Eating*. New York: Washington Square Press, 1980.

Foster, Steven. *Herbal Renaissance: Growing, Using & Understanding Herbs in the Modern World*. Salt Lake City: Gibbs Smith, 1993.

Foster, Steven, and Yue Chongxi. *Herbal Emissaries: Bringing Chinese Herbs to the West*. Rochester, VT: Healing Arts Press, 1992.

Franke, Wolfgang. *Nutzpflanzenkunde (Crop Science)*. Stuttgart: Thieme, 1997.

Fuchs, Leonhart. *De Historia Stirpium Commentarii Insignes (Notable Commentaries on the History of Plants)*. Basel: Michael Isingrin, 1542.

Fyfe, Agnes. *Die Signatur des Mondes im Pflanzenreich (The Signature of the Moon in the Vegetable Kingdom)*. Stuttgart: Verlag Freies Geistesleben, 1967.

Glob, P. V. *The Bog People: Iron-Age Man Preserved*. Frogmore, St. Albans: Paladin, 1971.

Grieve, Margaret. *A Modern Herbal: The Medicinal, Culinary, Cosmetic and Economic Properties, Cultivation and Folk-Lore of Herbs, Grasses, Fungi, Shrubs & Trees with Their Modern Scientific Uses*. New York: Dover, 1982.

Grimé, William, ed. *Ethno-Botany of the Black Americans*. Algonac, MI: Reference Publications, Inc., 1979.

Grimm, Jacob. *Deutsche Mythology (German Mythology)*. Frankfurt: Ullstein, 1981.

Grimm, Jacob, and Wilhelm Grimm. *The Complete Grimm's Fairy Tales*.

Grimm, Jacob, and Wilhelm Grimm. *Kinder und Hausmärchen*. Leipzig: Turm, 1907.

Grimms Märchen. Marburg: N. G. Elwert, 1922.

Grossinger, Richard. *Planet Medicine: From Stone-Age Shamanism to Post-Industrial Healing*. Berkeley, CA: North Atlantic Books, 1995.

Halpin, Anne Moyer. *Unusual Vegetables: Something New for This Year's Garden*. Emmaus, PA: Rodale Press, 1978.

Hartmann, Thom. *The Last Hours of Ancient Sunlight: Waking Up to Personal and Global Transformation*. New York: Three Rivers Press, 2000.

Hegi, Gustav. *Illustrierte Flora von Mitteleuropa (Illustrated Flora of Central Europe)* vol. 6, issue 1. Vienna: A. Pichler Verlag, 1918.

Heil, Alexander. *Gartengestaltung mit essbaren Stauden (Landscaping with Edible Perennials).* Berlin: Institut für Oekologie und Botanik, 2001.

Höfler, Max. *Volksmedizinische Botanik der Germanen (People's Medical Botany of the Germanic Tribes).* Berlin: VWB, 1990.

Hollerbach, Elisabeth, and Karl Hollerbach. *Kraut und Unkraut zum Kochen und Heilen (Herb and Weed for Cooking and Healing).* Munich: Hugendubel, 1998.

Hsu, Hong-Yen. *How to Treat Yourself with Chinese Herbs.* Long Beach, CA: Oriental Healing Arts Institute, 1986.

Jarvis, D. C. *Folk Medicine.* New York: Crest Books, 1961.

Kaminski, Patricia, and Richard Katz. *Flower Essence Repertory: A Comprehensive Guide to North American and English Flower Essences for Emotional and Spiritual Well-Being.* Nevada City: Flower Essence Society, 1996.

Kölbl, Konrad. *Kölbl's Kräuterfibel.* Munich: Reprint-Verlag Konrad Kölbl, 1973.

Kolisko, Lili, and Eugen Kolisko. *Agriculture of Tomorrow.* Stroud: Kolisko Archive, 1939.

Körber-Grohne, Udelgard. *Nutzpflanzen in Deutschland (Crops in Germany).* Stuttgart: Konrad Theiss, 1987.

Koschtschejew, A. K. *Wildwachsende Pflanzen in unserer Ernährung: Über 800 Rezepte (Wild Plants in Our Diet: Over 800 Recipes).* Leipzig: VEB Fachbuchverlag, 1990.

Lehane, Brendan. *The Power of Plants.* New York: McGraw-Hill, 1977.

Levy, Charles Kingsley, and Richard B. Primack. *A Field Guide to Poisonous Plants and Mushrooms of North America.* Brattleboro, VT: Stephen Greene Press, 1984.

Lötschert, W., and G. Beese. *Pflanzen der Tropen (Plants of the Tropics).* Munich: BLV, 1992.

Lurker, Manfred. *Lexikon der Götter und Dämonen (Encyclopedia of Gods and Demons).* Stuttgart: Kröner, 1984.

Mabey, Richard. *Das Neue BLV Buch der Kraeuter (The New BLV Book of Herbs).* Munich: BLV, 1993.

Magister Botanicus. *Magisches Kreutherkompendium (Compendium of Magic Herbs).* Speyer: Die Sanduhr, 1995.

Mansfeld, Rudolf. *Verzeichnis Landwirtschaftlicher und Gärtnerischer Kultur-pflanzen (Directory of Agricultural and Horticultural Crops)*. Berlin: Akademie Verlag, 1986.

Marzell, Heinrich. *Wörterbuch der Deutschen Pflanzennamen (Dictionary of German Plant Names)*, vol. 1. Leipzig: S. Hirzel Verlag, 1943.

McIntyre, Anne. *The Complete Herbal Tutor: The Ideal Companion for Study and Practice*. London: Gaia Books Ltd., 2010.

Mercatante, Anthony S. *The Magic Garden: The Myth and Folklore of Flowers, Plants, Trees, and Herbs*. New York: Harper & Row, 1976.

Mességué, Maurice. *C'est la Nature Qui a Raison: Secrets de Beauté et de Santé (It's Nature That has Reason: Secrets of Beauty and Health)*. Paris: Robert Laffont, 1972.

Moerman, Daniel E. *Native American Ethnobotany*. Portland, OR: Timber Press, 1999.

Most, Alfred. *Von Aubergine bis Zuckermais: Spezialitäten aus seltenem Obst und Gemüse (From Eggplant to Sweet Corn: Rare Fruit and Vegetables Dishes)*. Leipzig: VEB Fachbuchverlag, 1990.

Müller, Irmgard. *Die Pflanzlichen Heilmittel bei Hildegard von Bingen: Heilwissen aus der Klostermedizin (The Herbal Remedy in Hildegard von Bingen: Healing Knowledge from the Monastery Medicine)*. Freiburg: Herder, 1993.

Hortus Sanitatis (The Garden of Health). Mainz: Jacob Meydenbach, 1491.

Panati, Charles. *Extraordinary Origins of Everyday Things*. New York: Harper & Row, 1987.

Patnaik, Naveen. *The Garden of Life: An Introduction to the Healing Plants of India*. New Delhi: Aquarian/HarperCollins, 1993.

Pelikan, Wilhelm. *Heilpflanzenkunde, 3 Bde., Bd.1. (Herbalism: Three Volumes, Vol. 1)*. Dornach: Phil.-Anthro. Verlag, 1975.

Pollmer, Udo, Andrea Fock, Ulrike Gonder, and Karin Haug. *Prost Mahlzeit! Krank durch gesunde Ernährung (Happy Meal! Health Through Healthy Eating)*. Cologne: Kiepenheuer & Witsch, 1994.

Pötschke, Werner, and Harry Pötschke. *Gärtner Pötschkes Großes Gartenbuch (Gardener Pötschke's Big Gardening Book)*. Kaarst: Gärtner Pötschke Verlag, 1945; Augsburg: Weltbild, 2001.

Rätsch, Christian. *The Encyclopedia of Psychoactive Plants: Ethnopharmacology and Its Applications*. Rochester, VA: Inner Traditions, 1998.

_____. *Indianische Heilkräuter: Tradition und Anwendung (Indian Medicinal Plants: Tradition and Application)*. Munich: Eugen Diederichs, 1996.

Robbins, Tom. *Jitterbug Perfume*. New York: Bantam, 1984.

Rohde, Eleanour Sinclair, *A Garden of Herbs*. New York: Dover, 1969.

Röhrich, Lutz. *Lexikon Abendländischer Mythologie (Lexicon of Idioms)*. Freiburg: Herder, 1993.

Sahlins, Marshall. *Stone Age Economics*. New York: Aldine, 1972.

Schwanitz, Franz. *The Origin of Cultivated Plants*. Cambridge, MA: Harvard University Press, 1966.

Scotto, Elisabeth. *Les Légumes Oubliés (Forgotten Vegetables)*. Paris: Éditions du Chêne, Hachette Livre, 1995.

Simpson, Beryl B., and Molly Conner-Ogorzaly. *Economic Botany: Plants in Our World*. New York: McGraw-Hill, 1986.

Storl, Wolf D. *Culture and Horticulture: The Classic Guide to Biodynamic and Organic Gardening*. Berkeley: North Atlantic Books, 2013.

Storl, Wolf D. *Der Kosmos im Garten (The Cosmos in the Garden)*. Aarau: AT Verlag, 2001.

Storl, Wolf D. *Götterpflanze Bilsenkraut (Henbane, Plant of the Gods)*. Solothurn: Nachtschatten, 2000.

Sturtevant, E. Louis. *Sturtevant's Edible Plants of the World*. Edited by U. P. Hedrick. New York: Dover, 1972.

Tabernaemontanus, Jacobus Theodorus. *Neuw Kreuterbuch*. Frankfurt: Erstauflage, 1588.

Tacitus, Publius Cornelius. *The Complete Tacitus Anthology: The Histories, The Annals, Germania, Agricola, A Dialogue on Oratory*. Bybliotech, 2012.

Tergit, Gabriele. *Kaiserkron und Päonien Rot: Kleine Kulturgeschichte der Blumen (Crown Imperial and Red Peonies: A Brief Cultural History of Flowers)*. Munich: Verlagsgruppe Droemer Knaur, 1963.

Thurneysser, Leonhard. *Quinta Essentia*. Münster: Johann Ossenbrück, 1574.

Townsend, Benjamin. *The Complete Seedsman: Shewing, the Best and Easiest Method for Raising and Cultivating Every Sort of Seed Belonging to a Kitchen and Flower-Garden*. London: Printed by S. Powell for R. Norris, and T. Whitehouse, 1726.

Treben, Maria. *Health Through God's Pharmacy: Advice and Proven Cures with Medicinal Herbs.* Steyr: Ennsthaler Publ., 2009.

Uyldert, Mellie. *The Psychic Garden: Plants and Their Esoteric Relationship with Man.* Emeryville, CA: Thorsons, 1980.

van den Toorn, Piet. "Heilpflanznefamilien: Doldenblütler—Apiaceae/ Umbelleferae" in *Naturheilpraxis.* Munich: Pflaum, 2002.

van Wyk, Ben-Erik, and Nigel Gericke. *People's Plants: A Guide to Useful Plants of Southern Africa.* Pretoria: Briza Publ., 2000.

Vogel, Virgil J. *American Indian Medicine.* Norman, OK: University of Oklahoma Press, 1970.

von Reinsberg-Düringsfeld, Otto. *Traditions et Légendes de la Belgique (Traditions and Legends of Belgium).* Brussels: Ferdinand Claassen, Libraire-Éditeur, 1870.

Walter, Hilma. *Die Pflanzenwelt: Ihre Verwandtschaft zur Erden- und Menschheitsentwicklung (Flora: Your Relationship to the Earth and Human Development).* Arlesheim: Natura, 1971.

Weil, Andrew. *Health and Healing: Understanding Conventional and Alternative Medicine.* Boston: Houghton Mifflin Company, 1983.

Werdin, Sitha. *Gemüse-Apotheke (Vegetable Pharmacy. Old and New Medicinal Recipes).* Munich: Irisiana, 1995.

Wheelwright, Edith Grey. *Medicinal Plants and Their History.* New York: Dover, 1974.

Willfort, Richard. *Das große Handbuch der Heilkräuter (The Great Handbook of Medicinal Herbs).* Hamburg: Nikol, 1997.

Wolters, Bruno. *Agave bis Zaubernuß: Die Heilpflanzen der Indianer Nord- und Mittelamerikas (Agave to Witch Hazel: The Medicinal Plants of the Indians of North and Central America).* Greifenberg: Urs Freund Verlag, 1996.

Zoller, Andrea, and Hellmuth Nordwig. *Heilpflanzen der Ayurvedischen Medizin: Ein Praktisches Handbuch (Ayurvedic Medicinal Plants: A Practical Handbook).* Heidelburg: Haug, 1997.

Index

About the Author

Born in 1942 in Saxony, Germany, with a green thumb and the gift of writing, cultural anthropologist and ethnobotanist Wolf Dieter Storl, who emigrated with his parents to the United States in 1954, has had a special connection to nature since childhood. His specific area of research is shamanism and healing in traditional societies, focusing on the role of plants in all aspects of life, including sacred symbolism, magic, medicine, foods, and poisons. He has pursued this interest in many parts of the world.

After finishing his PhD in Anthropology (magna cum laude) on a Fulbright scholarship in 1974 in Berne, Switzerland, he taught anthropology and sociology in Grants Pass, Oregon. During this time he also offered an extremely popular organic gardening course, as he was one of the pioneers of the organic/biodynamic gardening movement. While preparing for his doctoral exams in Switzerland, he also lived in an experimental community and helped tend a five-acre organic garden. There he had the good fortune to learn from master gardener Manfred Stauffer who specialized in composting any organic matter.

Storl is also an avid traveler and observed nature around the entire globe, spending time with people who are very connected to the nature that surrounds them. From1982–1983, he spent a year as an official visiting scholar at the Benares Hindu University in Varanasi, India. After returning to the United States in 1984, he spent much time with traditional medicine persons of the Cheyenne and taught courses at Sheridan College in Sheridan, Wyoming. He has traveled and conducted research in South Asia, India, Mexico, the Canary Islands, South Africa, and much of Europe, pursuing ethnobotanical and ethnomedicinal interests. He has written some twenty-five books and many articles, which have been translated into various languages, including Czech, Danish, Dutch, English, French, Italian, Japanese, Latvian, Lithuanian, Polish, and Portuguese. Storl is a frequent guest on German, Swiss, and Austrian television and has also appeared on the BBC.

After another visit in India and Nepal in 1986, Storl and his wife moved to Germany, where he is both a freelance writer and lecturer. They live on an old estate with a large garden in the foothills of the Alps.

Storl's books are unique in that he does not treat nature with cold objectivism. He is able to delve into nature's depths and supports his experience with ancient lore from all over the world that has been, for the most part, left on the wayside in the wake of objective science. He theorizes that science is not always as objective as it claims to be. He invites his readers on a journey into a world of nature that is completely alive and has its own rhyme and reason. Myths and lore from many cultures also have a prominent place in his writings, as he claims that the images portrayed in this way often tell us more about the true nature of things than dry facts can do.